AF655718

Displacement, Disillusionment and Disparity of

# Adivasi Life

A Critic of Indian English Novel

# Displacement, Disillusionment and Disparity of Adivasi Life

## A Critic of Indian English Novel

**Dr. Manoj S. Madavi**

*Foreword by*

**Prof. Felix Padel**

**T.K.Titus**

AUTHORSPRESS

Worldwide Circulation through Authorspress Global Network
**First Published in 2021**
**by**
**Authorspress**
Q-2A Hauz Khas Enclave, New Delhi-110 016 (India)
Phone: (0) 9818049852
E-mail: authorspressgroup@gmail.com
Website: www.authorspressbooks.com

**Displacement, Disillusionment and Disparity of Adivasi Life: A Critic of Indian English Novel**

ISBN 978-93-5529-157-8

Copyright © 2021 Dr. Manoj S. Madavi

All rights reserved. No part of this book may be reproduced or transmitted in any form or by any means, electronic, mechanical, photocopying, or otherwise, without the express written consent of the author.

Printed in India at Thomson Press (India) Limited

*In memories of all those Adivasi warriors who fought fearlessly for their indigenous claim on Jal, jangle and jamin against the mighty British Empire during colonialism.*

# Few Words from the Bottom of the Heart

This literary research and analyses on displacement, disillusionment and disparity of adivasi life and other issues of their existence should be studied in a very optimistic manner. I feel, though it is a harsh criticism of Indian English fiction writing but aesthetic values in their novel are worth praising. My findings shows that the Indian English fiction writers lack authenticity while presenting adivasi disorientation and social marginalisation but this positive literary investigation will open new approaches for the study of the novel dealing with adivasi life in Indian English. Upcoming new English fiction writers will be acquainted with adivasi problems like subjugation, exploitation, political and cultural alienation of adivasi community which will provide them new parameters of the social study of adivasis realism as we found in the regional writings of Mahasweta Devi and Gopinath Mohanty. Social and cultural alienation of the adivasi does not find proper presentations through the novel writings of Indian English.

This book believes that the voices of the subjugated adivasis have moved from the periphery towards the center in the last few decades. Indian English Fiction Writers lack authenticity while depicting the adivasi marginalisation, therefore, a revisionary approach in literary criticism is necessary for the discourse on Indian English Fiction writings. This reference book also positively comments that the intensity of racial dominancy of the elite classes over adivasi community seems weaker in Indian English fiction. Dalit literature has raised the question from a Dalit centric point of view just as the feminism has been studying literature through a gendered lens in the same manner Adivasi life, culture, problems and it should be observed through the spectacle of adivasiism.

This literary expression on adivasi issues of identity and existence as reflected in Indian English Novels, also opines that while depicting adivasi characterisation and the socio-cultural background of adivasis, Indian English fiction writers have exaggerated the adivasi life, culture and traditions. The original aboriginal community with its several hardships did not figure predominantly in literature. Displacement and disorientation of the adivasis have not presented appropriately in the light of postcolonial studies. The struggle of the adivasi for their rights on their forest and natural resources has not shown or even slightly discussed in the mainstream Indian English fiction. My observations on regional adivasi novel writings are more convincing, realistic and informative about the ground realities of the adivasis. The adivasi life seems alien and ethnic others in the presentation of the literature which endorses the concept of nation-narration in Indian English novels and other literary cannons.

Postcolonial Indian English Fiction writers have neglected the threatening results of Imperialism, Neocolonisation, Neoliberalism and Global Capitalism on Adivasi culture, identities and existential issues. Indian English Fictional World is promoting Neoglobal, Westernize values of Imperialism leaving behind the existential issues of mass common population of India. Multiculturalism and Cosmopolitanism have damaged the Indian way of humanitarian and compassionate writings about native-indigenous communities and massive marginal classes.

Needless to say, that no work is ever a solitary exercise. Innumerable debts have been incurred in the completion of this creativity. I would like to acknowledge some of them.

First and foremost I offer my sincerest gratitude to my mentor Dr. Sanjay D. Palwekar, Associated Professor, Department of English, Post Graduate Teaching Department of RTMNU, Nagpur who has supported me throughout my thesis with his patience and knowledge. He has been more than a supervisor to me. Apart from the academic guidance, his critical insight and humility have been a great source of inspiration to me throughout the years. I would remain indebted to him forever for his invaluable guidance and cooperation to me. I express my heartfelt thanks to Dr. D. M. Shende, Professor and Head, Department of English, R. T. M. Nagpur University, Nagpur who encouraged me and provided time to time insightful suggestions for the successful completion of my thirst area in adivasi studies.

I owe a lot to all the philosophers, thinkers, writers and scholars from regional adivasi writing as well as mainstream English novel writing whose contribution helped me to a great extent to understand various facets of the adivasi life and indigenous literature topic. I express my gratitude towards all of them whom I have acknowledged in the note and the bibliography.

I am thankful to my parents, senior writer and critic, T.T.Warkhade, Ashok Masram, Maroti Kodwate, Sukhlal Bhalavi, Haribhau Kulsange, Mr.Pralhad Meshram and Dadaji Gedam along with other likeminded friends who works for the adivasi upliftment and pedagogical programmes for adivasi community. I am thankful to my loving daughter Niharika and dearer wife Darshana for their encouragement and patients in all possible way.

Eventually, I shows my in-depth gratitude to Mr. Sudarshan Kcherry, CEO of Authorspress, Delhi (India) for his kind motivation and deep interest to publish my work.

Sincere thanks to all.

**Manoj S. Madavi**

# Foreword

It gives me immense delight to write a foreword to Dr. Madavi's book *"Displacement, Disillusionment and Disparity in Adivasi Life"*. Manoj S. Madavi, my former student, first came to my notice when he approached me one day expressing his concern as to how the students of the arts stream could compete with science and commerce students in an English elocution competition soon to be held. Students from rural and adivasi background learning through their mother tongue without sufficient exposure to the language will be at a disadvantage, he pointed out. I encouraged him and asked him to accept this as a challenge; also added that every student could become fluent in English with a little practice, devotion and inner motivation. In the competition, Manoj won the first prize and his clear articulation and won the hearts of the audience.

This foreword let me hasten to add, will in no way be influenced by my previous knowledge of the author. Borrowing T.S.Eliot's observation and slightly altering it, let me state here that honest criticism and sensitive appreciation of a book must be directed on the book and not on the author, it was none other than Eliot who stated that criticism is as inevitable as breathing and also reminded us of the separation between "the man who suffers and the mind which creates."

Let me now attempt to jot down my sincere thoughts and observation about this book, which is an outcome of the author's painstaking research at R.T.M. Nagpur University. I am happy to observe that this research book on adivasi's representation in Indian English novels is a significant contribution to the area of Adivasi Studies and Adivasi welfare. The researcher's critical acumen and deep concern for adivasi's well-being and empowerment are very much evident in this study. Madavi's first-hand experience of adivasi life and the exploitation of adivasis by various agencies and groups which is continued have enabled him to carry out this research in a competent manner. Madavi's findings that the mainstream Indian

English novels do not penetrate deeper into the lives of adivasis, their historical struggles and cultural vibrancy and ethos should be taken seriously. Most of the acclaimed novels which deal with the adivasi experience do not depict the subjugation and systematic marginalisation of the adivasis with concern and compassion. Many writers have a patronising attitude towards the adivasi way of life and therefore their portrayal of adivasi life lacks authenticity and universality. The adivasi experience is conspicuously absent even in novels that overtly dealt with nationalism. The author brilliantly exposes "the sophisticated conspiracy of silence" in selected Indian English fiction.

On the other hand, Madavi points out, the depiction of adivasi life in regional literature like Bengali, Oriya, Hindi, Jharkhand and Marathi is very positive and promising. Writers like Mahaswetadevi Devi and Gopinath Mohanty have been successful in giving "strength to the adivasi voice in regional literature".

Madavi's main concern is giving voice to the adivasis of our beloved nation and to empower them by ending exploitation and marginalisation. Writers have a great role to play in this endeavor as they are the conscience keepers of the race. I am sure that the author's research in this rather neglected area will open new vistas of thoughts and positive actions in the area of Adivasi Studies and Adivasi Welfare. The pictures on the cover page convey the cultural essence of adivasi life in all its simplicity, purity and effervescence.

07/02/2021 **Dr. T.K. Titus**

# A Greeting Message from Adv. Nicholas Barla

Dear Dr. Manoj,

I take this opportunity to congratulate and appreciate Dr. Manoj Madavi for writing the Book *"Displacement, Disillusionment and Disparity of Adivasi Life"*. First of all there are not many books found on Adivasis. Secondly though one may find books on adivasis, but written by some non adivasi origin. I have gone through many sociology, anthropology and history books as a adivasi student. But there always rose many questions within me on different expressions by the authors? In high school and college in fact I did not see a single book. When I read the history of others, I felt who am I, without any history? Today when I see, I feel the urge to have some books about my 'Oraon Tribe' and the other Tribes. Being an Adivasi/ adivasi I strongly feel that many of my brothers and sisters, children also have similar enquiry and interest.

During my Philosophy studies in Pune, I read lots of books on adivasis, but written by non adivasi scholars. I felt many of the points were not understood, or misunderstood in their expressions and interpretations. Often I raised questions to my professors about the wrong expressions on adivasis. I found the scholars did not grasp the adivasi way of life, their feelings and their world views right way ! As persons from outside the community, it is difficult to understand and express everything in right way. Those days there were no educated adivasis / Adivasis to write, or to record about their philosophy, world views, history or the traditions and cultures according to their perspective. This gap is very vivid in many of the books. For example Gotul of Gonds or Dhum Kudia of oraons. The non adivasi authors must have observed the boys and girls were found in the same hall, engaged in singing songs or dance or in story telling...*etc.* They would write about Gotul with negative meaning. Whereas there was nothing wrong. It was a system of educating the adivasis. Rather it was the 'first centre of education' system in the world, which no one knows. There used to be one learnt woman and man as teacher(s) who used to be in charge of the gotul. They would teach boys and girls songs, stories, dances, music's, skills...*etc.* The following morning they would teach the young girls weaving, or stitching the leaves and make leaf plates, or cooking.....*etc.* The master of the boys may teach how to make plough, kot, or pidha (wooden plank for sitting), machia (rope chair for sitting)....*etc.* They taught them systematic skill training in adivasi languages that were very practical and useful for life. They taught sowing seeds, weeding.....*etc.* Connected to life. This was a learning center for adivasis/ Adivasis community. But Non Adivasis author one day he/she observes and interpretes the same wrongly and mistakenly. Since he was with some degree and knew how to write and misinterpret, have money to publish book, and thus there were publications of books. But how he / she brought damage to a community is not considered.

Dr. Manoj Madavi in his book found similar instances. He disagreed to many of the writings of the authors, who thus without much and depth understanding have written about Adivasis/ Adivasis and the negative pictures have been created on adivasi/ community. I do not know many of the anthropologists and sociologists books are of such nature. But we need many Dr. Manoj Madavies to depict clear academic and intellectual works and corrections of the past.

After going through the book, I realise that the Adivasi/ Adivasi scholars also need to come with different publications/ books on their own tribes that would be authentic and original of culture or of a community.

Adivasis / Adivasis are with a distinct race and culture. One cannot put them into one dominant culture or a branch of culture. The Indian states were divided on dominant linguistic groups *e.g.* Maratha Community as Maharastra, Biharies as Bihar, Bengalies as Bengal, Keralian as Kerala. Why the Bhils did not have their state? They are found in Maharastra, Gujurat, Rajasthan and Madhya Pradesh. They could have clubbed very well as one Bhil State. Why the Chhotanagpur where Adivasis/ Adivasis were divided in West Bengal, some were kept in Odisha, some in Madhya Pradesh? If the Chhotanagpur state could have been made it was possible. Without much understanding the social, culture, traditions and history the political leaders of those time just divided the adivasis in many states.

It is right time to understand the values of language, culture and a community.

I wish all the readers to read and all our Educated Adivasi Sisters and Brothers to come up with literatures like Dr. Manoj Madavi.

Congratulations and wish you all the best for further steps

18/03/2021

**Adv. Nicholas Barla**

Adivasi Samanway Manch Bharat

# A Special Outline from Prof. Felix Padel

This book by Dr Manoj Madavi highlights the extent of marginalisation and disparagement of Adivasi or adivasi life by mainstream writers. The author's point is that fictional writers in English, even when trying to give a sympathetic view of Adivasi life and situation, have tended to fall into stereotypes and 'use' Adivasis as a backdrop to other concerns. By contrast, a number of novels in India's regional languages such as Bengali, Odia, Marathi and Hindi have given more sympathetic and in-depth portrayals.

As a non-fiction writer, I question also non-fictional writing about Adivasis and adivasi life. Too much anthropological writing about Adivasi communities *objectifies* them. This is the tendency outlined in the book *Decolonising Methodologies: Research and Indigenous People* (1999/2012) by Linda Tuhiwai Smith, who is a Maori scholar-activist in New Zealand/Aoteaora. No anthropologist now can easily write about Maori (indigenous New Zealand) issues without careful introspection of their own motives, checking the colonial-era tendency to write about indigenous peoples in a way that diminishes them by turning them into objects of study. At the same time, Tuhiwai Smith and many others have reformulated the education system in their country so that every New Zealander learns some Maori language and culture at school. Maori education has brought back their language, and every research student has the right to write their PhD in Maori.

Are such changes conceivable in India? Although Article 350A of India's Constitution guarantees every child the right to be taught in their mother tongue, in practice most adivasi schools still try to exclude adivasi languages completely, and often even punish or humiliate children found speaking them, leading to a situation bordering on linguistic genocide. Could we imagine a situation where all Indian school children learn some Santali, Gondi or other local languages, for example, or where Adivasis enter a classroom to teach some of their skills and tell their stories?

In my own writing, one way I try and overcome the tendency to marginalise Adivasi voices is by quoting words I have heard people speak. For example, in the Niyamgiri case, I remember a Kond elder who I met standing outside the Supreme Court when an Odia judge had spoken apparently in favour of Vedanta. This man said just four words that summed up the situation (and Indian philosophy!) – "*Taro karma, amoro dharma*" ("his sin/action, our duty"). A Kond elder in a village elder near Lanjigarh I remember saying "They are flooding us out with money". A woman I spoke to who'd just been displaced from another Lanjigarh village said to me "*Amoro devta bi nasht kole*" ("They even destroyed our gods") when they bulldozed her village. And Lado Sikaka, Dongria Kond leader of the movement to save Niyamgiri from bauxite mining, said at Belamba Public Hearing (loosely translating): "People say there's crores of rupees [to be made from mining the bauxite] up on Niyamgiri. It's not money up there, it's our Maa Baap and we'll defend her! It seems like the Asurs of ancient mythology have re-emerged in the form of these companies."

All these examples show a adivasi intelligence and wit that has an ability to go to the heart of a situation in fewest words. Why don't most people listen to such voices? Often, they don't even get the chance to hear them; and when they do, perhaps they are too conditioned to even notice what they are hearing, due to the bias and failings of their own education and reading that emphasises a view of adivasis as 'lacking' (in intelligence, education *etc.*) – what some scholars term 'deficit discourse'. We are used to seeing adivasis described through stereotypes as 'backward', 'poorest of the poor' – in terms of what they lack. My friend Abhay Xaxa, who I knew in JNU, and who completed his PhD in sociology shortly before he died (far too young!) early in 2020, wrote a powerful poem on these issues entitled "I am not your data"....

Every Indian citizen should understand the huge injustice, exploitation, dispossession faced by Adivasi and adivasi citizens throughout the country; as well as the positive aspects of indigenous culture and history, such as the disproportionate role of Adivasis in India's freedom struggle, and the beauties of adivasi dancing and village life where people still exercise a high degree of autonomy.

The situation of indigenous people in other countries – including how they are described in fiction – is strikingly similar to the scene

Madavi describes for India in this important book. For example, *Last of the Mohicans* (1826) by James Fenimore Cooper is now understood as an outrageous distortion of native American life that misrepresented history fundamentally, while creating a 'noble savage' image far from the truth.

The cultural racism still persists in so many countries. But in New Zealand, Australia, USA and Canada many fiction writers are more careful now in how they portray their indigenous people. In Latin American countries such as Ecuador, Bolivia, Colombia, Brazil, and indigenous activists are still being murdered, but they are also active in politics, and indigenous movements are taking back control of education and questioning the extractivist economic models that are displacing communities as well as devastating ecosystems.

In India the negative stereotypes are still deeply embedded in the education system and its hierarchies. There are signs of change however. In Madhya Pradesh, new Adivasi learning centres such as Muskaan and Adharshila are democratising Adivasi education. Madavi's book is another sign of this awakening!

11/02/2021

# Introduction

India, after having been through a turmoiling period of British dominion which lasted for centuries and has seen with its own eyes what it takes to be a Nation, with the achievement of independence from the British, has carved out its path towards purification, self-dependency and tremendous growth in agriculture, commerce and technology. The literary field could not be untouched from this 'elevation process'. Growth in the living standard of the people increased the percentage of the literate population which resulted in the rise in the number of writers. The output of the literary works grew tremendously by the Indian writers in regional as well as the English language. While the stalwarts like Ravindranath Tagore and his contemporaries took their inspiration from the freedom struggle and revealed the beauty of Indian philosophy for the first time to the world, the post-independence writers like R.K. Narayan, Mulk Raj Anand, Raja Rao and others sought their material amongst the common lot and endeavored to wear their pen for the common laymen of this country. Later on, hundreds of illumined minds in every decade chose writing as their profession and brought different colours of Indian life before the world. However, wittingly or unwittingly, knowingly or unknowingly, deliberately or not; the miserable life of the aboriginal community who have been away from any mainstream development for centuries and stayed relied entirely on nature for all their needs, remained un-inspirational for all these literaties, or at least they did not bother to take any heed of portraying the struggle in the lives of the adivasi. Because to do that, they would have to sacrifice the secure place in urbanity and tramp into the deepest uncivilised forests to know things about adivasi life. The postmodern writers too, except one or two, kept the adivasis as aloof from their works as rich keep away the downtrodden, or even if we find few adivasi characters in some works, it cannot be said to be a true representation of the adivasi life in the true sense of the term. The underprivileged and marginal remained underprivileged and marginal in literature too.

The adivasi culture has its beauties and colors different from the mainstream urban life and culture. Theirs is a distinct culture that does not come under the purview of commonly known religions and cultures. Their customs, conventions, faiths, festivals, and social system are all so distinct from us all that when an urban stranger happens to visit any of these adivasi Thandas or villages, they are considered as outsiders, though respected and welcomed cordially. The dwellers of the deep forests have always liked to remain aloof and untouched from the urban societies and this is the reason that the aboriginal could nurture and protect their culture for so long. However, the heavenly forests and their natural resources caught the sight of the greedy corporate houses and governments too sought their selfish material fulfillments in shaking hands with them which resulted at the beginning of the endless game of humiliating, persecuting the adivasis on the fake charges and hurling them out from their habitat. This unjust persecution by the governments and the Companies made the adivasis to see government as their enemy and to take arms in hands to avenge for the injustice done with them. This is the tragic saga of adivasi life that could have been portrayed and given true representation in the world language like English. But to our dismay, there happened nothing of the sort. Of course, there are a few writers like Arun Joshi, Malgaonkar, Kamala Markandeya, Geeta Mehta, Anita Desai, Upamanyu Chatterjee and Arvind Adiga, the novels of which have been explored and critiqued in this book by Manoj Madavi, who endeavored to give narrations of the tragic fates of the adivasi and bring in light some of the facets of their life. Some of them have succeeded in winning the world attention for their works either.

Some of these writers emphasised urban fallacy, rootlessness, East-West encounter, social justice and power struggle, while the others have focused on marginalisation or adivasis, violence by Naxalites and exploitation of the adivasi women. Having done an in-depth study of the 'Adivasi' novels of these English novelists, however, Manoj Madavi deeply regrets and expresses his feeling of discontent for not giving true representation to the adivasi life and culture, and concentrating only on some superficial matters related to aboriginal life. He intends to put forward his grievances by using a revisionary approach for this study, as he finds it necessary in mainstream literary criticism for the discourse on Indian writing in English.

Manoj Madavi first discusses the issues of adivasi ethos and identity highlighted in Arun Joshi's *The Strange Case of Billy Biswas* in the first chapter. He lauds Arun Joshi for his magnetic skill in handling the traumatic postmodern world, the sense of detachment, utilitarianism and craving for salvation. He finds The Strange Case as a great example of postcolonial sensitivities of generous hearts that focused on intellectual doubts, erosion of values. But he regrets that the crisis of adivasi life has not been reflected through the novel. He lashes Arun Joshi for portraying merely a romantic nostalgia of American and student life instead of portraying the non-corrupted, non-materialistic and non-corporate ideology of the adivasi folks.

Two novels of Malgaonkar and Kamala Markandeya respectively have been dealt with in the second chapter. *The Princess* by Malgaonkar is a story of a betrayal of the adivasi Bhil community by King Maharaja Heroji. The Bhils become a political victim of the state agenda having no sympathy or consideration from both sides. Madavi thinks holds that the scheme of modernisation, dam constructions and deforestation have caused havoc for the aborigines, but the present novel does not show any sincere concern regarding this vital point. He thinks that the novel could explore much about adivasi political illiteracy, grave political exploitation, threats to adivasi existence and identity issues, their failed political rights; but it merely plays with state merging and partition. Similarly, *The Coffer Dam* by Kamala Markandeya, which deals with the East-West encounter between a British group of engineers and local adivasi people of India, but fails to capture the degradation f adivasi culture, their glorious past and their role in the national freedom struggle. Instead, it gives much space to the romantic portrayal of Helen and Bashiam. Madavi regrets that in this novel of multiculturalism, the adivasis are nowhere. For him, the novel deals with issues like dying humanitarianism, the superiority of the West and colonial mentality over the indigenous, but it could not create a larger panorama of double disposition of the adivasis.

The absence of adivasi heritage, their struggle and their faith in primordial power are the issues in Geeta Mehta's *The River Sutra* that have been explored in the third chapter. This novel, though good in presenting a series of interlocking stories in which the novelist picturised the adivasi myths and rituals, is biased on giving too much importance to the superstitions of the adivasis. Madavi criticizes the novelist for not giving any space to the displacement, dislocation and marginalisation of adivasi and focusing only on their superstitious nature. Another novel by Anita Desai, *The Inheritance of Loss* has been dealt with in this chapter. It caricatures a distorted and dehumanized condition of poor adivasis. Though the novel has been acclaimed all over the world and has received the prestigious Booker Prize, Madavi brings in light a serious anomaly in it by maintaining that the novel does not present a true picture of the powerless adivasis, nor does it give them due to representation. The adivasis in the novel seem only leftover.

*The English August* by Upamanyu Chatterjee and *The White Tiger* by Arvind Adiga are two more novels explored in chapter four to study the disillusionment and subjugation of the adivasis as narrated in them. Madavi criticizes the former for the absence of adivasi life in it, though the novel is set in the adivasi-dominated territory of Madana. The novel focuses only on one particular problem of water of the adivasis neglecting the other fundamental need of food, wealth and education. Adiga's The White Tiger, too, though magnificently exposes the political corruption, cultural and gender discrimination and socio-political injustice, it fails to give due justice to the adivasi pathos, something which the author of this book laments.

The final discourse is devoted to 'Unearthing the Unexplored', which is giving a comparative discussion of some novels written in vernacular and regional languages like Bengali, Oriya, Jharkhandi and Marathi upon adivasi life and culture. The author opines that the adivasi novels in these regional languages grasp the right thread of aborigine life and highlight their culture, their exploitation and dehumanisation, their problems and their needs in a more authentic manner than the English novels. This comparison makes is think introvertly that still due attention to the adivasi life hasn't been paid by the authors and a great 'Unexplored' part of their life requires to be dug out.

27/01/2021 **Vikas Meshram**

# Contents

# CHAPTER 1

# Adivasi Life and Culture in Postcolonial Literature

White man tells the children
That their ancestor "settle" here
When the truth is that, they invaded us
They murdered us and they raped us
Until we barely existed.
But we, the native, warn you
When your people came to our land
It was not with open arms but with
Bible, guns and disease and they had
The arrogance to call us Godless Savage
If there is a heaven and it is filled with
Christian, Then hell is the place for me.

– Anonymous – Native American Adivasi Warrier

Why shall I not resist,
can they do as they please
dense forest to desert fruitation to barrenness
Estrange us from the land of our birth
Enslave our women, Blind our vision
Put an end to creation
Neglect and humiliation causes anger
the blood surges through my veins Breaking Barriers at every stroke, the fury of youth pierces the sea of Consciousness, I become myself Why shall I not resist?

– Kavita Chakama

## Postcolonial Literary Responses across Globe

Postcolonial and Fourth World of Indigenous Literary responses are ever giving sources of inspiration to the Global World Literature in the contemporary scenario. These are the voices of native cultures and struggles which were once treated as inferior, savage and primitive by Eurocentric literary canons. Noam Chomsky is very much optimistic about the cultures, works of Literature and identities of native, aboriginal and indigenous communities when he says that all over the world, those we call *'primitive'* are trying to save those of us we call *'enlighten'* from total disaster. Postcolonialism addresses centuries of painful subjugation, wretched marginalisation and shrewdly planned deculturation of history of the third world countries which might not be washed out very quickly. The struggle against the colonial mentality is an unending process, but the humanitarian literary writings can give sharp tongues to these ideological struggles.

> Postcolonialism refers to the period after colonialism, the Post-Independence period of formerly colonised countries. A third world a possible usage of postcolonial associates it with writing and other forms of cultural production which display on oppositional attitude towards colonialism, which is to a greater or lesser degree anticolonial in orientation. Such usage makes it possible to refer to text produce in the colonial period as 'Postcolonial' and discriminates between those that contest colonialism and those that exist in a relationship with it. (Thieme: 2000:02)

The History of the sociology of the world is the evidence that the Native American adivasi, Australian Aboriginal, African Adivasi, Maori Adivasi of New Zealand including a significant population of indigenous communities of Africa and Asia were brutally colonised by western imperial powers. These adivasi communities have faced wretched subjugations and tolerated dehumanising pains from white-masters who looted their valuable natural resources, their land, forest, water, and mountains. British imperialism has snatched everything along with the chastity of indigenous women and sons in the name of slavery and white supremacy. These dark phases of human slavery were never treated sympathetically in Indian English Literature.

The white settlers tried to prove that they are the omnipotent and the whole world is their colony, the people of the third world are their markets and the indigenous communities are their unpaid slaves and laborers. In the name of *White Man's Burden,* Britishers tried to civilise the orient or indigenous communities. These white colonisers distorted the adivasiism and native-communal cultures. Imperialism has disoriented them from their natural-environmental rituals. Along with many long protests and resistance movements against colonialism, these communities of Asia, Africa, Australia, and New Zealand got emancipation from the bloody claws of imperialism. Once these colonized communities started writing about their ethos pathos, predicaments, protest, resistance and deprivation under imperialism and then these kinds of Literature came to be known as *Postcolonial Literature* or *Commonwealth Literature.* It is a serious question if the historical exploitation of colonies and indigenous communities is called Postcolonial Literature, then what is the terminology for the historical exploitation of Adivasis of India who are the ancient inhabitants of this land? Adivasis in India are those touched souls who were multiply colonised - internally, externally, psychologically, and economically. When we study the History of adivasiism in India, we can relate adivasi life with every theory of Literature from classical to post-globalisation. However, still, we do not find such discourses in Indian English Literature which can give justice to the adivasi world of disillusionment.

When a profound peep was executed into anthropology and in ancient Indian History, we come to know that colonisation of the adivasi is an old phenomenon. The adivasis are colonised and exploited from the ancient period of the *Varnashram* system by the Aryans. Adivasis were defeated by Aryans and sent to the forest with no hopes of life and upliftments. From the 11th to 17th centuries, they were colonised by Mughals, later by Rajputana and finally by the British East India Company. In the contemporary period of Neocolonialism, they are again robbed and subjugated by oppressive state policies. If this is the present ground of adivasi existence in India, then it must be admitted that Adivasis are *Multicolonised* in India for the last many centuries. In the western countries, a novel comes forward as the criticism of society, but in India, the elite classes considered it as inferior because it hammers on their established hypothesis of the superiority of being ruling classes. After Independence, because of the concept of modernity, the themes of metro life dominated on rural life of India, so in the Literature. That was the starting point that Indian English Literature has gone away from the rural sensibilities of common masses.

The Neo-liberalism or Neo-colonisation of the Third world is a capitalist process to minimize the humanitarian feelings among human beings. Therefore after the 1980's, we find very few novels that deal with Indian agrarian life. The agrarian novels deal with the resistance against imperial bosses, but Indian English novelists could not familiarize themselves with rural India. The Broken Identities of the adivasi culture and pangs of untouchability of Dalit have been rarely presented through the Indian English novels. The village identities became weaker in Indian English fiction, because the writers consider themselves as urban and metropolitan, having no relation with poverty and more impoverished life of the village culture. In the ancient Vedic Literature, we get glimpses of adivasi life. The regional Literature of India is very enthusiastic about adivasi life, therefore; we find their references in Indian epics. This tradition of adivasi's representation was not continued in postcolonial mainstream Indian English Literature. Anand Mahanand in his volume, *Adivasi India in Fiction* opines:

> Adivasi participation in sub-puranic and epic traditions of myths and folktales gives evidence that they were not an isolated lot. One can see the impact of epics heroes-heroines such as Ram. Sita, Laxman, Ravan, Bhima on some of the tribes in central India in their myths and lore. The present-day Gonds call themselves children of Ravana. In the same way, ancient Sanskrit literary works such as Panchtantra, Kathasaritasagar, Vishnu Purana, Kadambari and Harsha-Charita give descriptions of the adivasi which clearly show the interaction between the adivasi and the non-adivasi traditions. (Mahanand: 2011:23)

In the postcolonial Indian English writings, man, became the center of writing; earlier were the community, nation, and society. The Indian English Fictions deal with the issues of identity, existence, anxiety, and suffocation of individuals having no place for suppressed communities as its central theme. Adivasis faced the same crisis in the postcolonial scenario of Indian English Literature. We can take examples of novels. *The Suitable Boy, The Glass Palace, In an Antique Land, and The Inheritance of Loss* where characters are taken from different nations and cultures. These novels deal with cosmopolitanism and globalisation but not with the nativity, aboriginality and the other significant causes of India's poverty and various disparities. Though in mainstream writings, nostalgic feelings toward motherland come spontaneously, in reality, they know very little about their own country and the fundamental existential problems of marginal communities. Therefore famous critic, Shambhunath, foregrounds:

> Indian novels are writing in English to deal with cosmopolitanism where a character does not restrict to a particular geographical territory. There is the globalisation of characters and situations in such fiction writings. Such novels are the example of faceless and identities generations in cosmopolitanism. These novel writings project faceless as facefull because, in the concept of Global Village, only faceless – identities can establish themselves as cosmopolitan. This Indian English novelist looks at India far away from their territory and tries to assume that how is India? (Shambhunath: 2016:206, Translation)

While writing about the circumstances of the development of India, during the colonial and postcolonial periods, it seems that multicolonialism of the adivasi, their loss of cultural identities and distorted adivasi territories, do not find a prominent place in the mainstream History of Indian English Literature. Their adivasi and non-adivasi writers sustained the oral traditions of the Literature of the Native American tribes and the tradition of African adivasi Literature, but a rich heritage of adivasi oral Literature was not Literaturized by the postcolonial Indian English Fiction Writers. In this regards, Vibha Chouhan, comments:

> The Adivasis have been kept out of the social-cultural and literary History of India; they have also been not allowed to play any meaningful role in the contemporary agenda of development. There has been a growing feeling, particularly among the Adivasis, that mainstream intervention does not mean much in terms of social and cultural upliftment of the Adivasis who continue to be made the easy target of exploitation. This anger gives rise to get articulated through the construction of identity at variance with the forces that exploit them. The Adivasi see themselves as original inhabitants who lived before settled society came into existence but have not been given their due. (Edt.Devy: 2012:61)

The novelist and readers of India should not forget that the concept of *Global Village* is nothing but the process of *Reestablished Colonialism* or *Internal Orientalism*. The protagonists or heroes in postcolonial Indian English Fiction, deal with the themes of migrated generations, diaspora cultures, and identities personalities, as we can see them in the novels of Arun Joshi. The characters like Billy, Sindi, and Ratan Rathod, always lie in existential dilemmas, belongs to no culture and no society. The global village is the wonderer's village and a touring village, where nobody is serious with other "s pains and sufferings. The Mainstream writing culture of India is unsympathetic towards the suppression and marginalisation of broken communities of the adivasi and the Dalit. Indian writing in English is the best example of the writings of the diversion from native agrarian sensibilities to individual grief, isolation, anxieties and in toward worlds. Adivasi disorientation and subjugation are still never seriously represented through literary ways by the academician and governmental authorities of India since independence. This emotion of deprivation is crisply presented in the following Adivasi poem:

> Can you tell us when Shiva was born? Can you tell us when Jesus Christ was born?
>
> We were here even before that, and they were born much later they were born amidst human being, we were earlier than them

> Its seems that the tribes have the sole responsibility of developing the country
>
> Why are all dams' factories and firing ranges built only in the adivasi area?
>
> I also want to ask them, Is this the only way you have to develop the country. (Edt.Devy: 2009:13)

The novel is the studies of criticism and various possibilities of the national and individual life in a culture. The novelist vision should be broad enough to capture the gloom of the marginal communities which are outside of the central periphery. Such comprehensiveness rarely seems in the colonial minded postcolonial Indian English novelists. The process of novel writing cannot be separated from the historical and political realities of a nation and society. The Indian English novels in the contemporary period are full of fusion of histories and politics. The adivasi history in India is having the heritage of thousands of years. Their political exploitation is the most debatable issue in non-fictional and anthropological case studies in India, but still, our Indian English literary stalwarts could not present adivasi's history-political realities from their fiction writings.

In many countries, the novel is taking place in History. In History, its incidents can direct national policies. The historical senses can be strict towards a particular community and favorable for particular classes. Therefore, in Indian English Literature, we rarely get the depictions of adivasi life, but national mainstream life is at the center of literature writings. The novel has challenged the authenticity of the History of the world. The Postcolonial Literatures of Africa, Native America, and Aboriginal Australia have challenged the empirical power and recolonisation of the History of these subjugated nations through their postcolonial responses. The novelists like Chinua Achebe, N Gugi Wa Thiong, and Chimanda Achebe have challenged the stereotype colonial history through their literary writings. Regarding this reality, Shambhanath points out, "Novel is taking the place of History, it is filling the gap which remains empty by History, and therefore people are interested in reading novels than History. The novel can give real voices to the suppression and exploitation of marginal subjugated classes. It is collective reminiscences. It is the record of the unseen, unheard local life of the adivasi and native people." (Shambunath: 2016: 227, Translated).

Postcolonial Literature has provided a big platform to the native writers to describe their state of alienation, rootlessness, detachments, and homesickness because many of them have left their country and settled in Britain, America, France, Canada and experiences phases with of life. These postcolonial responses wanted to define the world in their terms because they no more wanted to be judged, to be identified by the western standards of literary creativity. Postcolonial Literature is heterogeneous products of various cultures and mentalities which should be appreciated with its differences and diversities both sympathetically and intelligently. The postcolonial Literature has broken the dominant Eurocentric racial monopoly of the white Literature and gave a high pitch voice of protest and resistance to native culture. In this regards, Mohit Ray, in his book, *Studies in Commonwealth Literature,* foregrounds:

> Eurocentric definition of civilisation refers to only those literates who understand the white man's burden, language and culture. Europeans have obliterated several native cultures all over the globe as a part of establishing political, social and cultural hegemony. In today's postcolonial and multicultural societies, the issues of native identities have occupied most of the postmodern and postcolonial debates, as a native of the colonies is the original inhabitants of the land. (Ray: 2003:76)

The postcolonial Literature shows the decolonisation of the mind of the colonial subjugated countries in which suppressed identities and marginal cultures started writing about their broken dignities which were distorted during the colonial ruling. Africa was the most broken and oppressed colony ever. Through poems, prose, biography, autobiography, and fiction, many African writers have given way to their stories of distortions. All these African writers have given importance to their native languages. Wole Soyinka's Nobel Prize-Winning novel, *The Interpreters,* is a dream of a new emancipated Africa. Christopher Kigbo was a poet of high emotions like W.B.Yeats or Ezra Ponds. His Story *Labyrinth* is the pathos of a tortured soul that has craved for identity. Chinua Achebe's *Things Fall Apart* and *The Arrow of God* is the classical study of the Ibo adivasi society and how they were crushed by imperial capitalism. N Gugi Wa Thiong wrote about Africa's brutal exploitation under dominant westernisation through his famous novels, *Weep Not Child, The River Between* and *A Grain of Wheat.* These novels are the postcolonial manifestos of the emancipation of the Third world kinds of literature.

Postcolonial Australian Literature flourished under the leadership of A.D. Hope, Judith Right, Peter Porter, Patric White and Thomas Kennelly. Peter Carrey has given richness and velour to Australian Postcolonial sensibilities. The stolen Generation of Australian Aboriginals is a dark episode in human history, and after colonialism, through postcolonial literary responses, these nightmare memories were written by the above Australian literary stalwarts. Canada is a rich territory that was brutally exploited during colonialism. Therefore the postcolonial literary responses of Canada are modern, rich and full of resistance against imperialism. A.J.M. Smith, Raymond Kninster and E.J. Pratt are the real pioneers of Canadian poetic tradition. Margaret Atwood filled variety and richness in Australian postcolonial novels. Alice Munro and Michael Ondaatje dealt with postcolonial social, political and cultural realities. Michael Ondaatje is famous for his celebrated novel, *'In the Skin of a Lion'* in which he presented and justified the Canadian National Ideology. Australia's aboriginal Literature about stolen generation is very much similar to the circumstances of adivasi's conversion in various religions and ideologies

The novel writing in New Zealand had flourished in the last decades of the Nineteenth Century. *William Satchell* dealt with the postcolonial women's sensibilities of New Zealand. Satchell created in his work the literary myths of New Zealand. Maori Adivasi culture and Pakeha culture finds its expression in his writing. The brutal crushing of natural resources, exploitation of nature, barren urbanisation, cultural revival, and feminist revolution all took prominent places in New Zealand's postcolonial literary voices during 1960-1980. Maurice Ghee and Michael Henderson enrich the postcolonial novel writings of New Zealand. A committed spirit of humanitarian attitude and values marks postcolonial New Zealand's Literature which serves as a paradigm for the multicultural future of its society. Adivasi Literature in India should be studied in the light of the spiritual enlightenment of Maori Adivasi of New Zealand.

The Postcolonial Literature has shifted the center of the Eurocentric dominant literary canons to the marginalised and oppressed section of societies of the third world. These Literatures have given voices to the suppressed feelings of being robbed and perished of the distorted communities of the world. Positively, these postcolonial literatures have influenced the Indian English fiction writings, and immediately after the east-west encounter, culture clash, racial discrimination, sense of alienation, homesickness, the deep-rooted concept of hybridity and nationalistic concern became the significant themes of the Indian English fiction writings. These voices of the Third world nations rejected stereotype norms of sophisticated European themes. This postcolonial Literature was literary, non-alignment towards western canon of scholarly presentations. These revolts of postcolonial sensibilities took central acceptance in many newly liberated countries in Latin America also. Requisitioning and rewriting of The History of the colonized cultures became the hallmark of postcolonial responses. In this regards Joseph Chandra, in his, *Classical to Contemporary Literary Theory: A demystified Approach*, observes:

> One significant outcome of postcolonial Literature is to undermine the universally acknowledge claims once made on behalf of Literature by liberal humanists. If Literature is said to possess a timeless and universal significance, cultural, social, regional and national differences and outlook are indirectly disregarded. The tendency is to judge all Literature by a signal, supposedly *Universal* standard. This universalism is rejected by postcolonial Literature. (Chandra: 2012:129)

The initial concept of postcolonial Literature is to focus on the rewritings of colonial slavery, several exploitations of the native cultures under imperialism but sometimes while presenting postcolonial views, we doubt old slavery codes. During the colonisation, the British have taken the advantages of Indian diversities. Caste, religion, and localities of Indian masses were different, so they implemented their policy of *divide and rule.* They successfully implemented their economic policies and tormented pre-Indian unity among the different Indian communities. In postcolonial Indian English Literature too, English writers have focused on elite themes and diverted the attention of readers from the national struggle of freedom towards popular themes. They tried to divert the economic, social, cultural and religious disparities of India, which evolved with growing globalised policies. The postcolonial Indian English fiction writers do not focus on Neo-colonisation and Neoliberalisation, which is bringing havoc to the identities of Adivasis in India. The Postcolonial Indian novelists do not speak about internal casteism and internal orientalism which is also a critical phase of postcolonial rewritings of the History of colonised countries. Mainstream proclaimed that there is neither scope of the struggle for neo-colonisation nor internal colonisation through Literature. They remain silent while deciding who is responsible for the Adivasis severe marginalisation. Mainstream writers keep mum on the topics and divert to debates on different directions. In this regard, Shambhunath foregrounds:

> Theorists and critics of postcolonial Literature do not claim that literature of India as national or democratic literature of India. They call these peoples Literature as postcolonial Literature. These theorists speak about histories and not about History. They observe this History that there is no correlation between them, but there is a difference between them. (Shambunath: 2016:229 Translated)

In India, After Independence, novel writing has flourished very swiftly. Experiencing from colonial exploitation, it was expected that the adivasi, Dalits, marginal, subaltern and feminist would have a new platform to express themselves in the Indian context. To some extent, Indian English Fiction writers have given justice to Dalit's and the marginalisation of women. The freedom struggle and caste-ridden Indian society peeps again and again through their writings but so far as the adivasi community which is to be considered as an ancient clan known by several names like *Adivasi, Aboriginal,* and *Indigenous,* finds no accurate depictions through the postcolonial Indian English Fictions. First of all, we must know the meaning of the word *Adivasi-Adivasi,* their past, culture and their ancient civilisation. In this regards, Meena Radhakrishan, Opines:

> "It is not an accident that the word 'Indigenous', 'Aboriginal' and 'Adivasis', all literary means an original inhabitant. Terms like Adivasi, Adivasis, and Indigenous have genealogies which arise from the specific historical-political Indian context. Historicising and contextualising these terms is the only way to understand the significance of nomenclatures current at a particular period. (Radhakrishan; 2016:02)

Right from the beginning of human civilisation which is comprises the history of ten thousand years of human civilisations; adivasi-aboriginal finds their existence in many parts of the world. In prehistoric India, we find the references of the adivasi in the epic like *'Ramayan'* and *'Mahabharata'* and many other religious books. Some of the historians say that adivasi are the decedents of *"Sindhu" and "Harappa"* civilisations. They are the native and indigenous people of this soil. The human civilisations have gone through a rapid period of change for the last hundreds of years in the name of kingship, slavery, colonialism, castes, freedom struggle, women emancipation, modernism, postmodernism, globalisation and neocolonialism but the metanarratives of Indian literary discourse still unable to project the adivasi problems on the International platform of pieces of literature. The Adivasi community has shown its presence in every aspect of social transformation. In India, these transformations were hazardous in the case of adivasi people because, during the last three hundred years, adivasis have gone through the trauma of various domineering forces in the name of progress. It was expected that in order to understand the predicaments of Adivasi/Adivasi, novelists, historians, academicians, and journalists would check the consequences of mechanisation, digitalisation, corporatisation, neo-colonisation, and sanskritnisation on Adivasis but these realities of adivasi life remained unchecked. Under the term of development, by constructing several big dams, water reservoir projects, field firing ranges, wildlife sanctuaries, forestation, industrialisation and mining projects, adivasis are made the first and the foremost victims of the massive destruction forces of modernisation. The danger of industrialisation has resulted in becoming a adivasi community as marginalised, laborers, more impoverished and economically destitute.

## Bare Existence of Adivasis in Postcolonial Indian English Fiction

The distortion and displacement of adivasi in India are very much similar to the exploitations of adivasi Africa, native America, and aboriginal Australia. As the adivasi were robbed during the process of British colonialism, all these aboriginal communities were also suffered during the process of neo-imperialism. The meanings of modernisations for the indigenous communities are not much less than cultural genocide. This was not the exploitations of natural recourses, land, and water but also of their cultures, traditions, and women who were brutally spoiled and damaged. The postcolonial pieces of Literature of Africa, North-South America, Australia, Canada, and New Zealand speaks about these dehumanize exploitations, but in postcolonial Literature of India, progressive voices remain silent about several exploitative policies against adivasis. This is surprising that we do not make the literaturisation of adivasi's cultural distortion in fictions and poems. In this regards, Asha Susan Jacobs, in her essay, *Narrating Adivasi Identity,* observes:

> Imperialism has brought the deforestation and mindless consumption of natural resources. In the world of native, the living and non-living, the human and the non-human merged and are bound to each other: the natural elements and the native witness atrocities committed against nature in the guise of development. To make way for the plantations, they

> make the mountain bald. Both the landscape and the women are raped, discredited and despoiled. (Jacobs: 2015:293)

Postcolonial Indian English Literature and the novelists took delight in writing and rewriting on the subjects of poverty, partition trauma, Indian freedom struggle, east-west encounters, existentialism, Diasporas, and migration generations but the 9% of adivasi people which comprises around 12 core populations in India, seems invisible in their literary works. Though there are lots of case studies on anthropology, sociology, History and economic studies on Adivasi region literary silence on their exploitation and hardships always stun us. Adivasi's cultural and territorial displacement barely exists in postcolonial Indian English Fiction. These writers, who wrote about the British colonialism and its destructive effects on Indian subcontinents, find the imaginary perceptions through their writings about the colonial consequences on mainstream Indian society. These Indian English literary stalwarts could not become the mouthpieces for these Adivasi who are having the first claim of being an indigenous community of these geographical territories. In this context, B. Poovilangothai, observes:

> Indigenous is an umbrella term often refers to the heterogeneous groups of indigenous populations which include aboriginals in Australia, Maoris in New Zealand, First Nation In Canada, Native Red Indians in America and Adivasi-Adivasis In India. Aboriginal, adivasi, Indigenous are some of the legitimates terms used by different countries to refer to the indigenous peoples of their nations. (Poovilangothai: 2016:17)

During the period of colonisation, which was a period of slavery in India, Indian cultural, economic, historical and social upbringings were brutally tormented. In any colonised country, it took some span to write the Literature of resistance against the brutal exploitation by imperialist cultures. The resistance through literary writing was merely a dream for Indians during the colonial period but with the initiative of Lord Macaulay, Wood's dispatch was implemented in India, and the way of English education made way for Indians. The educational facilities have started but not for all social strata's of Indian society. It was expected with English education in India, Indian writing will give voice to exploited, distorted and broken communities but Indian fiction writers took much span to introduce subaltern pain and hardships of Indian society in their writings. Regarding the postcolonial literature critic Jha opines: "Like other subaltern theories of literature, postcolonialism stands for those who have been sentenced by history to subjugation, diaspora, and displacement, empowering the marginalised by retrieving the voice, space and identities silence by colonial power" (Jha: 2006:194).

If postcolonial Literature represents ruthless urbanisation, industrialisation, erosion of ethos and loss of cultural identities during the colonial period, we do not find adivasi and their smothered identities as a most distinct part of postcolonial Indian English writings. We find Dalit discourse, famine discourse, study of marginalisation and the subalterns, but in these significant discourses, we do not find adivasi History, their indigenous customs, and aboriginal traditions. They have vanished from the postcolonial waves of Indian English writings. Nobody thinks about their multicolonialism. In this regard, Gourishankar Jha, comments:

> With the reform in the freedom movement of the nineteenth century began the primary phase of anti-colonialism which sought the tradition to be re-examined in the modernism of fifties and sixties, there was also a pan-Indian shift insensibility, for instance, the Dalit movement the women's movement, *etc.* In modernising postcolonial tension and anxieties are visible the colonial education, ruthless urbanisation, human industrialisation, loss of faith, erosion of ethos, challenges to the identity, *etc.* (Jha: 2006:194)

Actual Indian English writing flourished and noticed by International literary platform with the writings of the stalwarts like Mulkraj Anand, Raja Rao, R. K. Narayan, Bhabhani Bhattacharya, Manohar Malgonkar, Kamala Markandeya, Arun Joshi, Chaman Nahal, and Khushwant Singh. They were the harbingers of the literary prosperity of Indian English. These literary eminent checked social, political and economic aspects of Indian society during the colonial period and gave way to their observations through their postcolonial outlooks towards India. The concept of Nation, Poverty, East-West cultural clashes, hybridity's and gender issues was delineated through their pen and painted a larger canvas of humanitarian values through their writings. During these periods of Indian English Literature, writers look very ignorant about the indigenous communities of India which were brutally tormented under this social turmoil of freedom struggles and various land policies of the British Administration.

The postcolonial Indian English fiction writers of India have never taken colonisation as a severe subject for creative writing. A novelist like Salman Rushdie, Anita Desai, Kiran Desai, Arvind Adiga, Geeta Mehata, Menorah Malganokar, Arun Joshi and Kamala Markandeya, wrote about the east-west encounter, but they lack serious comments on colonial exploitations. They are westernised by their outlooks, mentalities and subject selections. Romanticism, glorification, superstitions, kingships, kingdom and sophisticated manners were predominated themes of their writings. They loved to westernise the pattern of literature writings. They write about Indian culture, which soothes the eyes of western readers. In this sense, Indian English writers are the sparrows of having golden wings. The mainstream concerns of Indian writings are not favorable with the ground realities of neglected sections of society but with the concerns of western attitude towards India. There are the majority of such readers of these writers in India. The prominent literary festivals are arranged for them. This writer, without any hesitation, distorted the Indian History and presented it according to their wishes. Their observations of India as Indians have lost their credibility. In Indian English literary scenario, they are legging back, but when they speak about minority adivasi and exploited women section of society, secularism and vernacular, they seem opportunist. Adivasis are the most victimized communities during the colonial and after the Independence period. We find only hope for their betterment through literature writings which give priority to adivasi's problems and its solutions. Regarding this observation, Vibha Chauhan criticizes:

> Historians have recorded the 1855 uprising in from detail, especially the active participation of the sepoys and the peasants. The protest by the Adivasi community and their resistance against the colonial regime, however, has not found adequate space in the historiography of the protest movement. This is apparent retention of marginalisation of the Adivasis in all spheres. The partial historical ambrosia has its roots in the epistemology of historical methodology and its implicit collusion with the socio-political power structures. (Edt.Devy: 2012:60)

The second wave of Indian English writers includes Allen Silly, Rohinton Mistry, Mukul Keshvan, Vikram Seth, Salman Rushdie, and Palash Mehrotra. These new generation writers checked postcolonial India in its real senses. They explored the consequences of colonialism, postcolonial hybrid Indian society, upcoming neocolonialism and the growing ratio of materialism. The feminine issues were checked again and again through the writing of Kamala Markandeya to Shashi Deshpande and Nayantara Sahgal to Arundhati Roy. These women writers have given voices to the voiceless and marginal. Many women novelists of Indian English established a strong rebellious voice against bias patriarchal mentality and found a significant base of women studies which was as strong as the feminism of the Western world. We do not find expressions, concern, and sympathies for Adivasi women in mainstream feminist writings. Adivasis are very much neglected from their gaze. Critic M. K. Naik says:

> Indian English Literature began as an exciting by-product of an eventful encounter in the late eighteen century between a vigorous and enterprising Britain, and a stagnant and chaotic India and is now nearly two hundred years old. It is the Literature written originally in English by authors Indian by birth, ancestral or nationality. It is no part of English Literature more them American literature or Australian literature since its difference is the expression in it of an Indian ethos. (Naik: 2007:01)

In India, adivasis are considered as ancient inhabitants of this land. We find their references from the pre-historic period. In ancient literature, we find the resistance of adivasi. In India, we find adivasi existence in *Ramayana, Mahabharata,* and *Panchtantra.* Banbhatt depicted the adivasi life in *Kadambari* during the seventeenth century, but modern Indian English Literature has not taken these adivasi issues and mythology into considerations while projecting them through mainstream Literature. By noticing their presence in this ancient Literature, A. K. Chaturvedi observes:

> Nevertheless form Sambara, a hero of Rigveda, to Eklavya and Matangaka, Adivasi has proved themselves brave, adventurous, courageous, stout devoted loyal integral, honest, unintentionally, skilled and well organised. Nineteen-century writer, John Malcolm verifies these qualifies and makes this statement more convincing when he writes about the adivasis. They are faithful, honest, active, capable of significant fatigue, devoted toothier master, quack and having a kind of instinctive sense of danger and are full of art and evasion (Chaturvedi: 2008: 19)

During the feudal period (400-1000 AD), adivasi territories were invaded by non-adivasi and soon after the process of conversion and sanskrutnisation took place among adivasis. During the Mughal dynasty (12-18th century), the Gond dynasty faced defeat at the hands of Mughals and converted to Islam. Along with Mughals, The Huns, The Sakes, The Greeks and Persians disturbed the adivasi regions. With the coming of the British East India Company in India, the British entered in adivasi areas and captured natural resources and Green forests for economic benefits. While reading the History of the last two thousand years of ancient historical writings and in modern Literature too, we can conclude that Adivasi of India is the hardcore targets of subjugations, conversions and many kinds of victimisations. Noticing their victimisations, Anand Mahananad points out:

> The Grand Trunk Road, which was built through adivasi labor, helped in business, and there was the anal inflow of outsiders dominated the adivasi's in many ways. Most of the adivasi families lost their agricultural lands and lived in a state of starvation. The adivasi were also victims of a host of the middleman who operated between the new ruler and the adivasis. Among the outsider, some merchants and moneylenders exploited the adivasi's in different ways. (Mahanand: 2011:27)

The Indian English writer took much delight in delineating British elite classes and east-west encounters, through their postcolonial writings. However, a significant episode of adivasi revolt against colonisation and oppressive moneylenders remained voiceless because of the negligence of the mainstream writers. Between 1776 to 1930, nearby 450 Adivasi revolts against exploitative British administrative policies in the adivasi region were taken place. Baba Tilka Manzi is to be considered as a first adivasi martyr in the revolt against oppressive British policies. It must be noticed when other provinces, kingships, and landlords had accepted the slavery of the British Empire, considering them as their supremo, adivasi's of C.P. and Berar and adivasi regions of Gujarat and South India rejected their ruling. Adivasi revolted against them and got martyrdom. The social and economic autonomy of the Adivasis was attacked by the rude intrusion of the joint hegemony of the British and agrarian landlords, seeking to enrich their coffers. The Adivasi groups were forced to react to protect their livelihood, culture and natural habited. They were naturally hostile to the imposition of the new order that threatens the breakdown of their socio-economic system. Such interference becomes the reason for several Adivasi protests that took place at the time. We can take a look through some of the significant Adivasi uprisings which could be a larger theme of novel writing for mainstream English writers. The spirit of freedom listed below reveals that these adivasi revolts were not limited to any one region but were spread over a large geographical area inhabited by dominant Adivasi groups.

- Halba Rebellion in Chhattisgarh–1774-79
- Chakma Rebellion in Orissa
- Chuar Rebellion in Bengal
- Bhopalpattanam struggle in Maharashtra
- Khurda Rebellion in Orissa–1817

- Bill Rebellion in Rajasthan–1822-81
- Tarapur Rebellion–1842-54
- Bhil Rebellion in Banswara–1858
- Gond Rebellion in Aliabad–1860
- Maria Rebellion–1878-82
- Bhoomkal Rebellion–1910

The Indian English novelists are aware of their limitations and their responsibilities. They know the Indian issues of caste, gender, class struggle, Adivasi, Aboriginal, and their severe exploitation but they prefer only those subjects which appeal to the metro audience and readers of India and abroad. Now many Indian English novelists are writing scripts for movies. Money is the only God for such writers. Money brings them to popular stories of novel writings. Therefore *Ninety Rupees Literature* becomes a very famous term for an opportunistic novelist in the Indian literary scenario. They focused on controversies and metro-modern themes. They know that controversy can give them money, fame, and popularity as branded *"celebrity"* novelist. "Aestheticism is no more moral word for them, commercialism is god for them. They have set the norm in Indian English fiction writing that is salable is a celebrity". In the contemporary scenario of Indian English novel writing, most of the Indian English novel writers are inspired by the corporate and capitalist values in which policies of global capitalism corrupt the local sensibilities of the characters. That is very surprising that West considers the novel of colonial countries as national Literature and we have drawn the lines of national Literature where most of the broken, distorted population of indigenous never take their rebellious shape for their existential issues. This is the reality of Indian English Literature. Still, we consider this Literature as the decolonisation of mind from western norms of literary creativity. Indian English Writing is yet to be free itself from colonial mentality.

Economic suppression was the only motive behind the uprising during 1857 and the independence struggle of 1947, but the adivasi was fighting for their ancestral claims on land, water, and forest to which they are inherited. Across the world, where British imperialism was taking place whether it was native America, Africa, Canada, New Zealand or Australia, nobody dares to challenge the colonisers as the adivasi of India encountered. It started in 1776 with the martyrdom of Baba Tilaka Manzi and ends with the *Bhoomkal Adivasi Revolt* in

Chhattisgarh. The adivasi have cost their blood for their rights on their ancestral regions. They even fought for the right of each adivasi man. They were in a true sense of freedom fighter. The *Santhal Hool* which is to be considered as the starting of the uprising of 1857 remains in the Background, and postcolonial writer denied this glorious History of Adivasi revolt which was full of thrill, sensation, and tension with higher patriotic sense. About *Santhal Hool* of 1855 which is the unavoidable episode in the History of the greatest adivasi uprising against the British Empire, Sanjay Bahadur comments:

> When the old way of a peaceful but brave tribe is threatened by the arrogance of an empire, savagery of the civilised: and the greed of the affluent, the only thing left to do is a rise in rebellion. The year is 1855. The Tribe, Santhal. Moving through a whirlwind of Passion, greed betrayal, cruelty and sacrifice this gripping narrative of the first mass rebellion against the John Company brings to life a footnote in History that cast a grim shadow on our present. (Bahadur: 2013: Blurb)

## The Marginalisation of Indian Adivasis in Global Perspective

The Postcolonial Native American Literature deals with many different social, cultural, historical and spiritual perspectives. Native American Literature mitigated in the coral traditions of native peoples. Native American Adivasi writing began in the 18th century as Native Americans tried to save their nation themselves and their cultures from destruction by the coloniser. In this regard, Shriniwas Rao comments:

> By writing about their experience, Native American writers hoped to educate non-native Americans about Native American cultures and beliefs and their rights as sovereign human beings. They believed that their written work, including adivasi histories, travel accounts, and protest literature would help for better understanding between Native Americans and Non-Native Americans. Modern historical novels explore adivasi histories to educate readers of today's complex adivasi events. (Edt.Patteti: 2011 196)

In the historical scenario of India, non-adivasi fiction writers can revive the historical past where adivasi encountered with British military with their traditional bow and arrows ferociously. This brave History should be the part of historical novels of Indian English which will be path-breaking, the trendsetter for the postcolonial novelist but our Indian English fiction writers of the postcolonial era have explored the theme of colonisation, the theme of poverty, casteism, gender issues and theme of massacre and partition.

Feminine sensibility during the post-Independence period, subjugation and marginalisation of women also find realistic expressions from their creative writings, but we do not find realistic, ground base history, social writings about the indigenous communities including their several centuries of subjugations. Their brave revolts, their cultural socialism, adivasi's conversions, agrarian life, exploited famine sensibilities and hardship of life during the colonial and postcolonial periods have no expressions in mainstream Literature. The postcolonial Indian English fictions have given only a few glimpses of adivasi life. Sometime adivasis are presented in the novel just to create sympathy or to create hype. Here are some of the novels which show the adivasi life and their marginalised characters who are craving for their identities.

## Peeping through Indian English Mainstream Literature towards Adivasi Life and Its realism

During the seventies, Arun Joshi's *Strange Case of Billy Biswas* came on literary panorama which is to be considered as *Universal Myth of primitivism* where half of the novel deals with the sophisticated, mechanical urban life with it is monotonous humdrum and half of the novel deals with heroes dwelling in the forest with the Adivasis. Here Joshi tried his best to deal with adivasi life, culture and their way of survival, but the character of Billy is dominant in the whole story. It seems that the author is romanticising adivasi life and glorifying adivasi characters. The novel was written during 1971 which was the period of Indian Industrialisation in adivasi territories. Adivasi pathos, problems, and struggle of survival have no ground in this novel. Though Billy's alienation and identity crisis become an essential theme in this novel, the characterisation of adivasi, their authentic way of living life is neglected. Billy's adaptation of adivasi costume and his death is glorified in the ending of the novel. All the sympathy and credit go to Billy and his sense of alienation in postcolonial India. Adivasi life and their continuous sufferings remain in the background.

Another essential novel which was written in 1963, *The Princes* by Manohar Malgonkar has depicted colonial India and smothered identity of princely state during colonialism. The novel depicts the dilemma and anxieties of the Maharaja of Begwad around the turmoils of Indian Independence. A significant territory of adivasi in the Maharaja's state is loyal towards Maharaja which supports the maharaja not to merge the state in the Indian federation, but unknowingly Maharaja cheats to adivasi and ultimately merges his state in the Indian state union. In the novel adivasi are shown loyal and honest towards the maharaja, but Maharaja makes them fools for his political ambitions. In this novel, which has historical backgrounds of the Indian Independence struggle, adivasi's ancestral past; struggle for survival and idealism remain in ignorance. Adivasi become the political victims of the state. They have no sympathy from the state and also from kingship. There was much scope, for the author that he could create an immense panorama of the adivasi History of displacement but he keeps limited himself with political victimisation of adivasis.

Most of the novels of Kamala Markandeya deal with identity and east-west encounter. She is the champion to show the pathos of the downtrodden and broken communities. East-West encounters and racial segregations are the critical themes of Markandeya's novel. Her novel, *The Coffer Dam* deals with the culture clash of East and West, where white man's superiority and marginalisation of adivasi culture are shown. Does the novel show how the imperialistic attitude of Clinton is? It shows how prejudiced of white man takes shape about adivasi community. Markandeya was born and brought up in an elite society; therefore, she is not gripping and constant while dealing with culture clash in adivasi's locality.

Geeta Mehta has registered her name as a successful postcolonial fiction writer dealing with eastern spiritualism and western materials. Feminine sensibility is her strength. Mehta wrote the famous postcolonial novel *The River Sutra.* This novel is a collection of interlocking stories in which she captured adivasi myths and rituals. Hype and glorification seemed through her novel when she depicted adivasi life and characterisations objectively. While presenting Hinduism and spirituality which emerged and shaped on the banks of Narmada River, the heritage of adivasi's, their struggle and faith in primordial powers have not been presented with acute detail study. She has taken many efforts to show adivasi feminine sensualities, but adivasi women and her feminine sensibilities remain in the dark. The novelist is ignorant about adivasi culture.

In the booker winning prize novel, *The Inheritance of Loss,* Kiran Desai, dealt with minimal space to the marginalisation of adivasis. Adivasi's sense of dependence and poverty could not carry in the novel with the sympathy when *Saeed* disliking emerged out of the appearance of the adivasis at the gate of the bakery, suggest-as time progress with no possibilities of their departure. This novel got Booker prize for the presentation of beautiful themes of postcolonial identity crisis and presentation of multicultural characters but so far as adivasi as the community finds no place in her multicultural world. She could create a more astonishing panorama of adivasi pathos and gloom, but *Saeed's* disliking for adivasi seems strange, and the adivasi backgrounds seem illogical in the novel. Both the writers, Geeta Mehta, and Kiran Desai, have much focused on the themes of spirituality, puranic Vedic tradition, multicultural world with different identities. In both novel adivasi characters seem like puppets in the hands of the main characters of the novel.

Arvind Adiga came with prominence when postcolonialism and globalisation of Literature were at its height. All the futures of postcolonialism are presented in The *White Tiger*. The themes of nation, ethnicity, hybridity, sense of detachment, cultural discrimination, political corruption, the inferiority complex of lower classes and cultural deprivations comprise in the novel, but just like another writer, have taken the adivasi themes only for entertainment and amusement. The writer's seriousness about adivasis does not become visible in the novel. The place of adivasis in global culture and mall-media culture shows no hope of betterment. The maltreatment of adivasis, deprivations of their rights from political parties and their victimisations for the vote bank find no convincing presentation in the novel.

The feature of postcolonialism finds its full expressions in the novel of Upamanyu Chatterjee. The sense of loneliness, subjugation and marginal life of adivasi, finds a prominent place in his novel *The English August* which is severally reprinted and made into a film is useful for anyone curious about the reality of modern India. Chatterjee has taken the theme of insensitive political thinkers, violent naxalites, and exploitation of adivasi women, missionary and conversion of adivasis. There was an ample opportunity for the novelist to expose the folly of administration, and root causes of the adivasi problems as his hero, posted in the adivasi belt as the BDO but the author could not create more massive awareness regarding the issues of adivasi conversions and naxalite movement. A novelist could create a reasonable discourse between the willpower of bureaucracy and the problem faced by adivasi communities in the red zone, but the novel indulged in introspection and personal mussing of individual characters.

All the novels mentioned above were written after independence when postcolonial writing was in a full swing in Africa, Native America, Australia, and America. The colonial consequences, sense of marginalisation, sense of subjugation were powerfully presented by these postcolonial writers of adivasi identity and nonadivasi writers. It was expected, Indian English fiction writer will do the same justice with the significant predicaments of adivasis, but nothing happened like that in postcolonial Indian writings, still today, the Indian English writing is flourishing. Marginalisation, exploitation of adivasi is growing because postcolonial Indian fiction writers could not become the mouthpiece of this broken adivasi community. Another possible reason is that all these writers of Independent India having their elite urban backgrounds are insensible to feel the pain, predicaments, disorientation, and displacement of lower sections of the society. In this regard, critic A. K. Chaturvedi opines:

> To bring in the light, the lifestyle and social status of the scheduled tribe, in particular, a few Indian writers have depicted them in their writing. Although twentieth-century writers have profusely dealt with rural life, they have rarely touched upon adivasi as such in their writings. This fact testifies to the conspiracy of silence against a large chunk of our society which is doomed to remain marginalised and lead a life in its periphery. However, the references of the adivasi life one have and find in Indian English Novel. (Chaturvedi: 2008:01)

Indian English writing is following the western canons of Literature. Therefore, materialistic lifestyle, migration generation, fashion, and mall culture seem to peep through their writings. A big trend of popular writing and popular metro literature took place in the literary area after the campus novels of many new novelists. Nevertheless, such popular metro creativities inspired by popular culture across the globe cannot give foundational values to society and Literature. It lacks the authenticity of social realism. We do not find social thoughts or consents of the welfare state in such dry and sophisticated writings.

But on the other hand, regional writing is sharpened by the own experiences of the local writers of those particular regions. We can find the fact and reality of particular issues in regional writing. This is the main reason that we find the realism of adivasi life in the Literature of Jharkhand, North East, and Orissa but not in the glorified Literature of mainstream Indian English novels. Ramnika

Gupta, in her article *Adivasi Literature – An Emerging Consciousness*, comments:

> While adivasi writing in Jharkhand emerges from the movement for a separate state, similar writing in the North East evolved from British time as Literature of discovery for self-identity and self-respect. It enriched the writing of all northeast. Be it Mizoram, Meghalaya, Nagaland, Assam, Manipur, Arunachal Pradesh or Tripura, the search for identity chiseled the Literature. The writer in the Northeast draws extensively on the wealth that he found in his fold tales, songs, myths and stores. (Edt.Devy: 2012:197)

The novelist writing in regional languages does not present adivasi life romantically. They seriously deal with the problems of food, shelter, employment and constitutional rights as we find in the adivasi Literature of Jharkhand and Orissa. They do not present the picture of adivasi women so sensuously and romantically as presented by mainstream English writers of India. In regional Literature, adivasi speaks about social policies, food policies, rural policies implemented by governmental authorities. They know all these policies and their benefits to the adivasis, but in the mainstream Indian English novel, as Arun Joshi portrays them in *Strange Case of Billy Biswas,* they are very romantic and enjoying dancing, drinking and drumming. That must be admitted that the adivasi life and culture written by mainstream writers are written through sitting in their sophisticated air-condition chambers. They are not familiar with the simple routine of adivasi hardships. Therefore when they want to write about these marginal sections of society, writers take them for granted and pictures them from their point of view, which is bias at many times. Noticing the difference between regional adivasi writers and English non-adivasi writers, Anand Mahananad identifies:

> Adivasi writers are socially conscious and feel that it is their responsibility to make people aware of social-cultural reality. Adivasi writers are different from the writers in their representations of Adivasi India. They do not give a romantic picture of Adivasi life and culture, nor do they present adivasis as people rebelling against the system all the time, as Mahaswetadevi Devi tends to do. They also do not give priority or patronage to the adivasis over the communities, but present adivasi's as part of the larger society. (Mahanand: 2011:237)

Throughout this creative writing and research *Displacement, Disillusionment and Disparity of Adivasi Life,* we tried to question the mainstream Indian English writing about their romantic attitude, glorified parameters to evaluate adivasi life. The researcher tried to study why Indian English fiction writers could not give justice to the theme of exploited adivasi feminism, subjugation and marginalisation of the adivasi community for the last many decades. Why mainstream writers are neglected the major adivasi issues like proselytisation, land acquisition and acculturation of Adivasis? This research aims to prove that the adivasi characters and overall adivasi life depicted in postcolonial Indian English fiction are not appropriately treated. They are shown as marginalised as compare to the civilised and white ruler's world. This research strongly argues that adivasi, ancient heritage, the struggle of survival, their characterisation and several types of exploitations are not merely a comic theme and scene to fill up the gap of story development of one's fiction. It is no more part of one's amusement and entertainment. Adivasi's life, ethnography culture and their place in liberalisation, privatisation and globalisation deserve much attention and literary writings. To bring this research into light, the novels of the selected author are studied, analysed and interpreted to arrive at the hypothesis of the study. In these selected novels, the primary sources are investigated in the light of secondary sources and the criticism available in the form of hard copies. The primary method applied for the proposed study is of analytical and qualitative, primary sources are analysed and interpreted to prove the hypothesis.

Throughout this process of creative work, an earnest attempt has been made to be loyal to the hypothesis of the study. This study has tried to examine the involvements and understandings of the particular authors while depicting adivasi characterisation, socio-cultural background with the realisation of adivasi problems. This research tried to show that dealing with adivasi life and characterisation in the post-colonial literature, Indian English fiction writers lack authenticity. Because of the negligence of these mainstreams writing towards adivasi's identical issues and ancient adivasi heritage, a significant population of adivasi communities across India has been disappearing with their heritage, culture, dialect, and identities.

While summing up the introductory part of this proposed research, few lines of Poet Robin S. Ngangom, who is a famous Manipuri poet deals in an ironic expression with anger over the contemporary adivasi subjugations and several marginalisation, he has presented his poignant and pathetic comments about the system sponsor terror and subjugation over marginal adivasis. This reality touches to a sensitive social mind:

Let us wage war on innocent things,
On nature's children, on sons of the soil,
With knives, sticks and stones,
In this small patch of land,
She is forgotten by History, isolated by nine ranges, In ignorant bliss kangleipak lives.
Once prime land, beneficent and fabled
And now the playground of black-marketers,
A haven for fortune hunters where
Non misses a heartbeat
As you feed money, sell honor, paddle justice (Edt.Devy: 2016: 198)

## CHAPTER 2

# Adivasi Ethos and Identity in *The Strange Case of Billy Biswas*

### Postcolonial Indian English Fiction

It is to be considered that postcolonialism observes history as a complete framework of knowledge, observations and investigations, but it is also a moving account of historical senses with which individuals engaged it at different levels. We find our engagements with social, political, historical, cultural and literary issues undermined during colonial rule.

> "......in postcolonial writing, the historical records never get wiped clean."
>
> – Sage Wilson

India was a colonial state from 1750 to 1947 under British Imperialism. This was nearly 250 years – a considerable period, which was full of historical, political, economic and cultural exploitations along with humiliation of native Indian sensibilities in the history of the world civilisation. During this drastic period of colonialism, much of writing has done which presented an immense panorama of slavery in India and the degradation of Indian values. In English literature, novel writing started during 1868 and *Rajmohan's Wife* is to be considered as the first novel written in English. R.K.Narayan, Mulkraj Anand and Raja Rao gave a massive strength to Indian English novel writings depicting Indian realities on the dawn of Indian Independence. We can rely upon their descriptions of India, which can be called as the mirror on that particular time of struggle for Independence. This realism in writing is continued by Khushwant Singh, Chaman Nahal and Anita Desai in the Post-Independence period. The ancient adivasi communities with their historical heritage never peep through their creative writings.

The novel writing in India of the stalwarts, as mentioned above, actually deals with socio-political, cultural, economic and cultural marginalisation during the British period in India. These above writers dealt with East-West encounters and cultural clashes between Eastern and Western ideologies. These writers have proved the fact that colonialism has deeply rooted in the psychology of the people of that particular territory. They have presented the Indian ethos in the Indian literary writings and rejected the colonial slavery and Eurocentric literary canons. These Indian writers have rejected the dominance of one culture over another and dominance of one history over the others.

Nevertheless, still, we have scope to say that we do not get enough representation of subjugated communities like Dalit and Adivasi in postcolonial Indian literature. These marginalised communities are still in the clutches of internal colonisation. After Independence, the harms of this colonisation have been presented through the writings of the above writers. Indeed, a significant portion of the common man's struggle against imperialism in India remained invisible in their writings. In this regards, critic, Jaydeep Sarangi, opines, "Indian history is the stuff tragedies are made of. The history of colonialism in India needs to be told and retold not from an ideological standpoint, as is the case with the official project of writing and then rewriting history valorising religious or ideological constituents, but form a politically non-partisan point of view". (Sarangi: 2007:01)

Soon after the Indian Independence, our nation was struggling for development in every sphere of life. The nation was taking progressive steps in social, political, economic, historical and cultural areas. Soon after, globalisation and its global policies started to create a threat to particular communities like Adivasi and Dalit. They are still struggling for their fundamental rights of food, shelter, education, and health in the present state in India. It is crystal clear that India is now an open market for the European and American Multinationals. Everything that is to be considered as pious, harmonious in the Indian moral value system is now in the trap of multinational corporates which does not have gratitude for the moral heritage and sufferings of displacement of weaker communities. The Adivasi in India is the most targeted victims of the policies of neo-liberalism. In this way, globalisation has not erased, feudalism or casteism, but it has increased the wide gap of socio-economic disparities in Indian society. Mainstream Indian English Novelist are very silent in these issues of all kind of disparities to which adivasis are in co-relation with.

The subaltern historians have presented the discourses of marginalising communities, but they have not presented the role of colonialism in bringing marginalisation to the adivasi community. The branch of subaltern studies is nothing but the study area of those intellectuals who brought up and learned from foreign universities and gives their opinion about Indian subjugated communities through their Eurocentric points of view. On the surface level, it seems that they have decolonised their mind from Eurocentric social values. However, when we observe minutely, their decolonisation of mind has not played any significant role in the upliftment of adivasi and other subjugated communities of India. It indirectly helped to strengthen the neo-colonisation of the weaker section of society. Theories of postcolonialism and subaltern studies in India played a vital role in diverting the attention of common masses of India from neocolonial policies of multinationals to popular themes. In contemporary literature, we notice the significant theories of post-globalisation, cosmopolitanism and statism, but these theories with metanarratives are hardly efficient to depict the distortions and anguish of the common masses of India. The adivasi life has vanished from mainstream social pages of literary discourses. In the Indian literary context, the subaltern theory does not speak about the subjugations of Adivasi from literary points of view.

In the post-colonial period of India, particularly in postcolonial Indian English literature, the mainstream novelist could not give proper justice to the disorientation and decultarisation of the adivasi society. If postcolonial literature deals with the historical aspects like subaltern studies, marginalisation, social-political and economic disparities of Indian society, then this postcolonial Indian observation seems very weak in the case of the Adivasi upliftment of post-independent India. About the historical sense of postcolonialism, critic, Gregory Castle, in his encyclopedia *The Blackwell Guide to Literary Theory,* foregrounds:

> The postcolonial refers to the unpresentable in the colonial, racial difference, legal inequality, and subalternate, all of the submerged or suppressed contradictions within the colonial social order itself. In this sense, the postcolonial present itself in the colonial epoch, especially during the period of decolonisation, when social contradictions are

> expressed in the intensified nationalist organisation and anti-colonial struggle. (Castle: 2007:135)

Indian English fiction writing flourished after the ending period of Indian colonisation. During this period, Mulkraj Anand's *The Private Life of an Indian Prince*, Kamala Markandeyas, *The Golden Honeycomb*, *The Coffer Dam*, Manohar Malgonkar's *The Princess*, Attia Hussain's, *Sunlight on a Broken Column* deal with the postcoloniality. Arun Joshi, *The Strenge Caste of Billy Biswas*, *The Foreigner* and *The last labyrinth* shows the postcolonial nexus which affected Indian socio-political, economic and cultural issues. Feudalism, racism, ethnicity, political victimisation, hybridity, nation- narration and alienation became essential themes in postcolonial writings of Indian English fictionists. Historical tragedies and rememorisation of the past were the most appealing literary materials for the novel writing of postcolonial Indian novelist. Therefore Ania Loomba says that history does not just provide a background to the study of text but forms a vital port of textual meaning. Most of the postcolonial fiction writers delved into the history of India and tried to fictionalise it according to their decolonised mind. In this regard, Gregory Castle, in his *The Blackwell Guide to Literary Theory,* points out:

> The postcolonial study includes those social and cultural situations in which domination takes on specific characteristics of widespread social services, the reaction of populations and suppression of native traditions, languages and cultural practices postcolonial studies is profoundly involved in a project of historical revisionism that makes possible the representation of historical subjects and conditions of existence that had been ignored or suppressed by European historians. (Castle: 2007:141)

The postcolonial literature of the third world became the voice of the protest of suppressed cultures from various colonised and marginalised countries. These countries strengthen their resisting voices, delivered the circumstances of exploitation and attempted to reassert their past, visions, traditions and harsh realities of historical hegemonic suppression. These things were later found out in fourth world literature of Indigenous communities including Africa, Native America, New Zealand, Australian Aboriginal and Adivasis of India. The Postcolonialism speaks about the internal colonialism, double colonialism, internal racial discriminations, cultural hegemonies, the dominance of power and language. However, in the Indian context, a significant part of the aboriginal population never became a part of this postcolonial resistance literature. Adivasis comprise 9% population of the country, and these 12 crores of the Adivasi population are living with their varieties of customs, rituals, nature worships and continuously facing dehumanising problems like poverty, political victimisation, and displacement cultural alienation and rapidly following physical and mental genocide due to capitalism. The postcolonial Indian English fictions show the little concern about adivasi's struggle for survival. This significant population of Adivasi is invisible in pre and post-colonial literary writings of Indian English Fiction writers. Regarding these issues, Dr. Ashok Mashale opines in *The postcolonial perspective In Indian English Novel,* 'The importance of nationalism plays a vital role in postcolonial literary outputs. The concept of the nation has become a curious debate in the postcolonial study. It broads on the concerns of gender, ethnicity, race, religion, caste, language, tribes, class, region and so on. Nevertheless, particularly, the above factors are absent in some postcolonial writings" (Mashale: 2011: 34).

These postcolonial Indian English responses became more vibrant during the 1980s with the emergence of the new novelist in the history of Indian English fiction. Salman Rushdie's *Midnight Children*, *Satanic Verses*, *Moors Last Sigh*, Vikram Seth's novel *The Golden Gate*, *An equal Music*, Joydeep Bhattacharya's, *The Gabriel Club*, G. V. Dasani's, *All about a Hatter*, Amitav Ghosh, *The Circle of Reason*, *In an Antic Land, The Hungry Tides, The sea of Poppies* and *The Great Derangement* derived the impressions of postcolonialism to multiculturalism and universalised their approaches. The literary sensibilities and literary pedagogy of these writers were more globalised. Their literary maturity and observance qualities were more integrated with all the sources available in religion, decolonisation, legends, mythology and symbol of global concerns. In this regard critic, M.K. Naik comments, "Several strategies-linguistic, literary, cultural and even political have been employed in the attempt to prove the utter redundancy of Indian literature" (Naik: 2009:168).

It was expected that the postcolonial senses of Indian English fiction writings would give justice to the issue of ethnicity, caste, marginality, subjugation and the disposition of weaker sections through their writings. These communities are very close to the agrarian society of the Indian village culture. Though India got emancipation in 1947, the East-West cultural encounters and caste-ridden mentalities were still flowing through the minds of the particular social strata of the Indian society.

After independence, we find a narrative of the middle class where we do not find the broad participation of marginal and broken communities of India. The postcolonial writings do not show it's concern about adivasi sections, which played the most crucial role to sustain ecological aspects and the biodiversity life. Our literature in English could not present the adivasi's contribution to ecological sustainability. They remain outside of the mainstream literary expressions. In postcolonial Indian English fiction writings, much effort was taken on political, cultural and economic shaping of India, leaving behind anthropological and ecological concerns of marginal communities. The mythology of the adivasi community, oral culture, landscape and the ideologies are barely found expressions in the Indian context of postcolonialism. In this regards, Bijay Kumar Das, in his *Critical Essays on Postcolonial Literature*, observes:

> Postcolonialism means something that has concern only with the national culture after the departure of imperial power. Like colonialism, postcolonialism is a "state of consciousness", a crucial stage in the continuum of our cultural process and self-awareness. Colonialism involves two types of imperialism-political and cultural. Therefore, myth and history, language and landscape, self and the other are essential ingredients of postcolonialism. (Das: 2007:07)

The colonial subjugations of India which forcefully emerged in postcolonial writing after the Indian Independence gradually shifted its center from east-west encounter to social realism. The themes of hunger, poverty, drought, broken village culture were predominant themes in the writings of Bhabhani Bhattacharya and Kamala Markandeya. The partition and partition holocaust became a significant theme in later postcolonial novels of Khuswant Singh, Chaman Nahal and Salman Rushdie. The concepts of nation and nationalities were discussed through their writings. During the 1980's Amitav Ghosh, Vikram Seth, Shashi Tharoor, Shobha De, Bharati Mukharjee and Manju Kapoor tried to provide strength to postcolonial responses through the themes like migration, globalisation, magic realism and imaginary communities. Indeed, they are the writers of great stature, but it was expected from them that they would give justice to native's cultures through their international literary experiences, but it seems that adivasi and their adivasiism remained alien to them. Adivasis pain could never become their pain.

Strangely, India has a postcolonial history, but America, Britain, France and Russia have not postcolonial literature and histories. The colonised countries have fragmented histories, and colonisers have not fragmented histories and literature. When we go through the fiction writings of Indian English novelists, it seems that Indian English Fiction writers have never thought about this westernised postcolonialism which was favorable for the neo-colonisation of third world countries, especially the weaker section like adivasis, Dalit, women and laborers. In the postcolonial literature of India, imperialism has entered in its new form and shape. Literature is not the exception to it, but this neo-colonisation of literature could not identify correctly by mainstream writers in India. In this new imperial era, shining is new, but the weapons of destruction are old. In the postcolonial literature of India, subaltern writers have written histories from a decolonised point of view. They are still writing the histories of adivasis, dalits, women and laborers including all those deprived sections of society who were never the center of mainstream kinds of literature but still their writings about subaltern classes could not bring any improvements in life of adivasis and the native communities of India. Regarding this truth, Shambhunath identifies:

> Postcolonialism observes history with a particular outlook. It claims the period after nineteen forty-seven as the postcolonial period of India. This study brings out suppressed voices of the marginalised, but while focusing on these issues, fundamental problems are neglected. It became a discourse of the elite section. This is a thought-provoking question that why India in this market of history is becoming a selling product of nationalism. (Shambhunath: 2016:264) (Translated).

Prominent narratives of dispossession, political victimisation and cultural subjugations of adivasis have been excluded in postcolonial Indian English fiction. It is to be said that history is the record of cunning passages and fragmented stories. Today we are the witness of the historical valor of mainstream society, but the bravery of the adivasi community is not there in historical writings of India. This disadvantaged community is still at the margin in the contemporary scenario. In this regard, Hamid Ansari, in his *Marginalisation of Adivasis in India*, explains, "In comparison to other disadvantaged communities and groups, the Adivasis have been less effective in constituting themselves as pan-Indian interest groups and in articulating their grievances through the formal political system. This could partly be attributed to lack of national homogeneity in the context and mechanism that has to lead to the exclusion and oppression of the Adivasis" (Xaxa: 2012:21).

This is very interesting to know that what the starting point of postcolonialism or postcolonial studies is? The answer is astonishing. This study becomes a focus area of study in Third world nations where the intellectuals of the Third nations comes to the First World's posh educational institutions and make their opinions about the rest of the world. In this case, knowledge becomes marginal to power. This is a question before the whole literary world that what will be the validity of postcolonialism and for what time it will keep colonialism in its background? Though after a few years of colonialism and postcolonialism will disappear, it can never be rooted out from the psychology of colonised and colonisers. The western world might consider themselves superior to other countries in a matter of racial superiority, but the reality is that there is high racism in such developed countries. Neoliberalism is controlling the life of the common masses. Therefore it is considered that the opportunity of new historical writings is possible to only those countries like Africa, Asia and Latin America where colonisation has shown its destructive phases and faces. In comparison with postcolonial responses of other countries like Africa, Native America, Australia and New Zealand, it was expected that Indian English writers would give voice to the Indian Adivasis, their struggle for land, forest and mountain will become a source of inspiration to the other postcolonial writers of Third World, but the aboriginal life with its severe pathos, suffering and cultural genocide could never achieve that height in our Indian literature as the Indigenous writing of Red – Indians and Maoris could be reached. In this regard, Felix Padel, on the cover page of his celebrated volume, *Out of this Earth-East India Adivasi and the Aluminum Cartel*, comments:

> Copping the most prominent mountain in South Odessa; are some of the world's best deposits of bauxite. It was expected this aluminum mineral would bring prosperity to one of Indians most unsatisfactory state. Nevertheless, for the adivasi people, who have lived around them since history began these mountains are scared not a resource to be exploited, but a source of life itself through the water they store and release in perennial streams. So metal factories, built-in adivasi areas to mine the mountain summits, are seen as a new colonial invasion, to be resisted. Thousands of Adivasis have already been displaced, in the process of cultural genocide. (Padel: 2010: Blurb)

The Postcolonial Indian English literature primarily deals with mainstream society and their emancipation from colonial rule. The broken identities and sacrifices of adivasi's throughout their various pre-colonial revolts could not take a dignified place in mainstream Indian English writings even after so many years of Independence. It strengthens our assumptions that Adivasis are the victim of internal colonialism in contemporary India. The writers of India, writing in English belong to the middle classes and upper-caste society; have not gone beyond their limited scopes in writing about the Indian reality. If at all they have written about adivasis, it is to romanticise them and their lives.

## Postcolonialism in the Novels of Arun Joshi

Indian Independence did not bring many opportunities for a dignified living for adivasis. In new India, we have an industrial and globalised culture with its popular moll industry on one side and destitute, colorless, poorer and suffering India on another side. This shows that in the theoretical debates of modernism, postmodernism and post-colonisation, adivasi life holds no literary place. Adivasis are the honest and poor community across the globe, so they are as in the same situation in India. Global capitalism has not left them other choices of good living; therefore, many of them embrace the violent ways of revolution for their rights. In the central part of India, adivasis are protesting against many developmental schemes and projects because of the fear of their displacements. Will our mainstream theorist and their theories can mingle between developmental policies, sustainable development, and adivasi survival? Adivasis are the farmers in most parts of India. Tilaka Manzi, Birsa Munda, Telang Khadia, Sidho-Kanho and Gundadhur fought for their adivasi rights on land, water, forest and agriculture. "Post-Independence Indian English fiction is postcolonial Indian English fiction because it continues to evoke colonial legacies in the contemporary society and seeks to complete with English language fiction for International prizes commonwealth fiction prize, The Booker Prize, *etc.*" (Das: 2007:172).

Joshi's the first novel; *The Foreigner* is the story of rootlessness, eccentricity, inconsistency and above all, ignorance towards life. The main character, Sindi Oberai, always, finds himself in a confusing state of identity. He finds, cultural clash between Eastern spiritualism and western materialistic values and considers himself as a byproduct of this predicament: Babu and June, the other character in the novel. Sindi considers himself responsible for their death. He is always with a feeling of guilt in his mind. When he returns to India, he works in the industry. Ultimately the other workers face ruin because of the fraudulent boss. Sindi plays a vital role and discovers his humanitarianism in such a situation. This unexpected change from the feeling of rootlessness to humanitarianism seems unconvincing. Regarding this perplex state of mind, M.K. Naik comments, "This sudden transfer matter is unfortunately neither adequately motivated nor prepared for earlier. The ending thus appeared to be botched up a weakness. Joshi's presentation of his hero's alienation is evocative enough" (Naik: 2009: 230).

Arun Joshi's novels are full of spiritual longings and philosophical aspirations. Postcolonial elements can be noticed when he shows East-West culture clash and westernizes mode of living in Independent India. His situation shows a postcolonial India which has gone through a massive state of change, but at the same time, he has depicted India which has lost a cultural pride because of the adaptation of the policies of the rapid growth of industrialisation and westernisation. His novel imparts knowledge that in the name of progressive civilisation and progressive development, materialistic values, wickedness, and corruption are rapidly creating chaos. Throughout his novels, his viewpoint seems that human rationality and consciousness are praiseworthy, but it seems very useless if it fails to give contentment and peace to the human mind and soul. The following line shows the philosophy of the life of Arun Joshi:

> I am, of course, talking mainly of the so-called upper classes. I did not get to know others. I don't think I have ever met a more pompous or more mixed up many people. Artificially, they were dry as dust. They could no better than mechanically mouth ideas that the west abandoned a generation ago. Their Idea of romance was to go and see an American Monitor or to go to one of those wretched restaurants and dance with their wives to a thirty years old tune. (Joshi: 1971:128)

Arun Joshi's novel, *The Strange Case of Billy Biswas,* presents his complex, sophisticated and intense analytical habit of mind. Here, his search for realisation abruptly ends. Billy, the central character of the novel, looks at modern civilisation as a monster who corrupts human co-existence. He observes the modern way of living and looking at objects creates socio-economic disparities. Money minded society and corrupt machinery weaken man's moral fiber. Billy selects for himself, adivasi life in Satpura Hills of Madhya Pradesh and adopts the adivasi lifestyle. It really seems unconvincing that an America returned, a Delhi Professor of Anthropology, sacrifices everything and embraces a forest life far from the madding crowd of industrial worldliness.

Postcolonial literature deals with identity crises and craves for nationhood. Cultural hegemony, economic disparity and racial segregation make the foundation of postcolonial writings. Arun Joshi's novel gives an authentic treatment to the issue of self-realisation when confronted with the barrenness which is spread by modern sciences. It is the novel that depicts the evil of technological development and the opportunism of commerce that has widened the gap between Indian societies. Joshi's primary concern is to show how to westernise blind values corrupts the soul of a moral man and is the theme of the Arun Joshi's critically acclaimed novel, *The Apprentice*. This novel again slashes modern snobbery, sophisticated manners and false image of a successful life.

Today we are not only ruling by British imperialism, but also we are living in the throat cut competition of globalisation where adivasi territories are the innocent victims of so-called progressive civilisations. This is happening with Adivasis in post-global India. The exploiting machinery against adivasis is well planned and unites in their policies. In the concept of Indian nationalism, adivasis are not holding a significant place than to display their culture in Republic parades. New global policies of India focus on the minerals, metals and resources which are lying under adivasi geography. Multinationals have only concerned with these uncountable resources. Adivasi's poverty and displacement on the cost of these resources is the only farce for the corporates. In the opinion of many revolutionary poets, writers and Indian novelists, adivasi's are the only symbol of carrying bow and arrow, but these stalwarts are not ready to give a literary voice to Adivasis through their English literary crafts.

The novel *The Apprentice* speaks with the reader in a confessional mode. Ratan Rathod, a representative of much Indian youth and central character in the novel, belongs to a middle-class family. Ratan, who is the son of a freedom fighter, wants to live a healthy life but suddenly circumstances changes and his life changes too. Despite being a poet and an athlete, he becomes a clerk and knowingly or unknowingly, he indulged himself in corruption. He shows a real post-independence Indian society, which is full of webs of hypocrisy and corruption, infected with the decadence of materialism and corruption. He presents a society where elites and cast conscious minds never hesitate to torture and taunt the broken sections of the society.

His understandings of the modern humdrum of life can be seen in the following lines, "I had become at the age of twenty-one, hypocrite and a lire, in short shame from morning till night, I told more lies than truth. I had become a master taker. An all this had happened within a period of six weeks" (Joshi: 1974: 27). The *Apprentice* is a powerful monologue of self-assurance. After indulging in corruption and materialism, the protagonist seeks solace in the company of God. Finally, he confesses that there is no remedy for his endless greed for his sin. We can notice here that his detachment is different from the detachment of Sindi Oberai of *The Foreigner*. When the self-realisation of his wrongdoing admits by him, he takes the penance in the shelter of God. He takes the polishing the shoes of the devotees in the temple on his way to the office. Rathod confesses:

> Life might well be a zero, for all I know, but it seems to me that it needs not to be negative. Moreover, it becomes harmful when you take out of it your sense of shame, your honour. I beg forgiveness of a large host; My father, my mother, the brigadier, the unknown dead of the war of whom I harmed, with deliberation and with cunning, of all those who have been the victim of my cleverness, those whom I could have helped and did not. (Joshi: 1968: 143)

The adivasi territory is on the prime target of urban corporates and landlords. Global capitalism, like a sweeping eagle claw, is attacking adivasi's natural resources and ancient adivasi heritage. Partially it seems that during colonisation and in post-global India, adivasi life seems the victim of British imperialism and internal Indian colonisation. It was the lebal given by colonial mentality that adivasis were considered as uncivilised and barbaric because they don't know greed, and they never surrender before exploitation. There are factual hardships in a adivasi culture that in this crowded age of post-globalisation, many regional writers are writing about adivasi life. Regional writers have done justice with adivasi life. The exploitation of adivasis through the hands of corporates and foreign multinationals has been presented by them. Regional writers of India justified adivasi revolts. In this regards, Shambhunath, opines:

> Novels on the local native's cultures bring with them indigenous values. One can notice an indomitable spirit in them. They promote the struggle for survival of native communities and doubts about modernity. They doubt urban morality, market and political hierarchy. Every novel is indeed born from doubts. It is a doubt that highly lacks in contemporary literature and society. (Shambhunath: 2016:32 Translated).

In postcolonial Indian English fiction, we frequently read words like broken identity, deprived section, Adivasi exploitation or Dalit marginalisation. However, the novelist does not give much exploration of internal colonisation and internal discrimination in Indian society through their critically acclaimed novels. In the post-colonial period of India, it can be noticed that there is material progress taking place in India along with gender discrimination, Dalit marginalisation and disorientation of adivasi farmers. Global capitalism has strengthened the exploited machinery directed by the corporate world. *The Apprentice* is a story of the salvation of a corrupt soul that holds a mirror to the world of materialism. We are shocked when Joshi makes the ending of this novel is very positive notes, seeking solace in spiritual life when his character, Rothod comments:

> The crookedness of the world; the crookedness of oneself. How to get rid of it? Revolution of God? The Sheikh had said, but what do I know of either of them, my friend? Revolution or of God? I know nothing.
>
> That is the long and the short of it. The superintendent's God it nouse. of what I am. Sure whose God then? The God of Kurukshetra. And who's Revolution? The Russian, The Chinese? The Americans? Coinciding at some point, I get bewildered, as you can see.
>
> Moreover, do not know what to do? Where to begin but time is short, and one must begin somewhere…consider me as an apprentice, and you will perhaps understand. (Joshi: 1974:142)

Throughout all the novels of Arun Joshi, we can come to know that he is the champion of the causes of postcolonialism where Eastern spiritualism and Western materialism dashed against one another. His celebrated and Sahitya Academy Award-winning novel *The last Labyrinth* deals with the crannies of his character's sartorial and Jungian struggle for the realistic modes of life. The novel shows that his personality is Labyrinth and so are his life, existence, reality and ambitions. Arun Joshi was deeply influenced by the *Bhakti Movement.* Again Joshi tries to show through his character, Som Bhaskar, that colonial and elite education has transformed modern man to ninety in cultural values. Som Bhaskar is a successful industrialist who craves more wealth and finds no faith in spirituality. He craves for the quest of both physical and mental fulfillment in life. His modern outlook towards materialistic social comforts takes him nowhere. Som is a successful industrialist and his greed for money is incomparable. Therefore the reasons for Som's monotonous and erratic way of life are numerous and varied. To crave for salvation, Som finds soothing in the company of Altab,

Anuradha, and George. Anuradha helps him to ignite a flame of spiritualism and inspire joy in him. Som noticed her beauty on the day of Janmashtmi, "She looked like a medieval courtesan around whom war might have been fought. There was a diamond in her nose. Which had not been there before….thee was Mehandi, on her hands? All this preparation I knew was of Krishna" (Joshi: 1981: 121).

Today the adivasi life is caught in the dangers of violence and fear. The caste system in India is also a danger that has not been uprooted yet. There is the uncertainty of life among the adivasi community because of the corrupt policies of bureaucracy and corporate tycoons. Now the voices of protest of adivasis and Dalits have taken place in mainstream regional literature. Indian English fictional writings do not have taken these writing seriously, but these voices have created the new discourse of *Resistance Literature*. Mainstream literature of Indian English is away from this *Protest Literature*. As Som is befriended with Anuradha, he feels an intense feeling of rootlessness, inadequacy, a sharp feeling of the rudderless boat which is missed and tossed on turbulent waves. The novel gives some spiritual, religious examples to find salvation and so Som Bhaskar ultimately starts believing in God, spiritualism and religion. Like the other themes of novels, Som Bhaskar also goes on-mountain in search of salvation and purification. It is a journey towards the mountain in search of Krishna, symbolises, his journey towards the knowledge of his soul:

> Its perfect stillness. I had heard of peoples who were staring into such flames had enjoyed the eternal bliss. Others had discovered their oneness…..with Bramha, A man I once traveled with one of the most sophisticated I have ever met - claimed he had seen in such a flame his previous incarnations. This title flame of mine, however, yielded nothing beyond an ounce of tranquility which of course was not to be laughed at. (Joshi: 1981:194)

Arun Joshi, a writer of magnetic writing skill, dealt with the themes of the traumatic postmodern world, sense of detachment, utilitarianism and craved salvation in his complete writings. His novel justifies the post-colonial way of writings, which is a means of the transformation of different cultures. The themes of his novel deal with spiritualism and eastern religious ideologies which are still rooted in Indian society, therefore these values and systems play a vital role in cultural decolonisation. He addressed that westernisation and materialism corrode our soul and ideology, but native culture and tradition deeply lie in the subconscious mind and inspire us for the fulfillment of life. Spiritualism seems the only way to redemption for his characters. K. Naik opines, "Joshi is a novelist seriously interested in existential dilemmas and equally acutely aware of both the problems of post-Independence Indian society and the implications of the East-West encounter. He is a skilled narrator and can even make an entire novel a long monologue without losing his hold over the reader's attention" (Naik: 2009: 271).

The continuous series of Arun Joshi's novel shows the changing human values, growing materialism, barren urbanity, and the rootlessness of the postcolonial world where everyone seeks his destinations to gain material progress, wealth and reputation. Having all the amenities of life, his characters like Sindi Oberai, Ratan Rathod and Billy Biswas, feels alienation about this modern money-minded world where human compassions and spirituality hardly matters. *The Strange Case of Billy Biswas* is an excellent example of postcolonial Indian sensitivities of generous heart which focuses only on intellectual doubts, erosion of values, and the crisis of faith. The novel is a satire on follies of modern and sophisticated values where everybody wants to seek the meaning of life but fails to find tranquility and spiritual regeneration. Regional writings in India put the adivasis at the center of debates and represent the fact of Adivasi struggle. Indian English fiction writers seem to project themselves as secular as they can show. In their writings about nationalism, freedom struggle, gender treatment, agrarian life and feminist studies, we have never found their contemporary approaches to strengthening the marginal voices of Adivasis. It seems that there is a competition between the orthodox religious forces and nationalist well-wishers for who will bargain better of adivasi territory and natural resources with multinationals. Therefore, Shambhunath points out:

> For economic prosperity, corporates are targeting forest and a river of adivasi land. From previous centuries, landlord and commercials were used to come here and cut the trees, making mines and used to exploit the Adivasis young girls. In the 21st Century, there is dashed between Adivasi Identity and the concept of nationalism, particularly from those periods when multinationals and governments have to interfere in adivasi's life and environmental issues. (Shambhunath: 2016:329, Translated)

Undoubtedly, the language of the postcolonial text is different from the language of power and cultural dominance. In postcolonial language, the novelist finally makes himself free to convey his expression adequately. When we go through the novel of *The*

*Foreigner, The Last Labyrinth* and *The Strange Case of Billy Biswas*, we are assured that Arun Joshi has decolonised the English language and presented the alienation and his monotonous life in a postcolonial way, when he says, "If life's meaning lies not in the glossy surface of our pretensions but in those dark mossy Labyrinth of the soul that languish forever hidden from the dazzling light of the sun, then I do not know of any man who sought it more doggedly and, having received a signal, abandoned himself so recklessly to its cell"(Joshi: 1971:08). Arun Joshi's novel also shows class consciousness and oriental elements of Indian society where the hero of the novels finds themselves engaged with cynicism, corruption, frustration and cultural dilemma. Arun Joshi has given a new meaning to the novel-writing of Indian English during the early Post-Independence period. His most adequate contribution to the Indian English novel is his art of characterisation. K. A. Iyengar gives his valuable remark about his contribution to strengthening the postcolonial base of Indian English writings when he opines:

> The issue between detachment and involvement, differences and commitment, going it alone and communion, is posed prominently enough but not consumed adequately in the action or the characterisation. There is a colorless cosmopolitan quality about the novel that is somewhat disconcerting; or rather, the novel fuels to evoke a sense of place convincingly. These are rootless people tossed about by the wind of chance and the uninvolved and blindly involved alike find themselves prisoners of one or another kind. (Iyenger: 2007: 504)

## Depiction and Characterisation of Adivasis in *The Strange Case of Billy Biswas*

*The Strange Case of Billy Biswas*, which is to be considered as the universal myth of primitivism presents marginal adivasi life where characters from the adivasi community play a secondary role. We are hardly able to know the psychological realm of their minds. Throughout the novel, a significant effort has been made to show Billy as a tortured soul who ultimately meets his tragic end and wins the sympathy of readers as well as of the critics. However, the novels take a condescending attitude towards adivasi life, their paths and ethos, where characters are not so free to deal with the theme of existentialism. The novel does not show any imprint of colonisation of Indian society though it was written in postcolonial India. Again novel is set in the adivasi village of Malaika hills, but the agrarian reality and economic survival issues of adivasis do not focus on the novel. The issues of adivasi land disposition do not find a single word in the novel. In adivasi history, many revolts took place in the Central provinces of India, but the themes of land acquisition by British or internal colonisers do not appear in the novel. The novel does not speak about the inseparable relation between Adivasi and *Jal, Jangle* and *Jamin.* Bangya Bhukya, the famous critic of adivasi rights, observes:

> The colonial state did not respect the traditional land rights of the Adivasis. Ironically, the postcolonial state has been continuing colonial practices to deal with Adivasis land acquisition. The only way out of this problem that the state should buy all land under LTR cases from non-Adivasis and distribute these to Adivasis. (Bhukya: 2012:77)

Billy's anxiety, suffocation, urban fallacy and rootlessness are shown powerfully, but the gloom of adivasi life does not come out through the adivasi characters like Dhunia, Belasia and other adivasi's in the village. The novelist could create a larger panorama of colonial adivasi life in Postcolonial India in this novel, but he fails in such representation. The novel was written during 1980, which was a particular period of adivasi's fight for their rights but the novel is far away from this hardship of adivasi life. Everything is romanticised and glorified in the novel. This novel is the only one-sided presentation of modern, materialistic, sophisticated and westernised life and personal musing on it. This novel and its adivasi themes remind the lines, not for Billy but the adivasi characters in the novel, "was he free, was he happy? The question is absurd, had anything been wrong. We should certainly have heard. (Auden-The Unknown Citizen). When we go through the novel *The Strange Case of Billy Biswas,* we find no hope and no identity for the native adivasi characterisation in the novel. Characterisation is one of the central aspects of the novel, but on the same ground, this novel does not seem convincing. When we studied the characterisations of Belasia and Dhunia, we can hardly call these adivasi characters as real. Colonial mentality peeps through the writer's mind when we read Billy's opinion about: "Bilasia, "I stated to the knot and all the time I was thinking of Bilasia, the fever rising within me once and my chest beginning to chock. Finally, I stopped clutching the ball in my hands as though it were a limb of Bilasia, her head, her breast" (Joshi: 1971: 17)." The Bilasia's characterisation in the novel seems to the victimisation of patriarchal thinking. The whole thought process of Billy shows his attitude of male dominancy and stereotype patriarchal thinking when he reveals his inner self by putting up questions to himself, "What do you think is going to happen to you? Are you going to run away with Bilasia may all you want is to get her into bed. Anyway to you think, you have survived more than a day in this wildness even with the help of ten Bilasia." (Joshi: 1971: 95). Both the sentences, above mentioned, are clear enough to show the typical mentality of internal colonisers towards the native adivasis. Billy's sexual desire is intense in this novel. There is no respectful approach for adivasi women in Billy's mind. His opinion about Bilasia is the perfect example of a body celebration of adivasi women just happened in the popular literature by famous writers. Billy, as a professor of Anthropology, could not share with us the concept of the matriarchal system of adivasis where women play a predominant role in every adivasi custom, rituals and decision-making processes. On the other shore, Bilasia's character seems very submissive, romantic and full of longings.

This is surprising that the leading feminist of India who throughout their writings have been supported the concept of women empowerment did not study this novel or the character of Bilasia from a feminist point of view. This is also a significant failure of our responsible literary consciousness that our concept of women empowerment and women emancipation focused only on urban or modern sophisticated women. The depiction of adivasi women in Indian English mainstream writings has been very demeaning. Our notion of women emancipation focuses only on an urban or modern and sophisticated working-class woman finding no space for the adivasi girl like Bilasia. In Vijay Tendulkar's drama *Kamala*, protagonist Jaysingh brought a adivasi woman from the flesh market of Lohardaga of Jharkhand. We have many references to women trafficking from the adivasi area.

Nevertheless, the forum of women empowerment or elite circle of sophisticated mentality could never raise their voice, nor could they create an echo on the international literary platform, through their celebrated writings. This novel of Arun Joshi presents adivasi as primitive as he can show. The images of drum beating, drinking, and ambitionless identities of adivasis have been created through the novel, but issues of displacement find no touch in the novel. The novelist seems unaware of the industrialisation in adivasi areas started soon after the independence. Regarding this concern, G.N.Devy comments:

> Development, as envisaged by the Indian state, has more often than not turned out to be a nightmarish experience for the Adivasis, leading to a disruption of their tradition. The different projects including large irrigation dam, hydroelectric schemes, open cast and underground coal mines, thermal power plant, mineral-based industries have displaced a large number of Adivasis from their traditional habitats and constantly shrinking economic base has led to their increased preparation. (Devy: 2009:62)

Bilasia is a marginal character, but one more adivasi character of Dhunia is shown in the novel, who is the chief of the adivasi village but his leadership qualities, his ancestral musings are not presented adequately. He is a character who does not speak about the industrialisation in the adivasi area. He just observes everything that is going to change rapidly. Being a chief of a adivasi village, he claims Billy as an avatar of God for adivasis who have come to save them. Notice the statement of Dhunia, where he excessively praises for Billy, "He is similar to rain on parched lands, like the balm on a wound. These hills have not seen like him since the last of our kings passed away." (Joshi: 1971:115). He praises the way Billy stands and holds people with his eyes, saying that the Devi would not have returned If Billy had not been the King himself. These are imagined stereotyped responses that a middle-class author would perceive in adivasi society.

The statement of Dhunia is suggestive enough that the mention of adivasi territory of Satpura Hills of Madya Pradesh was 'parched' and 'wounded', it means something was missing, everything was not going properly in that area. The wounded history and struggle for survival in that remote place has not taken place in the novel, nor has the novelist shown any interest in local adivasi problems. Most of the issues of adivasi's in that region remain unexplored. Adivasi wounds were kept aside. The character of Dhunia is used to glorify Billy but not to explain the circumstances of adivasi life. The statement of Dhunia shows the mouthful praise of Billy, "Have not you seen the way he stands? Who else but asking can hold you with his eyes, the way he does. What is more, the Devi would never have returned if he had not been the king himself" (Joshi: 1971:112). Dhunia being the adivasi leader, his knowledge about the adivasi way of life, about their glorious past, their various adivasi customs have not been appropriately presented. He is just a bard in the novel, who praises only Billy and of his miracles. Dhunia, in a real sense, is a marginal character which does not leave any impression on our mind. As the characterisation is concerned, Billy's alienation is sharply presented by the narrator Romi but the subaltern, subjugated life, disposed culture; several wantings of adivasi life and barren adivasi territories have not been presented in the novel. The glorious adivasi tradition of oral songs, scriptures and lifestyle also seems significantly weaker in the novel. In this regard G.N.Devy foregrounds:

> Centuries ago, Adivasis were driven into the jungle by the Victorian Aryans. They lived in the union, sharing its beauty. They were devoid of the notion of property and possession. There was not even a gender bias. Though the British gave them literary and a script, they had until then preserved their folk literature through oral traditions. They adopted the written words only about a hundred years ago. They not only preserved their literature through a united endeavor of community living and cultural traditions but added to it according to the needs of the times while keeping the original intact (Devy: 2009: 193)

There is a lack of idea of justice in Indian English Fiction writings. These fiction writers have neglected the adivasi issues for strengthening the ruling elite corporate policies. They are eradicating the adivasi roots of ancient cultures. For developing the particular zone of the nation, another part of the nation is colonised in Independent India. In advanced India, today we have the media, digital culture and moll industry. We have high-tech cities like Delhi, Bengaluru, Surat, Ahmadabad, Mumbai, Nagpur and other side cities like Ranchi, Gumala, Palamu, Jagadalpur, Narayanpur, Singhbhoom and Gadhchiroli which are exploited day by day in the name of development. This is the farce in the name of adivasi upliftments in the adivasi heartland. These changing global scenarios have been well known to our novelist, but they want to live in an aesthetic hallucination of academic progress. Modern feudalism, barbaric colonialism and luminous globalisation have made the adivasi situation like hell on earth. To control the anger of adivasis, NGO plays their role as mediator between broken adivasi resistance and multinational policies. These whole situations have opened up new ways for adivasi uprooting and disposition. The dehumanisation of adivasi life, human rights violation can be noticed very poignantly in the major adivasi territories of India, but the English writing in India, particularly fiction writing is silent about the state oppression over Adivasi. Regarding these hardcore realities of adivasi land, Gladson Dungdung opines:

> The fact of the matter is that the villages in Chhattisgarh were vacated for the corporate houses in the name of killing the Naxalite and the operation green hunt will be extended to those areas where there are high chances

> of exploiting natural resources in the name of development. Since there have been a series of protest against displacement in the mineral corridor, therefore, the government are attempting to get the land cleared for the corporate houses through legislation, manipulation and legal guns. (Dungdung: 2013:147)

The Adivasis are the indigenous communities of this land. They are the ancient inhabitant of this land. Their struggle to sustain their identity and resources is very ancient, and these ancient histories of indigenous struggle have been presented so vigorously by the regional writers like Mahashweta Devi, Gopinath Mohanty, C. K. Janu and Gladson Dungdung. All these leading writers have written about the issues of indigenous identity, deculturation, the cultural genocide of Adivasis and dislocation from their homeland. Bhujang Meshram is one of the leading adivasi poets and adivasi critics of Maharashtra. In his poem, he calls upon Birsa Munda – the revolutionary leader of adivasis in the nineteenth century to come again to lead his people's struggle, "Come! You must come to us Birsal come from wherever you are, my Birsa comes as the scythe that cuts the grass. Come as they are that cuts the wood come from here or there East or West North or South come as the wind blows through the field Birsa come as people wait" (Devy: 2015: 193).

These are the expression of an adivasi poet about adivasi martyrdom which shows the struggle and subjugation of adivasis on this land for the last many centuries. Nevertheless, on the other hand in the present novel of Arun Joshi, we do not find a single utterance about the adivasi's heritage loss and the disaster of Adivasi life. The global revolution of adivasi revolt does not find expression in the novel. Arun Joshi's novel, *The Strange Case of Billy Biswas* is excellent and artistic only for those who fully believe in imaginative flight. M. K. Naik, the famous academician and critic of Indian English literature, comments on the novel as follow, "The novels to be a major fictional achievement because it is not, in the final analysis, informed with sufficient imaginative power to make so unusual a narrative convincing, especially in its picture of adivasi society in which Billy finds himself king, its belts and practices and its apotheosis of the professor" (Naik: 2009:230). Though, Arun Joshi has tried his best to project the post-colonial dilemma of Indian society. As a novelist, he is successful only in showing the barrenness and the psychological emptiness of the individuals. The adivasi life, their characters and hardships, plays only a secondary role which is subordinate to the main plot of the alienation of Billy Biswas. The famous critic, Anand Mahanand, commented on this one-sided representation of the theme of alienation and growing materialism, where adivasi is invisible with their genuine problems. He criticizes:

> Joshi fails to notice social alienation, the bare existence of adivasi in mainstream subjugation and disposition of adivasi and more of internal colonialism upon adivasi life and provides only a partial view of indigenous aboriginals" life which is convenient and easy for writers. In sum, as Hansdak points out, the novel fails to portray longer issues of Adivasis life and remains romantic and glorified in essence, and the adivasi society is reduced to a picaresque backdrop against which Billy Biswas's tragic destiny is enacted. (Mahanand: 2011: 07/83)

The voices of the marginalised have moved from the periphery towards the center in the last few decades. Therefore a revisionary approach in literary criticism is necessary for the discourse on Indian writing in English. Dalit literature has raised questions from a dalit centric point of view, just as feminism has been studying literature through a gendered lens. This truth must be commonly accepted that the discourse about marginalisation and women's empowerment will never achieve their objectives until the mainstream literary canon will include their voices in mainstream literature and show their intensities and involvements with subaltern issues. While depicting this Fourth world of Adivasi Indigenous ethos with their social, cultural and communitarian background, these discourses should include the realisation of adivasi's survival problems. Finally, it's imperative to convey the message of Garden Brotherstone to mainstream English writers of India:

> Redefining of native – aboriginal myths, culture, customs and way of life through their available oral literature is an essential source of understanding and listening to the ancestral voice that instructs to find their connection with their pre-historic cultures. The evaluation of the fourth Indigenous world is a reflection of socio-economic, literary and cultural circumstances that affected the lives of aboriginal or of first citizens which are needed to be explored by mainstream writers. (Brotherstone: 1995:37)

When we read the depiction and characterisation of adivasi in *The Strenge Case of Billy Biswas,* it seems far away from the actual reality of adivasi life. The whole story of the novel covers Billy's alienation, finding no scope for adivasi life and its expressions. In the novel, adivasi's life has played only a supplementary role. The attitude of the protagonist towards Bilasia or adivasi women, in general, is condescending and demeaning. He imagines the sound of the adivasi drums at night after night and a girl in his arms, a warm, full-body, a adivasi girl. Here the man women relationship is not based upon the individual. Bilasia is just a body, erotic, exotic and adivasi. This is a kind of internal orientalism, how the upper caste, the educated, look at adivasi society as romantic and exotic. Adivasi women who live in the forest faced several problems, but in the novel, we find only body celebration of adivasi women. Billy is very much passionate about Bilasia. The entry of the outsiders in the adivasi territory is a much debatable topic from ancient literature. Billy Biswas is also an intruder in the novel but presented as a savior of adivasis. Such outsiders could not understand the tradition and psychology of the natives; therefore they could never be a part of adivasi life. Bureaucracy, officialdom and politician often take the benefits of the illiteracy of the adivasis. Adivasi women always become the victim of sexual exploitation of these outsiders who comes there to protect Adivasis in the name of national security. In this regard, Felix Padel explores:

> Many officials see their presence in a adivasi area as a punishment. The hierarchy that they impose over adivasi is reflections of the hierarchy that is imposed over themselves, which pervade the system inherited from the British. Some of the IAS officers with their elite exams and family background have serious concerns. However, there is such a gap between them and lower officers in terms of status and education that to confronts the issue of corruption requires the greatest courage and integrity. (Padel: 2015:296)

The novel *The Strenge Case of Billy Biswas,* set in a adivasi territory of Malaika Hills of Madhya Pradesh during the 1980s which was a period of adivasi unrest. Adivasi's movement was at its peak regarding the adivasi right of land, forest, and Constitutional rights. The interesting thing is that the adivasi characters and situations, as shown in the novel do not show any similarity with the actual ground reality of common adivasi man. While reading the novel, we do not get any information about the livelihood of the adivasis. Everything is romanticised about the adivasi in the novel. Arun Joshi could not catch the gloom and struggle of survival of adivasi. He is more interested in showing the sense of alienation of Billy, who is the representative of his nature. About the realism of the adivasi life which could be a part of real writing of adivasi culture and their disposition, Dinesh Mishra, opines, "Globalisation resulted in more money pouring in for mining, oil drilling and many other disruptive enterprises. An ever-growing number of intestines usurped thousands of acres of precious land which had traditionally and always belong to the adivasi people, now ruthlessly being thrown out of their habitat, in a most unjust and inhumane way" (Mehra: 2015:144).

Adivasi life, culture and hardships should be read in the light of struggle against mighty British Imperialism. If mainstream Indian writing is making marginal to adivasi, then the concept of nationality will weaken. If there are exploitation and indiscrimination in society, romanticism and glorification will be there in the life and literature of the common man, but this romanticism should not let down the hardships of marginal life. The community which is aware of their social and economic position plays a vital role in national policies. The literature of those communities becomes popular, but this could not happen in the case of the Adivasi community. It seems that today not only information became a tool for entertainment, but literature also became a tool for popular entertainment. Writing history or writing literature means to free the agonise past of those sections of society which sandwiches between the concept of nationalism and imperialism. It is to be said that where there is no dignity of women, there is the destruction of a culture. It applies to literature also. Indian English novelist has not presented the dignity of the adivasi women in their fictions. Writing on adivasi history means to go deep into historical facts of feudalism, casteism and hegemonic structures of India. Therefore, mainstream writers possibly not wanted to write on real adivasi issues. They don't want to shake the hegemonic pillars of cultural domination, and the fictional writing of Indian English is strengthening to this reality.

## Glorification of Adivasi Ethos and Identity

Writer, Ramnika Gupta presents the contemporary adivasi situation though her few lines, without any glorification or romantics.

> Now adivasi have learned to speak
> Now hunger means food or beating means rod now,
> They want the account, for their mountains, river and forest.
> That has disappeared in concrete buildings of the town
>
> (Gupta: 2015: 202)

As we stated earlier, Indigenous history, adivasi culture and aboriginal identity could never become the predominant part of mainstream Indian English fictions. For the first time Verrier Elvin, the anthropologist-writer, took a keen interest in Indian adivasi and their customs, rituals and struggle for survival. He even marries a adivasi woman. Along with some anthropological books, he wrote novels like *The Phulmat of the Hill* in 1937 which is a tragic story of a Pardhan adivasi girl who is infected with leprosy, lives in her village and set a little shop at the distant village. Her lover leaves her and goes to a distant place. Stream of consciousness runs through the novel. The novelist has succeeded in dealing with the personal musing of adivasi girl Phulmat. Another novel written by Verrier Elvin is *A Cloud That Dragonish* in 1938 which deals with the suspicious death of an animal, bird in a adivasi village. The adivasi believes that it is the wrath of a witch but soon comes to know that Motohari and Gunia, the adivasi boy and girl are behind the scenes.

Verrier Elvin has given justice to the adivasis issues because he was an anthropologist and he lived, worked and married himself in the adivasi community. However, when we observe the representation of Adivasis in Arun Joshi's *The Strenge Case of Billy Biswas*, it looks romanticised and exaggerated. A lot of sentences and monologue shows the unwanted glorification of adivasi life, "nobody here is interested in the prize of food, grain or new seeds, roads or elections and the stuff like that we talk of the supernatural, violent death, trees earth, rainstorm, rivers, forest, animates, dance, singing and we talk about women and sex" (Joshi:1971: 83). The novel writing brings several social, political, economic and cultural hopes and doubts of a society. It should have a mirror of collective consciousness and experiences and not favoring a particular caste or class. Novels are the unheard and invisible voices that give voice to broken identities and distorted cultures. In Africa, Latin America, New Zealand, and Australia, postcolonial literature gave voices to marginal communities. Nevertheless, this marginal voices of Adivasi of the Indian soil seems bare existed in the postcolonial Indian English fiction writings.

Billy's observation of adivasi life seems very unreal. The main reason for the adivasi revolt in history was illegal taxation and encroachment of their land and on agrarian territories. It must be admitted, adivasi life is not only the life of singing, dancing and drinking but it is a historical subject of the struggle for the right of self-dignity and their ancestral right over their territories and forests. In this regard, A. K. Chaturvedi comments, "Industrialisation and deforestation are playing havoc with the lives of the adivasi. Technological advancement and developmental projects that may be beneficial to the civilised world are causing irreparable loss to the adivasis" (Krishna Singh: 2015:289). When the adivasi territory of central India was in a state of insurgency during the 1980s, Joshi is presenting adivasi life as very cool, nothing to do with worldliness. Billy's anthropological knowledge shows no similarity with existing adivasi life. His insufficiency of knowledge reveals when he comments about the Adivasi life, "What kept us happy, I suppose were the same thing that has kept all primitives happy through the ages. The earth, the forest, the rainbows, the liquor from Mahua, an occasional feast, a lot of dancing and lovemaking and more than anything else, no ambition, none at all"(Joshi:1971: 86).

Both the statement mention above, from the novel, shows a novelist's arrogance about adivasi ethos. The novelist comments that the adivasis have no concern for rising prices of grain shows the limited thinking of the novelist about adivasi life. The novelist conceders adivasis as ambitionless but he ignores the fact that the Jaipalsingh Munda, a foreign-educated adivasi during pre-independence India, created awareness among the adivasi community about the exploitation of adivasi culture and existence. He aroused self - dignity among the adivasis. Adivasi writer and philosopher like Ramdayal Munda started a mass movement against the adivasi exploitation. A glorious tradition of adivasi revolt took place in India's colonial history, leaving behind the examples of several Adivasi martyrs like *Tana Bhagat, Tilka Manzi, Birsa Munda, Sidho-Kanho and Gundadur.* However, on another side, Billy Biswas says that the adivasi are engaged in drinking, lovemaking, sex and superstitions. Billy's opinions about adivasis are the perfect example of *Internal Colonialism* and *Sympathetic Cultural Hegemony.* Regarding this attitude of Billy, Anand Mahanand, foregrounds:

> It is surprising that a novelist writing about the adivasi in the 1970s fails to see any adivasi movement or struggle active in the regions and portrays the rivals as a quiet and peaceful allot. One also gets the sense that the adivasi world, as describes in the novel is an isolated one and that there is no-connection between adivasi's and civilised society. Billy gets into it and appoints himself its savior as it the adivasi's required Billy's intervention for their well-being. The adivasis of the seventies were not isolated totally from the mainstream. (Mahanand: 2011: 82)

Some of the statements and incidents in the novel, *The Strange Case of Billy Biswa's* seems the example of cultural hegemony and internal colonialism which reminds us of Rudyard Kipling and his *'Jungle Book'.* Arun Joshi painted the character of Billy as the savior of Adivasi by strengthening him with supernatural power which Billy performs several miracles which create tremendous respect in the minds of adivasis for Billy. There is an example in the novel of how a tiger was roaming in the forest and Billy spoke to it, and it went away, "A tiger had been roaming in the jungle for a week, killing our cattle's. Billy bhai went into the jungle and spoke to the tiger, and the tiger went away. That was when we first come to know of his powers." (Joshi: 1971).Many incidents and situations in the novel seem very unconvincing. If Billy had the power to control the man-eater of that region as Dhunia has narrated, then he could also save the adivasi from the drought-like situations. Billy could undoubtedly save them from the drought-like situation. Billy could equally be saved them from the poverty-stricken life. In the whole narrative, nobody is ready to speak about the gloom and paths of divorced Bilasia. Nowhere in the novel, we find the reason for her divorced life, but romanticisation and body glorification of this girl has been given by the novelist. Adivasis are the forest dwellers, they worshipped the forest and mountain, but the novelist could not adequately present their faith in their ancestral heritage. The adivasis in the novel do not appear to be a worshipper of nature, but are full of materialistic, superstitious and having cultural amnesia. Adivasi was never a pleasure seeker. Their past is full of struggles and humiliations.

> Since the Adivasis are nature people, their life is an infusion with the life and rhythm of nature and season. They cut the trees, but they break the stone, but they do not destroy the hill. There is a subtle difference between the way the Adivasi utilises the hill and forest and the way the non-Adivasis makes use of the forests and hills. Due to modernisation and expansion, an extension of town and cities and in the name of developmental works the Adivasis are driven out of their homes, which is forest and hills, Koel Karo, Narmada project are some of the examples of this. Because of all this, the Adivasis are displaced in their own country. (Pateti: 2011: 423)

If Arun Joshi has taken creative liberty while glorifying adivasi, equally he could have connected the adivasi predicament with their past including their historical revolts against colonialism. These adivasi revolts are the inspirational source not only for the adivasi community but also for all people of the country. The novelist could explore their revolt for the claim on their ancestral forest, resources and mountains, their claim for indigeneity, which was magnificently presented through the regional Indian Adivasi literature. While delineating adivasi life and culture in this novel, it seems that Joshi swiped out the history of colonial revolts of adivasi, which were fought for their existence. Adivasi life in the novel seems unconvincing because it is hard to believe that adivasi life is so smooth and without having any idea about the problems of livelihood and survival, against the deadly industrial policies during the seventies. Novelists have entirely missed the significance of adivasi revolt during colonialisation. Postcolonial India and Postcolonial literature also remained ignored toward, these native people's struggle. The adivasi's revolts were an unforgettable episode in colonial Indian history if without remembering those revolts; we are attempting to write their literature, it means we deny our history of colonial exploitation. In this regard Crispian Bates and Alpa Shah opines:

> The conflict over Indians forests has been one of the most important forms of protest as ascribed to adivasis, and it has played out all over the subcontinent, since colonial times. In these conflicts, the experience of those labeled adivasi's was no different from those of the broader categories of poor peasant living in the same area. Ultimately the crucial issues underpinned the conflict was revelry between the needs of local communities and the demands of communal forestry sponsored by the colonial government which, as Ram Chandra Guha argues, were embedded in a very different understanding of the social role of forests. (Bates/Shah: 2014: 04)

Arun Joshi has presented the areal picture of adivasi life in his novel *The Strenge Case of Billy Biswas.* If he could explore adivasi, marginalisation and their way of survival with their custom and primordial beliefs during the 1980s, then there were many possibilities for other Indian English writers to take these adivasi themes of the adivasi world and to show the social-economic exploitation of adivasi life which is continuing for the last many years. A thousand years of Indian history is the evidence that such type of adivasi glorification could never save them from the exploited machinery of the capitalistic world. Adivasi life is becoming a victim from both the side – the threat of naxalism and state-sponsored operations in the name of eradication of naxalism. Adivasis are often taken granted as Naxals when they raised the voice for his ancestral claim on land and forest. Their resistance is brutally crushed in the name of the destruction of terrorism and Naxalism. Nevertheless, this movement has not given any benefit to adivasi life in fact lot of innocents people, and younger died in the encounter. Commenting on these circumstances, S.N.Choudhary opines:

> The adivasi communities in all the areas of Naxalite operations had been gradually exposed to social, economic as well as political forces general by

> the larger society but they have not the clear concept of the exact motives and the causes of this struggle. Naturally, the adivasi participation in this movement was very marginal and segmental though the central leaders of this movement took the opportunity to control and led their operation in the adivasi concentrated area. (Choudhary: 2010:263)

From the inceptions of Indian writing in English, during the colonial period, Indian nationalism was important theme of literature. Anti-colonial sentiments were apparent in the writings of Raja Ram Mohan Roy, Aurobindo Ghosh, Rabindranath Tagore and Manohar Malgonkar, *etc.* In the Postcolonial era, Raja Rao and Mulkraj Anand took up the themes of the Indian freedom struggles. However, in the discourse of reconstruction of nationality and nation, which was the prime object of postcolonial writers, where were the Dalits and Adivasis? Indian English fiction writers, after Independence, started decolonisation of empirical power and decentering Eurocentric literature and gave reference to the voices of the native people of India. They described Indian freedom struggle, partition, poverty, the conflict between tradition versus modernity and the modern Indian Identity, *etc.* Despite this, the original, aboriginal population of India did not figure out prominently in literature. Indian freedom struggle, partition and poverty and feminism have been checked out through the postcolonial Indian English writings. In this regards, Gajendra Kumar in his *The Native Voices; A Case for the Second Tradition of Postcolonial Theory,* opines:

> Postcolonialism explains all those indigenous voices that resisted the ideological as well as a political invention by the colonial powers, in the interest of the oppressed – subjugated to enslavement and violence. Most of the thinker, like Roy, Gandhi, Tagore, and Ambedkar, encountered the impact of colonialism in different ways and prepared their narratives of resistance. The entire period of Indian freedom struggle is full of such invisible voices, of protest against the colonising powers. It is perhaps, high time we included those native voices in our vision of postcolonial theory. This is how decolonisation of theory may start in India. (Kumar Gajendra: 2003: 156)

One significant difference between Indian English fiction and the Regional Indian fiction or Bhasha literature is that in the former, we find glorified and over romanticised description of adivasi life, which are full of philosophical musing. These romantic, philosophical musings have been somewhat countered in Bhasha Literature where some writers have attempted to give a realistic picture of adivasi society. Novels written in regional writings seem more authentic about adivasi life, discussing problems of poverty, illiteracy and displacements as well as the struggles of adivasi people. One of the giants and most outstanding literary stalwart of regional adivasi writing is Mahashweta Devi, who wrote extensively about adivasis in her writing. Mahashweta Devi has written the novel, *Arenyer Adhikar* and *Chotti Manda And his Arrow*. These novels deal with adivasi movements to protect adivasi rights in forest, river and mountains. Regarding the adivasi theme and indigenous consciousness in her writing, Anand Mahanand in his book, *Adivasi India In fiction,* opines:

> Mahashweta Devi's choice of particular historical events, which is a neglected phase of Indian history, gives evidence of her social commitment. Through her novel, Mahaswetadevi Devi exposes, the exploitation of adivasi's and its effect on their lives, physically as well as emotionally. She makes an earnest attempt to give a realistic picture of the movement. She exposes the crookedness, exploitativeness and callousness of British Government authorities and the ruthless nature of non-aboriginal landlords, moneylenders and petty officials. (Mahanand: 2011:170)

When we compare the presentations of adivasi themes from *The Strange Case of Billy Biswas* and the novel of Mahashweta Devi's "*Chotti Munda And His Arrow,* then we can quickly notice that the mainstream Indian English fiction seems weaker than regional novel writings, particularly in bringing out the realism of adivasi life and struggle. Adivasi revolts were not only for their territory but also they wanted to reject the colonialism of their cultures and territories. *Santhal Hool of 1855* rejected the culture of imperialism. Their revolts were the freedom for human dignity. This Santhal revolt was the first massive public revolt against the British Raj, but in postcolonial India, threats were brought up on adivasi natural resources. Adivasi territories were again neocolonised in the hands of few multinationals. To counter the adivasi resistance, this time Operation Green Hunt and Salva Judum and many operations were started by influential policymakers.

Along with this reality about adivasi life, Billy tries to romanticise every aspect of adivasi life. Remarkably, he romanticised their customs and says that adivasi are much interested in drum beating, dancing, lovemaking and his observations about adivasi life seem glorified, when he comments, "These dances are an agony of sorts, just as walking into the rose garden or listening to twenty-four houses of jazz is an orgy. A bit of lovemaking, the frenetic drumming, the constant footwork, the making and breaking of formulations, the yelling, the folding of the women" (Joshi: 1971:101).

Adivasis, as represented by Mahashweta Devi, are not so romanticised or glorious, she focused on their day to day struggle, their ancestry, their sacrifice for this country. Her *Chotti Munda and His Arrow* show the rebellious martyrdom of Birsa Munda and the adivasi struggle for their ancestral rights. Adivasi peasants and their exploitation from moneylender comprised the core theme of her novels. About the realism of her novel about adivasi life, Anand Mahanand opines:

> Mahashweta Devi picks up the essential historical factors that were at work in this particular period in the history of the Munda tribe. Unlike other writers who were stimulated by adivasi exotica and chose to romanticise and idealise adivasi societies, Mahashweta Devi does not present a romanticised picture of the Munda tribe. Instead, she portrays the poverty-smoke and insecure lives of the adivasi people for whom rice remains an eternal dream where life meant wandering from one village to another due to ongoing eviction by the dikus whom land reclaimed from the forest way the basis of adivasi life. (Mahanand: 2011:171)

In the contemporary world, there is no natural process of colonisation over a weak country. European and American big nations cannot set up their colonies in any nation. Therefore internal and external multinationals or corporate houses are always in search of new territory having full of natural resources that could be neocolonised for the personal benefits. Today, as a result, most of the adivasi territory of Jharkhand, Chhattisgarh and Orissa seems the prime center of multinational colonisation. Regarding the colonisation of adivasi areas and adivasi's natural resources Abhishek Kumar Yadav, opines, "Capitalism has not stopped only in a country and looted the resources, but it had broken their centers of loot across the many nations of the world. Its main center is overseas. This multinational capitalism has captured media, newspapers, universities, organisations, intellectuals of the nation and set a big panorama of the fantasy world" (Yadav: 2015:148) (Translated).

Though *The Strange. The case of Billy Biswas* is to be conceder as a 'universal myth of primitivism', this depicted glorified and romantic life of adivasi and all the characters and situations depends on Billy Biswas when Billy is shot dead by the police, the novel ends without showing any concern of the adivasi characters like Bilasia and Dhunia. This novel shows adivasis as ambitionless but Anand Mahanand aptly critics this view and comments, "They were not without ambitions. Arun Joshi fails to notice all these aspects in their life and provides only a partial view of adivasi life. In cum, the novel fails to portray longer issues and remains romantic, and the adivasi society is reduced to a picturesque backdrop against which Billy Biswas's tragic destiny is enacted. (Mahanand: 2011: 83)."

The English writing fraternity of India, to some extent, possessed the hype, convenience and aristocratic values. Popular literature is in the focus of reading in the younger generation of India. In the era of social media, several what's app universities, facebook colleges and twitter schools are sharing the changing phases of the world. Bollywood, Hollywood, Tollywood, and Kollywood became the prime focus of interest and entertainment in the Indian mass population. However, the dying dialects and dying malnutrition generations of adivasi, exploitation from bureaucracy, loopholes in adivasi constitutional acts, seldom becomes the center of literary debates and creative writings. In India, this is how globalisation enchanted the conscious and subconscious of responsible writers and upcoming new generations. Globalisation has played a broader role in the living of the younger generation in real life, cutting from the ground realities. Indian new generation is becoming the butterfly generation and nothing doing with the displacement of the Adivasis and Dalits. *The Strenge Case of Billy Biswas* set in Malaika Hills in Satpura Mountain of Madya Pradesh, which are exploited areas for the last many decades. The adivasi movement is working for sustaining the rights of adivasi people. In the name of adivasi development, natural resources are being taken from those regions but Joshi's character, Billy Biswas, conciders adivasi as an ambitionless, drunkard and without dignity. It must be admitted that the novelist is talking about those forests which are very close to the Madya Pradesh border, full of natural resources, are always full of commotion and tension between local adivasi and state-sponsored authorities. Adivasi's situation in that particular region has shown by Gladson Dungdung in the following words in the book, *Mission Saranda – A War for Natural Resources*:

> Historically, the Saranda forest belongs to the Adivasis. They are the first settlers of the territory, and they have an undisputed symbiotic relationship with the forest. The British invasion resulted in alienation from their land, territory and resources which continues to this day. However, the Adivasis resistance to the denial of their ownership rights over their land, territory and resources has never ceased despite the state attempts to suppress them through brutal killings in so-called cross-fire, torture, sexual exploitation of their women. (Dungdung: 2015:231)

After Indian Independence, a generation has taken birth which is to be considered as a mass society. The society which is divided in the name of caste, religion, poverty and richness. This society was serving for the selfishness of the ruler class in which we do not find a place for the aboriginal community. In the competitive age of globalisation, modern Indian civilisation is running after western values and a matrix of sophisticated values. In the moll and media industry of modernisation, literature is also becoming commercial and granting the interest of ruling classes which ultimately seems incapable of the depiction of cultural and ethnic genocide of adivasi communities of India. Arun Joshi's novel, *The Strange Case of Billy Biswas* seems for away from the ground reality of adivasi. The novelist has taken much effort to show the internal, psychological conflict of Billy Biswas. The novel is full of philosophical musing over the barrenness of the modern world, but the adivasi life, depicted in the novel is not enough to present adivasi ethos and pathos of struggling account of their century's journey. Indian English fiction writer must study adivasi life, culture and their struggle for survival then novelists could present adivasi life from their natural spectacles, as presented by the regional writers like Mahashweta Devi, Gopinath Mohanty, C. K. Janu and Narayan.

# CHAPTER 3

# Adivasi Marginalisation in *The Princes* and *The Coffer Dam*

## Postcolonialism in the Novels of Manohar Malgaonkar and Kamala Markendeya

> It was white settlers who, as Britain did elsewhere, subjugated nonwhite indigenous peoples and took their land and natural resources. In other words, theorist argues, the inclusion of white settler cultures under the postcolonial rubric ignores the enormous difference race has played in the history of colonisation and continues to play today in the racist attitude that keeps third and fourth-word peoples economically oppressed. (Tyson: 2006: 424)

Postcolonial Indian Literature should be the literature of the oppressed and sabaltern people of this country, but in case of adivasi, they are double colonised after India's Independence. In our free state, adivasis are still marginalised. Post-Independence Indian English writing flourished with the decolonisation of the minds of Indian English writers. The Indian history was fictionalised with realism for the first time in the novels of Manohar Malgaonkar. Postcolonial historical fiction gave a new hight to Indian English writing. Through the historical analysis of Manohar Malgaonkar, capitalism, imperialist domination, social-cultural inequalities, poverty, exploitation, the tragedy of partition, the catastrophe of Muslim-Hindu commotion, revolutionary struggle of Independence and the disintegration of princely states, all have been discussed with acute detail. Because of his sense of understanding and analysis of history, he is to be considered as *The John Masters of the Indo-English Fiction*. K. R. Shrinivas Iyengars comment is more suggestive in this regards,

> "Malgaonkar is not an indigenous John Masters; nor is *Distant Drum* an Indo-Anglican variation of the Anglo-Indian *Bhowani Junction*. There is, on the contrary, an authentic quality about Malgaonkar and his novel that can stand scrutiny without reference to the master recipe" (Iyengar: 2007: 423).

The focus of Postcolonialism is the rewriting of history which unveils the enormous social, political, economic, religious and cultural transformation that many countries have undergone. These countries have rejected many orthodox practices while accepting others. The concepts and the effects of modern culture were responsible for accepting and adopting alien cultures, which have now got global identities. In the postcolonial nations, through migration and displacement of people, colonial expansions have been shaken. In other words, it can be said that these are the outcomes or consequences of colonial encounters. This colonial encounter finds its echo in the novels of Manohar Mangonkar. His novels deal with the Indian tradition, its hoary history which provides vivid information about India. Partition Holocaust finds very thrilling expression through his novel, which shows the real meaning of violence and non-violence. Issues of disintegration, communal harmony, violence and non-violence have been presented on an epic-scale through his postcolonial sensitivities.

> Unlike Khushwant Singh, Manohar Malgaonkar presents the political side of the partition from Gain, the ardent disciple of Gandhi and his creed of non-violence. Debidayal, the terrorist and Hafiz Khan and Shafi Usman, the communalist. Malgaonkar's account takes than something which emerges out of the characters themselves and their convictions. This detachment also marks his narration of the partition riots, when they are compared to similar descriptions by Khushwant Singh. (Batra: 1975: 41)

Manohar Malgaonkar was a master in the colonial history of India, so his novels cover the socio-economic, histo-cultural milieu of the Indian psyche. His tremendous novels packed with the historical panorama of India are *Distant Dram* 1960, *Combat of Shadow* (1962), *Princess* (1963), *A Bend in the Ganges* (1964), *The Devil Wind 1972 Bomdicoot Run 1982 and The Garland Creepers (1988).* Through his literary works, he focused on dangerous encounters of the struggle for homeland and separation of India. No doubt, his work contains the unique presentation of historical observations.

Today when we critically observe the adivasi life and their problems, we can say that after Independence adivasis are struggling for their fundamental rights. In this manner, they are the same in the contemporary period as they were in the colonial period. It happened because of internal orientalism and internal colonialism which is working on the adivasis of India. Regretfully, it can be observed that India has two pictures, one is shining, digital and globalise corporate

India and the other one is dark, dingy, struggling and malnutrition India. One portion of India is shining on the cost of other India. This first India of progressive communities has colonised the second India of suppressed and oppressed communities. Indian English fiction writers because of their urban and elite backgrounds can depict the life of shining India, but a larger reality of deprived India and multicolonisation of adivasi territories have far away from their literary visions. In this regard to adivasi distortion and displacement, Abhishek Yadav makes a hurtful comment:

> Adivasis were made the laborers in their land. They were forced to migrate from here to there, and this was the result of global capitalism. Their territory, which was full of minerals and metals, were captured and delivered to big corporate houses of the world for fulfilling their material pleasure. Native adivasis were now laborers digging their land to make the costly places of Worlds Business Tycoons, and while digging the land, they were buried in the same land. (Yadav: 2015:142, Translated)

*Distant Drum* was written in 1960, which presents a various facet of army discipline in India, during the last period of the British regime to the beginning years of Congress Rule. The hero of the novel, Kiran, presents an idealised picture of an Indian Army officer who is rebellious, spirited and brave. "We should have stopped all such waggish activities like dancing and singings. Copping the ways of foreigners I call it. I don't know why I have always been uninterested in dancing; it is nothing but a legacy of the British rule." (Malgaonkar: 1960:68). The novel covers the relationship between Britisher's and the Indians. The hardships of the life of a soldier find a prominent place in the novel. Again hardships of life and the sympathetic condition of laborers of the tea estate of Assam have been projected through the novel *The Combat of Shadow*. The psychology of the soldier, during post-independence India, recurrent evil and violence is the prominent theme of the *Combat of Shadow. A Combat of Shadow* is a novel that tackles the E.M.Foster subject of Britisher's alienation from the Indians and the corruption of the British by imperialism and their harm and ignorance of India" (Williams: 1987: 103).

The novel, *Combat of Shadow,* brilliantly presents British life and dominant cultures which have nothing to do with the moral values of the poor and exploited sections deteriorating their ethical existence shows the dominance by some rich people creating chaos in human relationships. It is a highly successful novel *The Princess* 1963 presents the picture of the disintegration of Indian states. In the novel, the political crisis dealing with the merger of the princely states in India becomes an essential issue of writing after Independence. Malgonkar tells the story very entertainingly, and his awareness of the political understanding gives his narrative a comprehensive dimension. The novel grippingly presents Indian national policy after Independence, regarding Indian princely states.

*A Bend in the Gangas* (1964) is to be considered as a sensational novel dealt with the struggle for freedom, the crisis of partition and the agony of post-Independence turmoil. Dealing with the Gandhian era, this novel sincerely presented the role of a terrorist in the partition holocaust. The story of the Great revolt of 1857 and the role of Nana Saheb Peshwa was brilliantly presented in the novel *The Devils Wind.* Here novelist shows much interest in Nana's characters than in the national struggle. The Malgonkar rewrote colonisation of India through the postcolonial Indian point of view. *Bandicoot Run* (1982), presents a historical substratum. This novel presents army life and national Platonism and honesty. The prominent theme of the novel is intense psychological perception and insight into evil. Extra constitutional authority, in this ordinance implementation of family planning, press censorship becomes a more critical topic for Malgonkar in his *The Garland Keepers.*

Adivasi life and culture are crucified in the name of development in the postcolonial world. To sustain the corporate loot, to sustain the casteist hierarchy, it is always better for the professional writers with the capitalist mentality to project adivasi as barbaric and as uncivilised as they can be shown. Adivasi culture, marital system, customs, rituals, communal harmony remains in the background in the race literary writings promote by global corporates. In every century, we are the witness that foreigner had attacked several on Indian land and settle here, but the British imperialism in India was a systematic structure of India's loot. To maintain British imperialism in India, English education was provided to Indians. Nevertheless, with the English Education, these new classes of educated India possessed with western values and westernised theoretical discourses. Therefore when we read the Indian English literature, mainly Indian English novels. We can meet a lot of literary stalwarts who directly or indirectly promotes western, colonial values through their writings. They seem unable to depict these adivasi values which were full of equality, brotherhood and liberty, free from all kinds of exploitation and inequalities. Regarding the inauthenticity of mainstream writers of India, famous critic, Bhujang Meshram, points out:

> Today's literary world seems class dominated. India's social-cultural disparities, cultural hegemony, devotion to foreign languages, the glorification of western colonisers and sophisticated elite culture were the realities of India, and the established elite class was aware of these issues. Literature became a playground for only a few elite classes. Therefore those who are underprivileged, broken colonised adivasis are considered barbaric. The elite literary stalwarts have presented them seldom through their literature just like leftovers. In this way adivasi's original representation becomes untouchable to the mainstream canon of Indian literature. (Meshram: 2014:56, Translated)

Through all this vivid theme of historical realism of India, Malgonkar has tried to present Indo-British relations and history from a postcolonial Indian view. Through most of his novels, he has shown that Indian is colonised by modern education and sophistical western values. He also warns that industrialisation is changing social harmony and humanitarian virtues. He alerts us to overcome the dominant and evil factors in society. In this regards, A. Padmanabhan foregrounds:

> Malgonkar is a writer who has made Indian history and consciousness intelligible to us more vividly and strikingly. The image of India that he presents is colorfully memorable. The most remarkable aspect of his fiction is the supreme value of human relationship attained through love. The message throughout his major works is that the division between races, classes and individuals can be resolved only through love. (Padmanabhan: 2002:136)

Postcolonial Indian Literature in English which has shown an imprint of resistance to the western canon of literature still shows the elements of internal colonial literature. Traditional Indian society, after Independence was sticking to nationality, so they oppose the western outlooks of life. This Indo-British relationship became a much-exploited theme in the writings of many post-colonial writers like Manohar Malgonkar, Geeta Mehta, Salman Rushdie and Kamala Markandeya. Along with the theme of hunger, poverty, humiliation and rural culture, the issues of native cultures versus western ideologies which were the main reasons for the conflict between the West and East have been explored by the Markandeya in her writings.

> Kamala Markandeya portrayed both ideal and ugly forces of Indian womanhood which have been part and partial of every society in the worlds as good and evil are yoked and travels together but the ideal character of the women that the novelist has presented in the guise of Rukmini can't found in the world other than India, but at the some have it

> also correct that in the present context of the society and worldwide view of feminism, the endurance of women to such extreme can't be uploaded of other. It would be deeply rejected. (Purohit: 2012:271)

Adivasi's revolt against British imperialism is a significant topic of literary writings because adivasis have paid the cost of Indian freedom by sacrificing their blood and bone. African literature and Native American literature were once looked down upon as tribes warfare. It was a systematic conspiracy against the aboriginal communities to judge them as barbaric. Nevertheless, still, N Gugi Wa Thiong and Chinua Achebe established African literature as resistance to British-American imperialism. Adivasi icon Birsa Munda has also fought bravely against cultural imperialism of external and internal exploitation. Birsa Munda, Tilaka Manzi, Sidho-Kanho and Gundadhur are also international adivasi heroes, but mainstream Indian English fiction adivasi writings have not even mentioned their names in their literary masterpieces. Cultural dualism, identical crisis, man-women relationship, finds a significant presence in the work of Kamala Markandcya. The theme of Ind-British cultural clash shown in some of the novel *Some Inner Funny 1956, A Silence of Desire 1960, possession (1963), A Handful of Rising (1966), The Coffer Dam (1969), The Nowhere Man (1972) and Two Virgins (1973).* Most of the characters in her novel deal with rural native culture and simultaneously present the British values of western culture. This clash of cultures becomes prominent themes in her novels. Her characters also seem bold and full of expressions. Md. Irshad says:

> Kamala Markandeyas characters are educated, well-mannered and highly sensitive. Nevertheless, all the characters are not the same. Uncultured characters have their class. The main aim of the uncultured is to improve their way of life by coming in contact with the cultured people but in vain. A few of them stand against the traditional way of life. This is an interaction between the two groups, the cultured reformed themselves in the light of outside influences, while the uncultured adjust themselves within their rigid traditional circle. (Irshad: 2013: 20)

Cross-cultural interactions, mutual love, cultural crisis, understanding of racial denomination and problem of the ruler and ruled finds prominent voices in all her fictions. Her novel tries to bring out the people of two different races and two different attitudes of living. The blending of eastern tradition and western materialism finds the acute study in her novels. Sometimes it seems that she is presenting herself through the mouthpiece of characters in her novel. Her personality is a blend of cultural synthesis.

Markandeya thinks that meeting of East with West is always possible and she tends to show through the relationship of Kenny and Rukmani in the novel *Nictere In The Sieve,* through the Richard – Mira's relationship in *Some Inner Furry*, in *Possession* through the character of Ellie and Vale, Bashiam and Helen in the novel *The Coffer Dam*, despite cultural, social, economic and political differences between two worlds or races. Markandeya's postcolonial sensibilities observe the merit and demerits of both cultures importantly. She was of the believer that the Indo-British relationship could be flourished only when both the culture respect each other's sovereignty. She explores the passive endurance, fatalism, superstition and economic backwardness of the nation despite her religious ethical, philosophical and traditional values. She admits the advantages of science and technology of the west through it is soulless and heartless. Markandeya showed her sharp cry against suffering and humiliation by racial discrimination.

The theme of cultural amnesia, rootlessness, sense of detachment and craves for materialism presented through the various novels of Kamala Markandeya. Decaulterisation becomes a striking theme in Markandeya's famous novel *A Handful of Rising*. Just like many other novels, this novel fictionalises the sociology of India. The protagonist, Ravi, feels a sense of alienation, who is a proletarian product and vagabond of the sixties. The mechanisation of rural tradition frustrates him, and he finds the rootlessness of his life in the materialistic urban milieu. Postcolonial Indian changes have been depicted very acutely by the novelist, through the character of Ravi. The theme of poverty and misery presents its picture through the mouth of Ravi. Kamala Markandeya opines, "He was alone in the jungle, and the jungle one fought or died. The knowledge was an incandescent light at the core of his being like the single eye set in the forehead of a demon. Lying, sleeping, walking, and even in his frenzied out of love, its beam scorched and excoriated him" (Markandeya: 1977: 217). The Adivasi life in India could be related and literature in the light of postmodernism, postcolonialism and post-globalisation. Indian adivasi life should be studied in the relevance of multicultural cosmopolitanism.

Nevertheless, during the one hundred and fifty years of British Colonisation and seventy-two years of Indian Independence, Indian Adivasis are still distorted and highly marginalised. The mainstream writers handling western literary craft have not given severe place to the Adivasis at the center of literary debates. Mainstream society of national life always used to loot adivasis natural resources for their richness, but adivasis are intentionally refuse to give space in the national, political, social and cultural life of nation and nationhood. This was a pre-planned conspiracy by the elite classes.

Markandeyas another novel, *Two Virgins,* shows the journey from adolescence to womanhood. The central characters are Lalitha and Saroja. Both the sister rejects the poverty and squalor of village life and desire for the prospect. Lalitha is bold, manipulative and outgoing while Saroja is timid, obedient and docile. Westernised values and traditional beliefs come to the forefront through the two characters of Saroja and Lolitha. Showing these two diverse polls, Madhavi Menon says, "The sense of identity of her characters always comes to be tasted against social values. The sense of identity operates within the social contest where the clash of different value systems and attitudes causes concern. In such a dilemma, conformity is the key to individual happiness" (Markandeya: 1977:133). *Two Virgin* presents identical postcolonial issues and the clashes between cultural values. Markandeya has delivered the changing values in Indian society after independence. This novel comes with the theme of agrarian, traditional values and its conflict with the modern, sophisticated and pretentious life of the modern period. Regarding these changing values and its representation in the novel, Madhavi Menon opines, "*Two Virgin* exhibits the preoccupancy of an Indian women novelist with tradition and modernity social evils and tension, the crisis of character arising from the changing values of modern civilisation concerning traditional Indian society" (Rao: 1983:139).

The novel, *Pleasure City,* also shows postcolonial Indian changing value in which Markandeyas hero, Rikki, is the culturally alienated product of English education. Meeting friendship and separation is the central theme of the novel. Rikki belongs to the fisher community, which shows the hardship and poverty of this community. After International Development Corporation has accepted the proposal of a resort building in the castle village of Rikki when he meets Tully, despite a wide gap between them regarding social status, they accept each other. The Indo-British relationship again becomes the central theme of the novel. About the writer of the novel Madhavi Menon opines:

> The situation of the novel is almost the same as in *The Coffer Dam*, the intrusion of technology into a nondescript fishing village jeopardise the

> traditional occupations of the villagers and imposes on them an alien set of values attitude and decision. It upsets the traditional system of thoughts and social behavior and scales of values. Commercialism, individualism and materialism enter the original lifestyle of the simple fisherfolk. (*Menon:* 1983:157)

*The Golden Honeycomb* shows the ancestry of the generation of Indian history about the maharaja of Devapur State Bawajirao I, II and III respectively. The novel is the window to the East-West encounter of postcolonial literature. The history of feudalism and common masse's deprivation comprises the central theme of the novel. In this regard, Usha Bande remarks in *Mothers and Mother Figures in Indo-English Literature,* "The English wanted to hold on to the country that they called "a gem in the British crown", and as the prologue to the novel records, they adopted all means fair or foul to frighten the noose around the native kingdoms. Consequently, the rulers of the state all over India remained weak and almost the mouthpiece of the British regime, whereby they alienated their subjects" (Bande: 1994:106). The deprived section of Dalit, Adivasi and Women were only utility objects for mainstream literary magnets, but in the last few decades, Adivasi-Dalit literature discourse has challenged the mainstream literature. Dalit literature has given birth to a mass Dalit movement, but it could not happen in the case of adivasi literature. Non-adivasi writers did most of the writing about Adivasi, therefore we notice a little kind of unauthenticity about these writings. About the non-adivasi writers, writing about adivasi life and culture, Vandana Tete observes:

> Non-adivasi writers writing on adivasi life are working from a significant period of their life, but they still do not know adivasi dialect and their oral literature. They want to impose their perceptions and observations of adivasi life in their way. Those writers who are writing in Hindi suddenly became the master of Adivasi literature. These famous nonadivasi writers are now accepting various literary prizes and holding respective places in various organisations. (Tete: 2013:55, Translated)

There is no doubt that the historical acuteness of Manohar Malgonkar is matchless to the other contemporary novelist of historical fiction. He is at home while depicting the Indo-British relationships. He has convincingly brought psychology of both the side through his entire observation of British and Indian culture. The dualism of conflict performs a significant role in his characters in the novel. While presenting the aristocratic scenario of kingship in his novel, he seems slightly ignorant about the common masses and their movements of India. Native cultures and characters hardly take any shape through his novels. Regarding this fact, L.C.Khatri, opines, "Writing history is not the purpose of Malgonkar as a fictional writer, rather writing fiction is his primary aim and history plays only a secondary role in his fictional art. Whatever Malgonkar has written, we find cultural conflict everywhere. It may be the conflict between the Indian and the western cultures, or it may be a conflict between the indigenous cultures of India like that of Hinduism and the Muslim" (Khatri: 2012: 187).

## Characterisations and Depiction of Adivasis in *The Princess*

Manohar Malgonkar's *The Princess,* is at once, an autobiography and an epic. It is an epic because it narrates the story of the State, Prince and Maharaja, and it is an autobiography because the main hero Abhay narrates it in the first person. *The Princess* is an epical saga because it presents historical events of state declining from 1938 to 1947 until their margining with the independence of India in 1949. We find a brilliant fusion of the British policy and Indian history of the freedom struggle during the last phase of the Indian Independence. The role of Maharaja, Princess and Congress Party is also very crusial. A.N.Dwivedi in his research paper *The Historian as a Novelist: Manohar Malgonkar: Perspective on Indian English Fiction* gives an opinion, "*The Princess* evokes a vivid picture of the partition days in India when the aristocratic rulers of the princely states were put to untold suffering and hardship owing to the changing political scene. The title of the novel is a pointer to these rulers in general and not to even one single prince of Begwad whose life-story forms its subject matter" (Dwivedi: 1985: 139).

This historical novel deals with the anxieties and dilemmas of the Maharaja of the Begwad during the period of Independence. Nearly 565 princely states were not ready to merge in Indian Union, but Congress was insisting them to be united. Begwad was a adivasi significant territory where nearly twenty thousand Bhil adivasis were living from ancient times. The Maharaja, as well as the Congress, wants the support of the adivasi for the power and the Maharaja also appeals to their traditional loyalty. Congress has done much to attract adivasi by giving them the plan of building dams and other modernising programs.

Nevertheless, as in many cases, adivasi often becomes a tool for political victimisation. Though adivasis in the novel are ready to die for Maharaja's loyalty, finally under the pressure of Government, Maharaja finally merged the state of Begwad into Indian Union. This adivasi political victimisation is going on through the Middle Ages to the contemporary period, but literary barrenness about Adivasis is an eye-opener reality of adivasi community. Regarding the adivasi victimisation Gladson Dungdung, in his famous volume, *Whose Country Is This Anyway,* comments:

> After Indian Independence, The perception, mindset and the behavior of the ruling elites towards adivasi remained the same. Politician's attitude towards adivasi was like if you are to suffer, you should suffer in the interest of the country, but the country does not care about their pain, suffering and sorrow. It seems that the Adivasis are born to suffer in their own country in the name of national interest, growth and development and the sunglasses are only born to enjoy their lives. (Dungdung: 2013:03)

In the novel, the characterisation of Bhil adivasis finds no hope to express themselves in this whole political melodrama. Adivasis are presented only as puppets in the hands of Maharaja, having no rational, having no culture and no raising voices against their displacement. It seems strange, when Malgonkar could build the strong canvass other characters in the novel, he lacks that authenticity while depicting adivasi as a community. Mohgonkar has not taken a single character from the dominant territory of Bhil adivasi for interactions. Whatever he wanted to present about adivasis, he presented them by showing as the mob. *Abhay,* the narrator describes the adivasis as follow, "As we approached, we passed a small group of men and women going towards the camp, all almost naked for little wisps of cloth around their middles, the men wearing twists of colored rope for turbans and the women chains of flowers on their heads"(Malgaonkar:1963:95).

The novel, *Princess,* does not focus on the characterisation of the Bhil tribe who are going to be displaced because of the big project of dam construction in their territory. Their agricultural problems, their use as mercenary soldiers, do not find any mouthpieces. A significant population of Bhils very calmly accepts the surrender before oppressive governmental policies in this novel. It is hard to believe. Novels present adivasi characters as only unpaid, soldiers who are always ready to die or to kill someone for Maharaja. When Bhil oppose the governmental policies and merging processes of the other territories, the rumour comes that Maharaja has used his private military of Bhils to show his power. Adivasi presence in the novel is only shown to create a riot and threatening public life. We can notice the degradation of adivasis in the novel.

> It seems that Kanakchand had organised what the Mandal described as grand rally. Bhil, who had come to the gathering, got into an argument with him. In the clash that ensued, thereof the manual workers were injured, and Kanakchands jeep was destroyed by fire. The incident was magnified and distorted out of all proportion. It was allied that the Bhils were the ruler's hirelings deliberately sent to break up the meetings, armed with rifles and spears. The state police, they accompanied, had turned their books as the Bhils were dancing round the burning jeep. (Malgonkar: 1963:277)

The Adivasi life is in danger from all directions, in the same manner, they are forcibly displacing from their homeland and also from their adivasi moral values. Those who migrated to big cities surrender to the mainstream system. Such severe deprivation of the aboriginal community is noticed through the regional adivasi novel writings. Adivasi writers have opened their wounded heart and shown they crave for indigenous identity. Such a depiction of the adivasi life could not take place in mainstream Indian English novel writings. Manohar Malgonkar's novel presents the characters of adivasi Bhils, who works for Maharaja, believing in violence, loot, and anarchy. This is the underrated depiction of the adivasis. Bhil's anxiety about their fields finds no sympathetic treatment in the novel. Referring adivasis as wild goons, Abhay says, "The next morning's paper came with prominent headlines "Outrage in Begwad State" was one of them. "Ruler Goondas attack cultivators rally was another" (Malgonkar: 1963: 277).

When the process of merging the Begwad state into the Indian republic comes to its ending phase, it leaves no scope for adivasi in this new republic. Adivasis come to Maharaja for their rights and security. They visit the Maharaj and Governmental Officers. They are not allowed to enter in king court. When they protest against Congress, the publicity is made about their weapons and violence. When Abhay goes to meet them in Polo ground, the novelist has described the chaos of adivasi people in the court as lacking the courtly manners, but we do not find the demands of adivasis who throughout their life and from many generations are loyal to Maharaja of Begwad. "The ground was a seething mass of bronze bodies, all wearing little coloured twists of rope as turbans and standing or squatting In separate groups according to their villages. The spearhead glinted in the morning sun. As I stopped the car and walked towards them, they raised to their feet and began to yell, and some of them hurt their spears high into the air and caught them again" (Malgonkar: 1963:324). In the novels, adivasis are ready to sacrifice their life for Maharaja and Begwad and want to rebel against the Congress party, but Maharaja and Abhayraj itself are not severe about the patriotism of Bhil adivasi about themselves. Conversation between adivasi characters and Abhayraj shows the intensity of patriotism of Bhil adivasis.

> *Abhay*: Why have you come to court?
> *Adivasi*: To be with you, we shall fight for you, die for you But why cannot we take our spears with as we are not going to kill anyone.
> *Abhay*: New government does not understand such a thing. They are city people, not jungle dwellers like you, and they do not understand our culture/customs.
> *Adivasi*: We do not want a sarkar of strange / we do not want any other rule but the Bedar"s
> ***Abhay:*** stop cackling like women "I yelled, Dammit, I can almost hear the Bengals." (Malgonkar: 1963:425)

Adivasi characterisation, as a community, finds no echo in the novel, though they are large in numbers. The process of dam construction, forest reservoirs, field firing ranges and other modernisation were started during the British Raj not only in Begwad but in the most adivasi part of pre-independence India and positively the adivasi of those periods faced the evil of deforestation and industrialisation. Here, adivasi as a culture-adivasi as the community finds the degradation of human values. The adivasi considers their land, forest and river as goddesses and worshipped them at but when they are displaced from their land, the novelist could create an immense panorama of adivasi decultarisation, but we find no illustrations of their predicaments.

> I now realise that the way things were going, it was a serious lapse on my part to have sent money to the Bhils of the Bulwara I can only say that I had meant well. The poor wretched still clinging to their land, but they had not been allowing cultivating them because they were to be taken over before the crops could be harvested. As a result, Bhil had no crops and nothing to leave on. On learning their plight, I had sent them ten thousand rupees to tide them over until they were paid the compensation for their land. For nearly a year there had been almost constant trouble in Bulwarwa Valley. No alternative holdings were being offered to the Bhils, and the authorities were unwilling to pay compensation until they have surrendered their lands. The Bhils had become increasingly truculent, declaring they could not move until they were given alternative sites. I don't know whether the government could have solved the problem. It

> was not going to be easy to find cultivate land to resettle twenty thousand adivasi-farmers crop, of course, it was impossible to find in it in one lot. (Malgonkar: 1963: 337)

The Adivasi of India is not capable of breathing freely in the social and personal life of this modern materialistic society. For the last hundred years, they are underrated and demeaned by mainstream canonical literature. Such fake social values and elite literature which is built upon the tombs of adivasis and subjugated communities can never sustain the strong pillars of the values of equality, liberty and brotherhood. The literature which does not comprises comprehensive humanitarian vision, how can such literature and writers become a role model and lighthouse for new aspirants of literary creativity. This must be admitted that those predicaments, thoughts, cultures and dialects become narrow-minded cannot become eternal. Its doom is the essential law of nature. Literature can be real if it derives from historical facts. Therefore historical adivasi rewriting is an essential condition to all adivasis and non-adivasi writers in India. In the present scenario, many Indian English novelists are bagging the literary prizes like Nobel, Pulitzer, Duff Cooper, Commonwealth, Booker and Man-Booker for literature. Surprisingly, they have not treated adivasi issues in their novels, having Indian social background. They have built up the floors after floor of sophisticated and materialistic values of cosmopolitanism where indigeneity, aboriginality and Asivasidom are invisible from their literary sights. Regarding this literary amnesia of mainstream writers, Dr. Yashwant Manohar, points out:

> The social mainstream ignores not only adivasi Dalits life but their historical facts are also distorted. History with the truth should be our prior movements. Crore of people are Adivasi in this nation, but the particular elite group feels insecure about claiming them as Adivasi. For their convenience, they introduced the word "Vanvasi".Nevertheless, why this wondering situation confronted with only Adivasis? This must check and rewrite. Mainstream historians have written histories from their comfort zone and with a hierarchical perspective. They hide the actual historical facts. Now, this attempt of historical distortions of claiming Adivasi as Vanvasi is continuously going on. This distortion of history must be stopped. When Adivasi will speak and rewrite history, he will break all the shackles of slavery, and new history will establish (Edt. Gare: 2005: 06, Translated)

In the climax of the novel, it seems that Maharaja of Begwad, literary sold to the adivasi honesty to the government leaving no hope of useful life for Bhil, after Independence. Maharaja's officials also ask for bribery in the name of the protection of their rights on their ancestral land. One of the adivasi character comments, "The compensation officer have been openly asking for money that what they want money where are we to get the money Maharaja? Your officers were quite satisfied with fowls and eggs whenever they come touring, and once a year, some honey and bananas or a bottle of rum these new officials want cash even before they do anything. (Malgonkar: 1963.338)." However, the Bhil of Begwad is poor, distorted and illiterate, but they are a die-hard worshipper of Maharaja. They do not want modern amenities and development. They do not want the ruling of a person like British Gour babu. They want to see Maharaja as their Maharaja and nobody else.

Nevertheless, Maharaja uses them as a mercenary weapon against nationalists in the Indian Congress. On this occasion, Abhayraj opines, "This was the first time I became aware of adivasis as a force, as a race of hunters who had barely settled down as formers and who live by instincts and emotions and a few adivasi laws and closer to the Bronze Age than to ours. Furthermore, it was this time two that I began to understand why my father had always regarded them or his special responsibility" (Malgonkar: 96: 1963).

Speaking for adivasi, writing about adivasi, is becoming a fashion for money, now a day. Romanticisation and glorification of their customs can be seen in various movies and media. Several agencies are doing an anthropological survey on adivasi, claiming to bring them into a mainstream social force. The process of sanskrutinisation and conversion by Christian missionaries, conversion by Hindu right workers are working with equal force to show that adivasi of this land are the inevitable part of their orthodox cultures. All political parties and cultural agencies want them to surrender before their cultural and political imperialism, but nobody bothers about their problems of displacement, deculturation and the problems created with the waves of globalisation. Adivasis are mostly ignored by the mainstream, including literary platform also. In literature, they are invisible. This is the need of the time that adivasi should be given their political and social rights without interference from outside deciding anything for them. Their demands of *MAVA NATE MAVA RAJ* (In my land, I am the ruler) should be sanctioned. Regarding the sheer corruption, bribery, political negligence of the politician and bureaucrats, Gladson Dungdung makes a severe comment in his book, *Mission Saranda – A War for Natural Resources,*

> Perhaps, Indian bureaucrats pretend to believe that whatever they decide is best, that is why they never bother to talk to the beneficiaries before planning a program for them. Consequently, we have not even had ten successful programs in our country for the last six decades. This should hardly make us proud. If we talk about any program like Indira Awas Yojana, *MNREGA*, then everybody has complaints about implementation, corruption. Nevertheless, still, the state fails to change how it operates. Corruption, immorality and favoritism have become part and partial of Indian culture. (Dungdung: 2015:241)

The way adivasi has presented in the novel *The Princess* the contemporary situation of adivasi is no more different than the previous period now adivasis show their honesty with a particular political party for the hope of useful life. However, every time, they are created by all the political parties. For all the political parties in India, adivasi is just a voting tool and nothing else. In the name of development, they are displaced. In the name of globalisation, adivasis are becoming the victim of cultural genocide. In this regard Gladson Dungdung in his famous book *Whose country Is This Anyway* criticizes the political lethargy in the adivasi territory of India in the following words, "Adivasi have mostly been victimised in the development process in India, but they are still untouched by development even after 65 years of Indian independence. The three buzz words compensation, rehabilitation and development are widely propagated during land acquisition for the dam, industries, mining companies, power plants and other developmental projects. However, one must check the states of displaced masses to understand the ground realities of these promises in the dark." (Dungdung: 2013: 83).

*The Princess* deals with the theme of feudalism, kings and his kinships and the melodrama of disintegration of states with the merger into the Indian Union which claims of democratic values. Kanaksingh, the anti-hero of the novel, explains the importance of the merger of the state in democratic values. Nevertheless, in all this process of democracy of the Indian state, adivasi finds no place. The novel does not show any strong comment about the identity and existence of adivasi in democratic India after colonisation. The novel ends with giving power to Kanaksingh, and other people of Congress are ready to marginalise the adivasi. Maharaja and Abhayraj were against democratic states because they don't want to lose their hegemony. In a contemporary scenario, we find some anti-social elements which do not believe in democracy and democratic rights of adivasis and Dalits, it seems, those anti-democratic peoples are ready again to go to the feudal period for reviving feudalism and sheer orthodoxy. Commenting on the adivasi victimisation in a democratic state, K. Sachidanandan explores:

> The challenges to Indian democracy have always come from sections that hate democracy as an idea. This hatred is rooted in a profound contempt for the people with their diverse natures and aspirations and manifests itself chiefly in four ways: one, intolerance towards India's philosophical and cultural plurality; two silencing of intellectual opposition; three, the enfeeblement of the federal polity any four, contempt towards those sections of the population whose welfare constitutes the very goal and measure of democracy including women, peasant, workers, Dalits, Adivasis and ethnic minorities. (Satchidanandan: 2016:12)

## Depiction and characterisation of Adivasi in *The Coffer Dam*

After Indian Independence, the History of the Adivasi community was written by those intellectuals who were paid servants in the court of British Imperialism. They focused on adivasis as uncivilised, drum beater, drunken, barbaric, rebellious and away from civilisation but while doing this, the pain of exploitation, revolts against colonisation, their role in ecologically sustainable development have denied. They have made a stereotyped picture of adivasis which was ugly and incomplete. Therefore, today also, the concept of Adivasi life is one-sided and very obscure. Common masses considered adivasis as uncivilised and violent. Because of neoliberal policies, adivasi displacement took rapidly in the adivasi area of India. Colonisers have exploited them. Capitalism took the benefit of adivasi's isolation in the social mainstream. Therefore adivasi revolted against colonial policies in the past. Well-wishers of Adivasi have strengthened their voice on the national and International platform but in a minimal sense. Indian society has taken a duel role in adivasi issues. Regarding the confused identity of adivasis and mainstreams expectation from Adivasi's, Tapan Bose editor of *The Other Media,* in his book *Who is Native? Who is an Adivasi,* comment, "On one front, it is expected from adivasi that they should accept the social and economic life of mainstream society by forgetting their past and on other front adivasi are looked down as obstacles in the social and economic policies of development of the nation" (Meena: 2016:34, Translated).

*The Coffer Dam* the most celebrated and literary articulated novel of Kamala Markandeya was published in 1969 when the process of urbanisation of India was at its full speed. Industrialisation made its way into adivasi territory with damaging adivasi culture, forest, rivers and dehumanises exploitation of natural resources in adivasi areas. Construction of dams in the adivasi area was often the prominent condition before the government. If corporate wants to set up their industries in India, adivasi areas are an easy target for them. Forest reservoir, dams and big industries are to be built in the adivasi area. *The Coffer Dam* is the story of such a big dam to control and channelise a turbulent river of south India. "River that rose in the lakes and valleys of the south Indian highlands and thundered through inaccessible gorges and jungles down to the plain with prodigal waste" (Markandeya: 1969: 09). The adivasi peoples of India do not want the lavish facilities of living. Their concern is with the basic amenities of life, but even after Indian Independence, they are struggling for essential needs of good living. This shows the failure of a big secular nation in the world. Adivasi's marginalisation in India in every sphere of life is an unwritten reality of India. Commenting on this biggest marginalisation of Indian Adivasi community, Gladson Dundung, opines:

> The Adivasis hardly needed new mud houses, bicycles or radios. If they are permitted to plan the development of their village, they would have emphasis on clean drinking water, a residential school, health, electricity and roads, *etc.* The main problem with the Indian politician and the bureaucrats is that they consider Adivasis merely as victims or beneficiaries but not as opinion-makers or rights holders. They are never made them part of the system as decision-makers. (Dungdung: 2015:189)

In the novel, for the construction of the dam, British engineer Clinten, Helen and their assistance came with their families and settled near the adivasi village shifting to wretched adivasis to some less convenient place. The initial processes of construction of the dam started with the displacement of tribesmen badly, as happens usually. This is the history of the sociology of adivasi in postcolonial India. In the name of the country's development, these big industries, major dams, water reservoir and coal mines all were purposefully located to the adivasis schedule area. For the profit of capitalists a considerable number of industry-mines, thousands of adivasi villages are disposed of. Adivasis who used to worship hills, water, forest and animals displaced because of global capitalism. They become alienated in their land. Compensation is not given to them. No substitute home and no substitute village was given by corporate to them who destroyed their huts. Their livelihood has been beastly crushed. In their nature land, because of displacement, Adivasi is going through the process of deculturation, disorientation and several disparities. Bashiam is a adivasi hero of the novel who is an educated and skilled technician, but for racial minded, Clinton, who has the superior sense of being English looks down to Bashiam as *Jungliwalah* having a low status because he belongs to the adivasi community. Clinton's outlook towards Bashiam is:

> Bashiam seemed to him to be riddled with fears, in thrall to the spirits of forest and rain like the hill tribesman, he was still at heart. Even the other Indians kept him apart, a stronger in their midst, calling him junliwallah as he had taken to doing. Jungliwallah. A man of a jungle. A primitive just come down off the trees. Englishman and Hindu alike looked down their delicate Aryans noses and overtly spurred the aborigines (Markandeya: 1969:24)

The antipathic behavior of Clinton towards adivasis is the exact opposite of his wife, Helen, who is sympathetic. Clinton looks down on adivasis as barbaric, but Helen considers them as a loyal human being. When Clinton charges hefty fine on adivasis, she strongly condemns her husband's mentality. Clinton could not understand why his wife took much indulgence among adivasis. Commenting on her wife's attachment towards the adivasi community, he says, "What if a tribe whose outstanding characteristic in his view was the severe retardation of its civilisation? Alternatively, of the glib communication, she had established with a people who presented to him only the blank capacities of their total incomprehension" (Markandeya: 1969:35). The character of the chief of the adivasi village shows the difference between the adivasi younger generation and older once. He holds responsible for the younger generation for the degradation of adivasi values and commonsense. He things younger adivasi runs after money. They are blind against western and industrial greed. His opinion about the evil of the adivasi community is very suggestive. He thinks that instead of relying on the forest products for their livelihood, they ran after money and lose their peace and tranquility of mind. His rejection of the materialistic system seems intolerable to the younger adivasi. Everybody ignores him though he is the chief of the village. Ideological differences between the younger and older generation of Adivasis have been shown by following the dialogue between Helen and the adivasi Chief:

Can you hear them morning? His voice a shrill bark came surprisingly.
Helen said, squatting down beside him, „I heard them in the camp. Here it looks, of ___ it looks. It is not. They mourn here too. They miss the money. They are becoming as money-mad as your foreigners are."
"It is a useful commodity."
"Useful, Useful you can say what for, I ask you, for that rubbish they buy from the camp shop?"
Tin cans, sand cupboards boots and scented pig grease to plaster on their hair for this, they moan."
"I have heard differently, said Helen. There are other causes of components.
"Ah yes" the old man confirmed with asperity, "there is short of food too, whose fault is it, the jungle is full of the game if they relied on that and not on the money which comes and goes, but what is the age of an old man talking. Keep away, I told them. I am their headman. I have To say these things, someone has to say them: but no. Now they are perished and are hurt, like small children. Like fools, whose fault I ask.

(Markandeya: 1969:72-73)

The character of Bashiam emerged as mature, fulfill when Helen tell him the opinion of other Britisher about him. He shares the way of adivasi living, to Helen and reveals his understanding of adivasi life.

"Once she said to him. Do you know what they call you behind your back?
"Junglywallah, he said at once without hesitation.
"Do you know what it means?"
"A man of the jungle, an uncivilised man."
"What it really means," she said cruelly, "he is someone who does not count someone who gets kicked around and does not do anything to stop it."
He said slowly, "Do you mean me?"
She said quietly, there used to be a village who's the bungalows are... Where your bungalow is a adivasi village."
"A small settlement, yes".
"When they were told to go, they went"
"Yes"
"Without protest, like animals."
I suppose you could put it like that."
Helen said, "You are a member of that tribe. It was their land they did not want to leave it. They were persuaded. Why did they allow themselves to be? Why did you? Without even protesting (Markandeya: 1969:49)

This is the small discussion about adivasi life between Helen and old adivasi chief of the village, but Kamala Markandeya has not presented the adivasi life of struggle, they had for their rights on forests. The novelist has shown them so submissive, forgotten their glorious past of revolts. Younger adivasis who show their presence in novels are unaware of their adivasi culture and indulged in materialism. Through the theme of displacement, the novelist could make a meaningful discourse for adivasis, but she engaged much dialogue to show the hanging romance between Helen and Bashiam. Helen tries her best to familiar with adivasi ethos but her sense of being alien, seen again and again. The postcolonial literature reinvestigates the idea of the nation, cultural assimilation, nationalism and patriotism written by the colonised country after colonisation.

Nevertheless, in the post-independence freedom of India, hardly we see that the adivasi is considered as the citizen of this country. Even after many years of Independence, they are struggling for their rights. Adivasis fight for the right is going on since the coming of the British East India Company to the present scenario but the adivasi in India hardly seen in literature written by Indian English writers. The way they are exploited, they are far away from the postcolonial themes of literature like nation and nationalism. Helen's visit to the adivasi village shows that their representation as a citizen does not find a prominent place in the novel.

Adivasis claims as Adivasi or Indigenous is formally rejected because an indigenous community comes under the International customary law. They have their self-determination rights. Adivasi proves the owner of their land, forest and river. Therefore the government considers adivasis self-determination rights as the conspiracy of the foreigner to destroy the unity of the nation. Therefore, we have to understand the meaning and co-relation between the worlds like "Indigenous, Native, Aboriginal and the Adivasi.

Along with tribes in English, Adivasi has some synonyms like Indigenous, Aboriginal, primitive, native, naïve and savage. Regarding adivasis as ancient inhabitants of this land Shyamcharan Dube says, "Adivasis are the representatives of the ancient community living in Indian Subcontinent. We can admit their ancient culture as the heritage of this subcontinent. (Dube: 2011:42).

In *The Coffer Dam*, during the construction of the big dam, when the explosive blast happened, thirty poor adivasi labourers die, but as a chief engineer, Clinton does not show any regret on their death. When the matter of disposing of their bodies takes place, he clearly shows his anti-adivasi attitude, which seems like an example of racial and cultural dominance. The adivasi chief, the older man in the village, laments a lot on their death. This shows the difference between capitalism and communalism, "He was dry, divided bones scraped thinly against each other, and flesh fell away from the bones as if dried out in some oven. He creaked when he moved. So he lay still, looking at all of them and listening to the voice in the hut and beyond to the calling and keening of women and beyond still for something which did not come" (Markandeya: 1969:165). This victimisation of adivasi labours during the process of industrialisation in India is an ongoing process. Inferior adivasi dies, mercilessly killed, disposed of, deploy and dislocated but nobody cares. The novelist has only presented one side of their exploitation that is corporate policy, but the problems are numerous. About the pathos of the adivasis A. K. Chaturvedi opines:

> Nobody agrees with Clinton's proposal of incorporating the dead bodies of adivasis into the structure. Everybody is of the view that the dead bodies should be disentangled from the machine that has ruthlessly crushed them. For this purpose, the boulder has to be lifted to raise the dead bodies. Nevertheless, who will dare to leave the boulder? When nobody is ready to risk his life for the sake of the dead adivasis, Bashiam, a courageous adivasi as he is, comes forward to do the adventure. However, Clinton is very well aware of the fact that the machine has developed a severe fault and that the one who lifts the boulder in this condition is sure to lose one's life. He allows Bashiam to lift the boulders. (Chaturvedi: 2008: 60)

The adivasi labourers who died on the construction site were Bashiam's fellow mates. He was from the same blood and the same community. Bashiam decision to leave the boulder shows his sublime qualities that characterise the culture of Indian adivasi, but on the other hand, Clinton's cruelty towards adivasis shows his capitalistic mentality. Basham, in the novel, presents a nobleman with adivasi background having imitable human values:

> And paused to gather strength, for it needed strength and said, I must do it, since they are my people, whom I cannot leave, although I have tried. My people who are the impediments as they have long been said are now proving themselves to be, which it is for me to remove. I will, he said and felt strong and looked at his young man's limbs which were smooth and strong but would twist so easily, frail under metal, breaking him with them for he possessed nothing except his strength.
>
> (Markandeya: 1969: 183)

While constructing the dam, one of the British engineers who have sympathy for adivasi, warns Clinton that if the coffers of the dam are not breached, entire land may be swept by the flood which will create a damaging situation for adivasis. Mr. Makendrick warns Clinton, "The Coffer will have to be breached, or the river will burst its banks. The whole land basin, where the adivasis are is at the risk of inundation. It is a matter of extinction of the entire land basin which will form the bed of a lake unless the coffers are breached. (Markandeya: 1969: 215). Overall depiction and characterisation of the Bashiam in the novel *The Coffer Dam* seem that adivasi life in the novel is not justified. They lack the basic amenities of life. We do not have the references for the struggling life of adivasi in the novel. Postcolonial India is India born and brought with capitalist and industrial mentality. Adivasi became the first victim of this wave of capitalism, but the novel does not focus on that issue nor finds any echo about the rehabilitation of adivasis who are displaced during the process of industrialisation. Bashiam plays an important role in the novel as well as a miner in many episodes. In the battle of love, he defeats the heroine's husband, Clinton. Bashiam is a bright star in the sky of primitivism. Bashiam presents the qualities of civilised as well as adivasi life. A.K. Chaturvedi says, "Despite his birth in a adivasi family he does not depend on the forest product for his livelihood. He chooses the technical education or his livelihood in place of living the life of a junglywallah as all adivasis do" (Chaturvedi: 2008:63).

The novel is a perfect example of internal as well as external colonialism. This novel is the case of multicolonialism, where adivasis find no voice. They barely exist. Jobs, bribes, and wages seduce poor adivasi labourers. Adivasi huts are destroyed, crops swayed away when the river gets wild, but Clinton has no sympathy, no concern for these adivasi which shows his colonial mentality on one side but the Krishnan, head of the Indian technician and Das who work for Helen and Clinton as their cook, also shows their detachment towards adivasis on the other side. They are the representative of the internal colonisation of adivasis in the novel. Adivasis are shown as the community which does not want good amenities of life. They are left to doom and displaced. For today's capitalist market, they are only victims and labours. They are considered as the biggest obstacles in the national progress. Nandini Sunder has commented in this regards:

> No doubt adivasi have now been become exposed to the market, bureaucracy, state and broader social and cultural groups, they had little knowledge of interaction and negotiation with them. Even if they had to interact with them, they did so only marginally. In fact, not only tribes

> treat them as outsiders, but tribes also consider others basically as outsiders and therefore not worthy of emulation. (Sunder: 2016:328)

Thus the Indian English fictions are very neutral and ignorant about adivasi issues. The literature of any nation or community should go beyond the visible word to show the realism behind the visual situations. Kamala Markandeya does not seem more about the adivasi issues and reality in *The Coffer Dam,* but the realism of adivasi life is covered in most of the regional adivasi writing under the term of *Adivasi Literature* or *Adivasi Discourse*. Ramnika Gupta points out:

> Adivasi literature is taking shape with their spirit of togetherness and freedom. This literature has proved quite cataclysmic in positively shaping the nation-Adivasis's perception of and attitude towards the Adivasis. Adivasi literature is about life. It is about man's co-existence with nature. It is about freedom, quality and brotherhood, about social integration and honesty. It is free from greed and acquisitive instinct. It favors social equality and is against injustice. (Ramnika: 2009: 191)

The mainstream novelist should understand that corporate policies and internal colonisation are the main problems of adivasis poverty. When this corporate machinery encroaches adivasi territory for their economic purpose adivasi protested against them. It is evident if adivasi wants to be free from the exploited clutches of globalisation they have to challenge positively to the governing policies, the corrupt bureaucracy which is in the lap of government. For their existence, adivasis are now becoming politically conscious and want their representation in politics also. It is to be said that globalisation is *Global Village,* but in reality, it increases the identity crises among Adivasi and Dalit. Globalisation has erased their identity as marginal and subjugated people. Now, this is the time of struggle to save their identity in this global multicultural pot. This is a big challenge before the Adivasi community puts on their cultural values to their new generation because the new generation of Adivasi looks at themselves as representative of mainstreams. In the light of so-called cultural civilisation and the propaganda of Adivasi development, Aboriginal Adivasi society considers themselves as deprived, outcast and humiliated by the mainstream society of shining India. Indian English fiction writers are the painters of this shining and colorful India, but they rarely depicted Adivasi existential issues in their mainstream novels.

## Adivasi Life in Cultural Clash – *The Coffer Dam*

## Adivasi Life in Cultural Loss – *The Princess*

Manohar Malgonkar is the champion of the cause of the postcolonial representation of India. Through his novels like *Distant Drum, Princess, The Devils Wind* and *A Bed in the Ganges*, he has shown how the colonial rule was dominant in the Indian society. Through all the novels he has tried to decolonise the set western parameters of literature. Undoubtedly, he was the master of characters making as Maharaja Heroji, Abhayraj, Charudatt, and Kanaksigh. All these characters from the novel *The Princess* show different ideologies on the eve of the disintegration of Begwad province. Nevertheless, in this melodrama of disintegration, the Bhil adivasis of Bulwara seem only sidewalkers. Bhil has a history of centuries. They are very loyal towards the Maharaja Heroji. Regarding the adivasis appearance as a bodyguard for Maharaja Hiroji, Anand Mahanand opines: The relationship between the Maharaja and the adivasis is very peculiar.

> Abhay, the Maharaja's son and narrator, feels that the adivasis have been kept in the dark to prove the Maharaja's supremacy. They are not allowed to get the benefits of civilisation or be assertive. He believes that the relationship between the ruler and the people is a kind of ritualistic bond. It is the only influence that holds the turbulent people together. (Mahanand: 2011: 94)

Throughout the many generations, Bhil adivasis were loyal to the Maharaja's legacy. Now the Abhayraj, the narrator is the Maharaja, and he does not know much about the Bhils, but he knows that the adivasis are serving his province for the last many years but still they don't have the light of civilisation. When the process of disintegration of the state starts, Maharaja uses them as political tools. Bhil supports to Maharaja, against the lucrative policies given by Congress. Indian Independence in 1947 came with the promise of assimilation for the marginal, Dalits and adivasis for a better future. The entire political leaders during the Independence era were promising to the adivasis to gain their forest and customary law, but even after 70 years, adivasi is going in darkness day by day. This is the history that the political victimisation of adivasis has never taken seriously by the mainstream writers. Politician says *In the name of countries development, they must suffer, and now they are suffering.* Regarding the adivasi's political and social mobilisation, Alex Ekka notices:

> Adivasis are the indigenous people of India have as much right to be owners and partners in the development process as other Indian,

> especially because they have protected and harnessed the resources being the original settlers in the country. Their concept of land is profound, and perhaps the general society can learn from it, Not only that the adivasi people's aspirations were belied in ensuring their governance of the state, but also in bringing about their socio-economic development as per their pace and ethos. (Ekka: 2012:60)

In the ending phase of the novel *The Princess,* adivasi seems in great conflict. They are considered as the mercenary gang of Maharaja Heroji and are against the merging of state in the union. When in public programs, Kanaksingh announces the benefits of merging the state, suddenly Abhayraj counters him, and then chaos took place in that meeting. People run here and there, so the police fires in the air and then the Bhil adivasi are considered responsible for this violence. Then the rumors are spread everywhere that the violence was supported and provoked by Maharaja Abhayraj and his private soldiers, Bhils. "In the Bulwara riots, the mob compels the threats, so police have to fire in the air. Some minor injuries took place (Malgonkar: 1963: 342) Then the next day news comes that the adivasi area in the main connection for the violence. Again they become the victim of feudal policies and governmental oppressions. The news comes in the morning in which adivasi is blamed directly for state-sponsored violence. Malganokar has explained the circumstances in the following words, "Your highness, of Begwad, Abhayraj has resigned from his commanding post. He decided to give up all the amenities as Ex-highness. He has to present before the committee to explain the circumstances of riots in which adivasis of Bulwara has taken active participation. He decided to give up all the facilities as a statesman" (Malgonkar: 1963: 342).

We find the strong literary voices of feminism in Indian English literature. Women writers like Anita Desai Kamala Markandeya, Shashi Deshpande, Bharati Mukharjee and Geeta Hariharan challenge the stereotype norms of canonical literature and establish rebellious literary voice against the patriarchic mentalities. Nevertheless, we do not find adivasi women's subjugations, distorted chastities of adivasi women and multicolonisations of Adivasi women in their literary writings. Their concerns seem only to the elite classes and educated women and not for the deprived section of society. Adivasi women are the victims of twice thrice colonisation. They are exploited in society by moneylenders, feudal lords, from the man at home, and they have to face several exploitations from the females of elite classes. Adivasi women are brought outside of their residents to the metro cities and are sold to the mediator. These mediators exploit them severely. They cut out their wages and exploit them physically. They are not secure in those places where they work for their family. Despite all fact, adivasi women are migrated to all the part of the country in search of employment. It is regrettable that in the exploitation of these wretched adivasi women, urban, educated women also perform their minor role in marginalising them. The novel, *The Princes*, ends with the note that the adivasis are violent and for creating commotion they are often used for political purposes.

Nevertheless, there is no explanation of the displacement of the mass number of adivasi of Bulwara Bhils. What happened to them after their displacement from Bulwara? The novelist has not presented the disintegration of adivasi, but the whole novel revolves around the theme of Begwad State, Maharaja Heroji, and his shrewd policies regarding merging the state into the union. He used the adivasi as the mercenary weapons. Maharaja Hiroji and Abhayraj equally were responsible for the political victimisation of adivasis. Abhayraj was aware of the duplicity of his father; therefore, he comments:

> Beautiful people, loyal and brave. They are fighting men, and this is their country, almost as it was since time began we don't want to take it away from them for the sake of putting up factories and mills somewhere generating electricity. They would have felt uprooted, sold like a slave – six hundred rupees per head or a patch of irrigated land. I lift it to them. The choice was theirs. (Malgonkar: 1963:101)

This is surprising that the history of feudalism in India considers adivasi the owner of the land, the owner of the country on one side and allows for bonded labour of adivasi, open labour market of adivasis on another side. Authorities, whether it is pre-independence or post-independence period, it was always playing shrewdly with the adivasi community. State and governments often give promises to them with romantic imagination of development, progress, higher living standard but never speaks about their constitutional rights. In the novel, *The Princess,* we came across some political tactics of double treachery of government and feudalism. Commenting on this the most corrupt part of the system, Felix Padel comments:

> A struggle between mining companies and the governments whose natural resources are exploited is a stable future of the history of mining. Naturally, companies get the lion's share of profits, but the struggle marginalises the people who have lived for centuries in symbiosis with the resources of mountains, forest and rivers, despite the promises always

> given at the start of pretty that they will get the fruits of development. (Padel: 2015: 321)

We can find that in the case of Bhil adivasi of Bulwara, they are a victim of the political holocaust and corporate and industrial conspiracies. They are becoming the epitome of sacrifice in the name of a progressive nation. A nation which will stand on their blood and bone but still government, bureaucrats, media and common masse expect from them that they must suffer for the sake of the nation's glory. What happened with adivasis in Bulwara seventy years back, now again happening in a ruthless, crushing manner? Under corporate policies, their forest, agriculture and water sources are all going under neo-colonialism. Still, a vast majority of Indian English writing chooses to keep silent on these destructive issues. This is the responsibility of the mainstream writer to give voice to the voiceless, to give eyes to the eyeless for the observation of the future. Nevertheless, the audit of Indian English novel during the last 70 years says that these progressive writings have not given expressive voices to marginal, ancient inhabitants of this land. Regarding this intellectual silence on adivasi deculturisation, disposition and subjugation, Anand Mahanand comments:

> The issue of deciding and speaking for the adivasis is relevant even today as we come across different agencies speaking on behalf of the adivasis and making attempts to bring them to their fold. The conversion programs of Christian missionaries, the Hinduisation process of the right-wing political workers are a few cases in these points. All of them, including political parties, are busy bringing them into their fold, but they don"t bother to find out what the adivasis need. These agencies largely ignore the adivasi points of view. (Mahanand: 2011: 97)

Several Non-Governmental Organisations are working in the exploited adivasi territory, but they are not serious about their aim of adivasi upliftment. They are getting benefits from governmental fundings whose runners are corporate tycoons. Therefore these NGO's are failed to bring any betterment in the distorted life of the adivasi. Suggesting the remedies on adivasi's upliftment, Ganga Sahay Meena comments:

> Understanding the solutions to the adivasis problem is an uphill task. At first, Non-adivasi society should understand the particularities of "Adivasiism". Their rights to self-determination should be decided. Issue of security of adivasi folk and communalism, Dialects should be given protection and rehabilitation. There should be a barter system of thoughts and ideologies between mainstream and aboriginal and not of one-sided exploitation with the strict implementation of the law.

> Generosity and sensitivity towards adivasis life is a must condition for mainstream society. (Meena: 2016: 68 Translated).

The novel, *The Princess,* shows the political, geographical and identical marginalisation of adivasi. The theme of displacement, demands of the adivasis are not pointed out in the novel. This is the melodrama of disintegration and the personal loss of power of Maharaja Abhayraj and having not any concern for adivasis. The final passage shows the disappearance and doom of adivasis in the novel when

Malgonkar comments, "Music was creating buzz, then followed commentary, I was listening carefully. I was catching each word of commentary. Nevertheless, I came to know, Bhil adivasi and myself in no more part of the commentary. A harsh male voice providing statistics of excessive production of newspaper and welfare policies" (Malgonkar: 1963: 382). Kamala Markandeya's novel *The Coffer Dam* which setting is given in the southern part of India but its appeal is universal. Just like in all her novels, Markandeya has dealt with the culture clash, the psyche of Westerners's and their outlook towards native culture. Colonialism still runs through the mind of Clinton, the Chief Engineer of the dam. Various discussions, sentences of the British characters show Eurocentric psychology while giving an opinion about the adivasi village and their cultures. Bashiam is an educated adivasi technician, but Clinton's calling him as '*Jungliwallah*" shows the empirical mentality" which has a historical sense, is not very easy to wipe out. We find a critical dialogue about the displacement of a adivasi village in the making process of the dam. A novelist could give a subtle touch of indigenous culture, their struggle for land and forest, memories of adivasi ancestor and their concern for natural objects. Nevertheless, this novel seems silence on these native – aboriginal themes, only the marital failure of Helen and Clinton, lovemaking and involvements of adivasi Bashiam and Helen, runs throughout the novel.

*The Coffer Dam* deals with numerous issues like dying humanitarianism, the superiority of the West, a rational attitude towards ecology, colonial and anti-colonial mentalities. The novel shows the dual reflection of the colonialism of the adivasi community. Perhaps this novel is the first one, who claims double disposition of adivasis. British engineers, Indian bureaucrats and officials also hate the local adivasis, claiming that adivasi is the obstacles in the path of the country's developmental policies. They want to dispose of adivasis elsewhere so they cannot interfere with the construction site. Clinton is the chief of the British Engineers team and boss of superior white mentality, who hates local from the bottom of his heart. His professional sense seems, when he comments, "My work, from mountain conviction, which loomed tall as a mountain now. "My dam, my business" (Joshi: 1969:127). The relationship of Clinton – Helen in the novel, seems not mutual. She wants to go further out of her marital responsibilities and wants to find an illusory world of freedom. She tries to take an interest in adivasi life and adivasi man Bashiam. A lot of cultural discussions take place between them. As Helen shows her interest in adivasi life, Clinton seems for away from these cultural assimilations. He is ruthless; the heartless symbol of white supremacy who wants to exploits nature without showing any morality and ethics to the adivasi landscape.

> Regarding sheer hatred of Clinton for adivasis, Kamala Markandyeya comments, "Clinton has no trust in the Indian adivasi as he considers them to be a people who worshipped birds and beasts and probably snakes, decking the forest with scruffy hutches which they knocked up out of driftwood and crammed with leaves and flowers for their defies"(Markandeya: 1969:76).

The theme of the novels runs with the East-West culture clash. The novel shows the concept of nationality, alienation, destruction of agrarian culture. In a real sense, this is a postcolonial novel. Nevertheless, the construction of the dam in this novel creates significant problems for the adivasi community. Though they are becoming homeless, though they are in the age of calamity like flooding, other characters like Helen, Clinton, Mackendrick does not show any sympathy for their indigeneity, their cultural and geographical loss, though they riched on the height of genocide. Those adivasi people are displaced from the traditional habitats that they have been still waiting for four centuries for adequate compensation or rehabilitation. Although large sections of these people are peaceful and silently accept the hardship imposed on them, a specific section has become political and occasionally resorts to violence. Degradation of the environment is due to the greed of consumers to overexploitation of resources and wanted damage to our ecosystem. The literary writing of India never tried to promote adivasi leadership. They never tried to explore the issues of adivasi education through their mainstream writings, it resulted in barrenness in social, political and literary arena. S.N.Choudhary has made an eye-opening comment, in this regards:

> The literature on adivasi studies reveals that reputational leaders have played a crucial role in the mitigation of problems faced by tribes for long. Many of them popularised corruption and red tappism, and gradually they became outsiders in their land. Panchayat and Block level adivasi elites and adivasi-dominated institution are insensitive to adivasi concern. Many emerging adivasi leaders have imitated the culture of non-adivasi established elites. Hence the inclusion of tribes in the developmental process remained at a distant place. (Choudhary: 2016:04)

Adivasis depicted in *The Coffer Dam* who faced the problem of disposition is not an old issue now. In contemporary scenarios also, a lot of dams, water reservoirs, field firing ranges and national parks are constructed by displacing adivasis from their land. This is the cultural and physical genocide of adivasis in India. A novelist could develop more severe issues regarding adivasi's struggle for surviving. However, an issue like growing materialism among adivasi youth, the theme of displacement, the conspiracy of officialdom, neocolonial state of mind of Clinton, Mackendrick and destructive aboriginal cultures, does not find good representation. Though the dam is constructing in the adivasi belt, there is nothing like development for the native adivasi, what they have in the name of development is geographical and cultural alienation including physical sufferings. Regarding this false concept of adivasi development, Felix Padel in his *In The Name of Sustainable Development -Genocide Masked as Adivasi Development*, opines:

> Development, as Gandhi said, when equality before the law becomes a reality and Adivasis or Dalits can go freely to the courts and expect justice, even when the perpetrator is a government servant or corporate executive, then the real development is guaranteed. It is hard to see this happing in the immediate future without confronting the most dangerous fundamentalism – neoliberal economics that is essentially displacing Adivasis and causing their cultural genocide. (Padel / Das 2010: 493)

*The Coffer Dam* was written in 1969, and *The Strange Case of Billy Biswas* is written in 1971; still, the life of the jungle is shown so entirely, so romantic, without any chaos, without any ambition for adivasi, nor any adivasi characters emerge in the 'Billy Biswas' who could become a spokesman for the drought-like situation of Malaika Hill of Satpura Region of Madhya Pradesh. In this romantic glorification, adivasis become the second in *The Strange Case of Billy Biswas. The Coffer Dam,* which came earlier in the publication, has the theme of displacement and genocide of adivasi life in South India, where adivasi characters like Bashiam, at least speaks about the displacement issues. Bashiam is a adivasi professional technician, who also seems culturally elevated who does not have the exact idea of adivasi struggle in that jungle but at least he wants to stand for his people. In this postcolonial novel, Markandeya tried to decolonise the English pattern of writing. She has given an intense Indian touch while showing the cultural encounters between East and West, and in between alien and aboriginal. Racial hatred can be noticed from the behavior of Clinton and his Engineer team towards the local adivasi. The machinery and other electronic apparatus which was shown in the novel, enough itself to prove that immediate after Independence, the adivasi area was chosen for the industrial growth of India. Mainstream literature always glorifies adivasi life in their novels. A adivasi girl and urban outsider love affair are shown, sometimes a British lady and adivasi youth take place in the scene, sometimes disturbed city officialdom comes into the adivasi territory to seek to refuse and come in contact with a local adivasi lady and exploits her. These are the stereotyped pattern of Indian English novelists. They decide themselves earlier what to shown and what to kept. So that the issue of industrial exploitation was not adequately presented through the novel *The Coffer Dam,* many scenes are focused on Adivasi Bashiam and British Helen, and they are eloping from contemporary realities. As Markandeya comments:

> Bashiam, the hill-man whom they called junglywallah or even more disparagingly the civilised junglywallha. He became her like-man, providing the information she sought of a country and a people who intrigued her, always had a curiosity with which she had always been liberally endowed. The curiosity grew with each encounter: no longer satisfied with watching, but wanting to know; entry achieved, now seeking performance. (Markandeya 1969: 44)

The exploitation of corporate machinery seldom becomes the theme of fiction writing in Indian English. Agrarian country life, the struggle of labourers never became the central theme of writing for Indian English writers. Therefore modern Indian English writers having the concern with metro and urban issues could not feel that agrarian ethos of villages of India where 70% population inhabited. This is the main reason that novelist sitting in sophisticated chambers could not observe the gloom of agrarian life. Adivasi life has its primary concerns with nature and its objects, but when British Imperialism expanded its wide roots in India adivasi territory, they exploited the natural resources as much as they can. Adivasis started to feel the threats from all sides seeking help from nobody.

Indian feudal lords, missionaries, British Imperialism and caste-the culture of India, played a significant role in disturbing adivasis in the colonial period. This exploiting machinery could not stop in the post-independence period where state policies and bureaucratic decisions played a crucial role in distorting poor adivasi communities. Through the pre-Independence to post-independence period, moneylenders used to rob them brutally. Women of the adivasi community were twice colonised, exploited by the British, Bureaucrats and moneylenders. Missionaries came with duel faces. They came with educations and a health agenda for Adivasis but their minute focus was the adivasi conversion into Christianity. They played an essential role in enforcing Christianity upon them and uprooted them from their native culture. All those values which are the validity of their identity, missionaries have tried to disconnect them from it. Because of this religious exploitation, adivasi life shook terribly. Resulting from several such exploitations, they decided themselves fight with different colored enemies. They united against them in history, but in mainstream scholarly presentations, they are nowhere. Today lives in the adivasi area have changed. Adivasi youth cannot cope up with the digital age. Even if they get the opportunity, working culture seems alien to them. Despite providing employment facilities in adivasi areas, their situation is still marginalised even after seventy-three years of independence. Regarding the frustration among adivasi youth, S.N.Choudhary says:

> Adivasi youth is the immediate victim of cultural disintegration. Many elements of their indigenous culture are today almost dead. In want of essential requirement alien culture is still not their own culture and therefore all the alien cultures benefits like English education, management mechanism, modern communication skill, interaction with police, courts are far away from them. They have largely failed to avail benefits of modernisation and development. (Choudhary: 2016:04)

Thus, flood-like situation, materialistic adivasi youth in villages, adivasis communion with nature, the sudden introduction of industrialisation in adivasi areas, Bashiams cultural dualism, Helens urban and sophisticated suffocation, Clinton extreme colonial mentality, adivasis dependency on alien Britishers have depicted by Kamala Markandeya. However, the adivasi life in the novel remains in the dark in the climax of the novel. The old adivasi man, his village and Bashiam remains silent, and Clinton, his superiority sense, dominant colonialism overpowers the novels. Therefore Anand Mahanand gives his final remark: As a writer with progressive attitudes, perhaps Markandeya expects

> Bashiam not to forget his people and adivasi identity and yet work for the progress of his region and people. However, one is disappointed to see the way Bashiam acts. All that Bashiam gets is the status of a loyal servant. It is to be noted that Adivasi Bashiam does not assume leadership. He feels happy that he can love Helen, a white who is his boss's wife. He volunteers to live the boulder because he feels for Clinton whose wife he has courted. This shows that Bashiam is loyal but not subservient, and this loyalty results in his destruction. (Mahanand: 2011:91)

An elite-Intellectual class seems unable to understand the global policies of New Imperialism. Multinationals have made a new map of neocolonisation of the world by erasing agrarian and aboriginal adivasi communities across the globe who are sitting on the top of the enormous storage of natural resources. Intellectual, socially responsible thinkers, novelists, are making possible ground for commercialisation through their writings. East is coping west in industrialism, therefore writing class is also working for the interest of corporates. Earlier they were robbed us by political colonisation, but in the new era, in the name of Democracy, they are making intellectual, emotional, social and cultural colonisation of India. First was British Imperialism now American Imperialism is bounded to colonise the world once again. Third world nation is their primary target for neo-colonisation. Natural resources, big dams, gold mine, coal mine and mines uranium mines are their interest, which is mainly found in hilly and forest areas dominated by significant adivasi population. Hence adivasi become victims in the name of developmental policies.

Adivasis are not only displaced by using NGO, military, local landlord's armies or by economic promises but a much cultural transformation is also forcing in those adivasi areas. The Indian English novelist never speaks about the cultural imperialism of multinationals, nor do they speak about the ideas of internal cultural imperialism which wants adivasi identity sweeps away. Do our nationalist novelists have any concern for adivasi poverty and several hardships of their existence? It fact it does not seem.

# CHAPTER 4

# Stereotype Portrayal of the Adivasi in *A River Sutra* and *The Inheritance of Loss*

**Postcolonialism in the Novels of Geeta Mehta and Kiran Desai:**

Geeta Mehta incorporated Hindu-philosophy, Jainism, self-realisation, blind faith, pain, love, desire, sorrow, disappointment, colonialism and adivasi myth through her some of the famous novels like *Raj, Karma Cola* and *The River Sutra.* Dialogism has been used to construct her narratives. Through her novel, postcolonial Indian society takes shape. In cultural and literary studies, postcolonialism has been used in a historical sense. Sometimes it lacks ideological formation, so it lacks unified critical perspectives. This umbrella term covers the distorted historical past of many colonies and their exploitation under white supremacy. Nevertheless, it omits the significant episodes of the subjugation of indigenous communities, particularly in the Indian social context. Adivasi in India seems out of the box of the concept of postcolonialism. About the silence on adivasi's disposition and cultural genocide, Felix Padel opines:

> Displacement for the Adivasi community means a psychic death. This is the sense in which Adivasis, through the invasion of their land by dam and mining projects, face a situation of genocide. Every aspect of their social structure is severely disreputed, and the people witness the death of the community's cultural securities and ecological system which their ancestors had always carefully maintained. (Padel: 2016:160)

Postcolonialism can be studied through the terms of national, historical and cultural aspects. Colonial experiences and colonial exploitation vary from culture to culture and nation to nation. Indigenous communities of various continents were crushed and destroyed through the process of colonialism. Indian tribes, African indigenous, American tribes and Australian Abongional were much-shattered communities during the colonisation; therefore, the postcolonial writings differ from nation to nation. This theory of postcolonialism has a broader perspective. The postcolonial novels of Geeta Mehata discuss social justice, power structure, gender and racism.

Her novels show the postcolonialism based on relativity. This relativity has checked between harmony and conflict, between ideas and practices between different people and their cultural modes. Issues of globalisation and migration also find prominent places in her writings. The central theme of postcolonialism is reclaiming the identity, which was smothered and marginalised earlier. The postcolonial voice shows resistance and misrepresentation of orients. Indian English Fiction writings tried to glorify the adivasi realities. They have shown adivaṣi characters as innocent as anyone can befool them very quickly. This is not the reality of adivasi land. The adivasi villages mostly find their location in forests which are in authorities of the forest departments. Governmental officialdom sometimes misbehaves with them. Indian Constitution has given significant rights to the adivasis, but the forest authority is not cooperative with them. Sudha Vason in the edited volume of Meena Radhakrishna, states:

> The interaction of the forest department with Adivasis lies in the crux of how the rule of law, particularly the idea of state properly encroached upon by Adivasis is often used in public discourse to justify forest department activities. The same concept is not applied concerning the working of the forest department. This ongoing historical disrespect of the state in Adivasi India erodes the imagination of the rule of law. (Radhakrishan: 2016:26)

In *The River Sutra*, India's cultural life and religious mythology which existed from the earlier period have been presented with excellent literary skills. In her novel *Karma Cola*, she presents contemporary Indian spirituality and western gullibility. Her next novel *Raj* is an interrogation about native princely India and Imperial British India. Geeta Mehta's alienation from her homeland allows her to develop her material from Indian mythology, history, culture and religiosity. Her experience of living on different continents provided enough scope to check the consequences of postcolonialism. In one of her interviews, she opines:

> There is a tremendous richness of living on three continents. The magic of America is enchanting; it gives me the belief that anything possible. Each time I finish a book and I think I will near write another America

> makes me think, "Yah, I will have another shot. London's great virtue is that, as the capital of an empire, its libraries have staggering material on India. Furthermore, Because of the British reticence, it's easy to be alone and write there. My heart is in India – so when I am there, I don't write. I just let it all seep through in my prose. (p. 53-54) (*Making India Accessible*)

In all her novels, Geeta Mehata is restructuring historical data by reordering it properly. For rewriting of history, she practiced revisioning and rewriting the past and situated the plot within socio-cultural contexts and discovered meaning in her history. Such type of ordering is postcolonial ordering where the author is granting importance to what the *Centre* once called *Margin* and what colonialism called *nature* and hence the *other.* Geeta Mehta, as a postcolonial writer, reinscribes her country's culture and past. In her political novel "*Raj*" she has drawn our attention to distressing experiences of racial and cultural violence of colonialism.

Nevertheless, the multicolonisation of suppressed communities seems out of her literary interests. Through her novel *Raj*, Indian feminine history is recreated. Through the novel, she has given voices to the marginalised. She had freed the history from a particular ideology and generated awareness of power relations and finally drawn the social-political dislocation of social relationships. But when the matter comes of the representation of Adivasis, it lacks authenticity and is limited in scope,

Truly, Geeta Mehta's *Raj* is a significant attempt to observe the cultural exploitation of colonialism through the postcolonial historical sense. Her postcolonial sensibilities are mature. In her writings, we can find the exact difference between "Superior – Inferior", and the center-periphery of the colonised – coloniser. The novel depicts the exploitation and domination of the colonised. Social injustice and power structure are exceptionally narrated. Mehta writes, "The sovereignty of the British crown is supreme in India, and therefore no ruler of an Indian state can justifiably claim to negotiate with the British Government on an equal footing. Our supremacy is based not only upon treatise but exists independently of them. The Angrez is worse than money lenders. They steal everything we have and still say we are in their debt" (2015:395). The other characters in the novel, like Victor, Tikka and Prince Pratap, suffer from cultural dualism. Though they are in a powerful position in the novel, yet they make others suffer from their community. Thus they are both victims and victimizers. Colonial mentality, cultural domination seems from her character's portrayal. Her characters are possessed with the western colonial mentality. Aestheticism, in her novel, is brilliant, but the marginal content comes very rarely in her literary creativities.

*The River Sutra* is the blending of ego, lust, love, renunciation and mutual evolvement. The novel is a representation of contemporary Indian psychology. We find very progressive dialogues about attachment against detachment, materialism versus spiritualism, love against hate and tradition against modernity. Finally, all the themes in the novel eulogise river Narmada. Geeta Mehta, who traveled on a different continent, has comprehensive experience of different cultures. She has incorporated her experiences with arts, mythology, identity and geography in the Indian context. The nostalgic feeling, theme of salvation and the tension between 'home' and 'no home' finds powerful expression through her post-colonial sensibilities. But the dual disposition of deprived communities, physical and mental abuses of adivasi and Dalits communities hardly takes any shape through her literary sensibilities. Postcolonial Indian English writing became rich because of the writings of Geeta Mehta. Renunciation always has ideal in Indian writing in English. Indian feeling of culture and life eventually comes through renunciation. In her novel, her characters renounce material possession, emotional bandage, desire, anger, ego, lust and passions. This provides retrospection to live once. Through her writing, Geeta Mehta is successful in finding a cultural identity to a certain extent. Kiran Desai came on the literary horizon of Indian English fiction writings when she got the Booker Prize for her magnificent novel *The Inheritance of Loss.* This tragic-comic novel spans the history of two continents and the different opinions of their generations. This postcolonial novel deals with marginal communities, clashing cultures and growing globalisation. The story of the novel hangs from Kalimpong to New York. Crave for identity and struggle for recognition finds the fundamental themes of her novel.

> The novel is narrated from the vantage point of a traveler who shuttles between New York and North-East corner, between the sense of loss and sense of deprivation, between the giant nation of colonialism and the small nation of intimacy, between the terror of insurgency and exhilaration of being alive in the world. The title of the novel is suggestive, and it manages to explore the kaleidoscope topography of majestic Kanchenjunga with the quaint British style structure of Kalmpongk's civic society highlighting the condition of non-Nepalies

> during the Gorkhaland agitation and the ugly aspect of this town famous for cheese and lollypops. (Ghanshyam: 2013: 213)

*The Inheritance of Loss* is a postcolonial novel on many grounds. It shows a broad canvas of socio-political events. The novel presents contemporary reality on discrimination, racism, eloping of Asian illegal immigrants in the Western-European country, a state of insurgency in East-India which covers a wide area from Kalimpong to Britain to the United States. Novel projects light on the collapse of faith, historical events, longing, love and loss so brilliantly that grips our attention. Most of the postcolonial writings have expressed their nostalgic feeling, incomplete longings and desperate regretting over the contemporary realities. Kiran Desai's novel powerfully tells the story of alienation, an individual's quest for identity in his own country and immigrant sensibilities in postcolonial India. Prasanjit Chakravarthy commented in this regard:

> The novel *The Inheritance of Loss,* prospects insights into many contemporary national and international issues like economic equality, globalisation, fundamental, multiculturalism, insurgency terrorist violence poverty alleviation and unemployment, corruption and the dying economy. The novel is set in the backdrop of rising insurgency in Nepal. It traces the memories on the contradictory terrains of East and West, poverty and wealth, the migrants and the residents. The novel deal, with a host of account both individual and national in the political backdrop of the Gorkha Insurgency in Kalimpong, a quiet and quaint hill town, now a bursting subdivision headquarters jointly administered by the West Bengal Government and the Darjeeling Gorkha Hill council. (Ghanshyam: 2013:213)

This novel shows the bond of love, mutual relationship on the backdrop of racial hatred and extreme nationalism. The novelist artistically interweaves characters. This is an intense love story between a boy Gyan, who is the mathematics teacher of Sai and the girl Sai, love between a father who is the cook of the retired judge Jemulal and his son Biju, love relation between a grandfather who is a retired judge and his grand-daughter Sai, living with her grandfather in the city of Kalimpong in the Himalayas. Sai loves Gyan who is the successor of Nepali Gorkha mercenary. His intense love for his motherland, his belief in violence for this sake is a significant theme that questions the memories of revolution. Another character, Biju son, of a cook working in a retire judge's home, is an illegal immigrant in New York and spends much of his time to evade the authorities. One common thread between all these characters is that they continuously feel that something is lost. Here is the loss of inheritance, loss of love, loss of human bonding, loss of nationalism, loss of aspirations and the loss of roots. Adivasis cultural loss, loss of their ancestry could never be treated with fair justice in Indian English novel writings. Major developmental projects have brought a threat to adivasi existence, but this native reality could not become part of writing by Indian English fiction writers. A novelist could show the concerns about these issues, but displacement, dislocation and dispossession of adivasis, their resistance to unnecessary developmental projects have not been taking serious concern in novel writings by, mainstream literary circle. Virginias Xaxa opines in this regards in his famous volume- *State, Society and Tribes in Postcolonial India:*

> The benefits of the developmental projects have not accrued to adivasi people. Hence resistance against such projects has increased in the adivasi regions in recent years. Some of the important ongoing movements are the struggle of adivasi people in Kashipur, Lalajigarh, Kalinga and Nagarnar. The key figure in these struggles has been the adivasis themselves. NGO and social activists have also begun to support these struggles. Another noteworthy struggle against the displacement in recent years is the struggle of the adivasi in Kerala, which is being spearheaded by a women leader called C.K.Janu. (Xaxa: 2008:56)

The feelings of rootlessness and homesickness are the very dominant themes of postcolonial Indian English writings. Everyone has their desire, ambition, but they could not fulfill it so finds themselves miserable. The retired judge now living in Kalimpong, wished he had been born European seems his intense longing for westernising culture. In a postcolonial situation, the judge seems pan-Indian in his longing, imagination, which shows his lack of attraction for his motherland. His company with Sai seems to fail to compensate for the loss has experienced in life. Notice the comment of G. A. Ghanshyam in this regards:

> The solitude became a habit, the habit became the man, and it crushed him into a shadow. For the entire day, nobody spoke to him at all, his throat Jammed with words unaltered his heart and mind turned into blunt acting things. He forgets how to laugh. To the end of his life, he would never be seen without socks and shoes and would prefer shadow to light, faded days to sunny, for he was suspicious that sunlight might reveal him, in his hideousness all two. (Desai: 2006: 40)

In *The Inheritance of Loss, the* novel speaks about the characters who feel powerlessness and humiliation. Gyan, who is in love with Sai, presents himself as the patriot of Gurkha land, who is ready to die or kill for his motherland. He is the promoter of the slogan,

*"Gorkhaland is for Gorkha only'*. His love for native land turns into anger and malice for those Nepalese who are snatching every opportunity of bread and butter from the local Gorkhas. In the novel, Gorkha opines that they are neglected and exploited though they are committed and loyal towards the motherland. For their love of the motherland, they have sacrificed their future. Gorkhas were treated as foreigners after they retired from defense services and they walk like labourers on barefoot in their motherland. These Nepalese remembered how in the past, Indira Gandhi asked for their support and how they voted their vote to India against the king of Sikkim to enrich the jewel-colored kingdom. The novelist accepted that despite their loyalty towards India, India does not show their rationale to the sensitivity and problems of the Nepalis. The novelist has commented on the demands of a separate homeland:

> The separatist movement here, separatist movement there, terrorist, guerillas insurgents, rebels, agitators, instigators and they all learn from one another, of course, the Neps have been encouraged by the Sikhs and their Khalistan, by UEFA, NEFA, PLA; Jharkhand, Bodoland, Gorkhaland, Tripur, Mizoram, Manipur, Kashmir, Punjab, Assam. (Desai: 2006: 129)

This postcolonial novel, *The Inheritance Of Loss,* tells us about the centuries of marginalisation, subjugation, and disposition by colonial economic, cultural and hegemonic forces of the west that derived the glob in the upsurge of social, political, historical and cultural disparities. The novel is compact with incidents and situations. Gyan realises the temporary hanging with Sai and indulges in being a martyr of his Gorkha motherland, but Sai remains in adolescence, always missing to Gyan. Biju's father is a postcolonial victim of a master-slave relationship who wishes to make his son, the Eastern Caliban separate from his master Jemubhai who is Prospero in black skin and white mask. Biju's intense longing and love for his mother and motherland in his immigrant sensibilities have powerful.Gorkha agitation shows no ending in the novel. It's an ongoing movement. The natural beauty of Kanchanjunga is celebrated by all the characters, only intense longings for Kalimpong finds the prominent stage of the novel. Adivasis in the novel, *The Inheritance of Loss* are suffering from racial discrimination. It's only because of their race, color and manners they are considered as uncivilised. The novelist has also presented their characters as marginal, having no voice of identity. The mainstream Indian scenario seems very unsympathetic about adivasi culture and rights. About the subjugation of the adivasis, Gladson Dungdung opines:

> Adivasis have always racially been discriminated against, exploited and disposed of the question is if you take away the livelihood resources of Adivasi without providing those alternatives discriminating against them and treating them like sub-humans then how can you expect their human growth. Today millions of Adivasi are struggling for survival. The Adivasi region lacks education, health facilities, drinking water, sanitation and shelter. (Dungdung: 2013:114)

In both novels, situations have taken from the globalised world. We are witnessing the adivasi Village of Vano, Narmada River, New York, Kalimpong and the life of the valley. Both the novel shows the barrenness of life and futility of existence even after having all the amenities of life. The novel indirectly as well as directly comments on the growing material values in contemporary society, whether it is East or West. Both novels present the higher values of life which are connected with material possessions, but the outcome seems that characters find some lacuna and bare ground in their heart. Characters find themselves isolated and aloof from their relationships. Both the novel convincingly brought the postcolonial identity crises to which all the characters hang themselves. Everyone tries to find their identity but seems a failure. Certainly, spiritualism, religious beliefs, myth and imagery took an essential part in the novels of Geeta Mehta. Spending much time abroad, she has taken her keen interest in the philosophical spiritualism of India. Probably, she might be the first Indian English novelist who extensively used the myth and gave them a place in the novel. Her spiritualism is the answer to the westernised moll culture where one gets boredom, after having all the amenities. The diversion of the Indian mind from spiritualism leads to the degeneration of Indian society. When we read her novels like *Raj, Karama Cola,* and *The River Sutra,* we remind the quotation of Aijaz Ahmad when he comments, "One did not have to belong, one could simply float, effortlessly, through a supermarket of packaged and commoditized cultures ready to be consumed" (Ahmad: 1992:82).

Mehta's observation of the colonial regime in India is not superfluous. She has shown her disgust about the Europeanisation of Indian traditions. She closely observes and satirizes the princely behavior of King's families who were the soft victimisation of western materialism having lost their faith in Indian spiritualism. Her postcolonial responses show how the colonial mentality of westerners was looking to India. East-West encounter as reflecting in her novel is different from the east-west encounter shown by Manohar Malgonkar and Kamala Markandeya. Her magnificent novel *Karma Cola* depicts colonial India and its merits and vices. S. P. Sawan, in his research paper *The Meaninglessly Meaningful: Geeta Mehta's Karma Cola,* opines:

> It is a poignant study of the sham and hypocrisy of the princely class in colonial India and the deceptive Gurus selling pseudo promises and vague foreboding in the name of enlightenment, to the occident coming to India in quest of meaning. Karma Cola satirizes the subterranean and almost absurd lives of the hippies from Europe and North America who came to India in the 1960s/1970s in the quest of spiritual bliss, in search of meaning to their otherwise meaningless and absurd lives. This is a confrontation and an encounter between the East and the West; the Orient and the Occident. (Patel: 2012:195)

Today, adivasis are becoming the victims of displacement, but tomorrow Dalits, and then farmers will be the victim of global corporate policies. Indian English writing is not aware of these upcoming hardships. Because of this intellectual silence, marginal questions are becoming more serious. The identical mass movement of feminism, Dalit Adivasi and farmers, are also going on at the edge of extreme marginalisation but Indian English writers seem still in darkness. They do not have a solution for how to give strength to the voices of marginal against neo-colonisation. What should be the parameter for novelist and public intellectuals for debates and writings? If our novelist could not make a progressive literary front against the world's neo-colonisation, then we will be on the way to self-destruction. No adivasi, no Dalit, no elite and no business tycoon will be served for an extended period in the mongering profit system of capitalism.

The issue of adivasi identity and existence is not only limited to Adivasi only but it's a global issue of surviving of humanity. If nature is distorted, all will have to face the circumstances. These ecological concerns and adivasi's efforts for environmental protection were never shown through their writings. Indian English novelist glorifies the postcolonial period and prepares a ground for liberalisation and globalisation under the theoretical them like cosmopolitanism, multiculturalism and hybrid society. However, the problems of the third world were related to food, shelter, education, health, justice prosperity and sustainable ecology then how can western parameters of literature writing enhance the realism of Indian fiction writing.

Glorifying the western cultural values cannot be a solution to give strength to marginal voices in literature. The novelist must be acquainted themselves with these realities.

## Representation of Adivasi Life in *The River Sutra*

*The River Sutra* came in 1993 to present the contemporary picture of Indian spiritual and cultural scenarios. The river "Narmada" is in the center of all incidents, activities and salvation of all characters. Her novel *Raj* presents the life and her making in postcolonial India. The struggle of princely India for disintegration separated identity and how that struggle brings the change into a small segment of sophisticated high culture society, have presented magnificently through the characters of Jaya Sing's story. Mehta has tried to blend historical time, narrative time, contemporary and mythological time unitedly in the flow of the river, Narmada. *A River Sutra* is much more than six stories. It tells us the story of life through the myths of the river Narmada. It is all about the Indian cultural, mythical values, adivasi pathos, ethos, arts and music.

Three chapters in the novel present adivasi life. However, the novelist has given her energy to remerge Indian mythological, spiritual identity in the postcolonial, globalised world. When we go through the presentation of adivasi characters and their development, we find a romanticisation and inauthenticity about adivasi life. Her presentation of adivasi, native feminism is not just different as depicted in Hindi films. The way, she tried to show the adivasi world with such grace and tranquility, in reality, adivasis life is not so idealistic. It is full of challenges of neocolonialism. Regarding her romantic representation of adivasiism in *The Rever Sutra,* Stella Sandahl opines, "Geeta Mehata does not of course entirely ignores the poor menace adivasis, but she maintained them only as a decorate dements like their appearance in commercial Bombay films" (The Toronto Review of Contemporary Writing Abroad: 2014:96).

In the initial chapter of the novel, *The River Sutra,* readers meet the adivasi village of Vano, situating on the bank of river Narmada. Though the novelist has not used a particular adivasi character still, it can be assumed that the village is adivasi-dominated. This is the first thing that surprises us. All the credit goes to a retired officer who works as a manager of the rest house. Again adivasi village and their way of living remain silent. Even the novelist has not shared the name of the main character of an ex-civil servant, who wants to live his life in tranquility with nature beside the bank of the river. When the narrator goes for a morning walk from the rest house to Vano, he meets with adivasi women who greet him. He surprises that these women behave very familiarly to the unknown person.

Nevertheless, he could depict this adivasi grace very positively, but we do not find much exploration about their manners. Some of the adivasi workers in the garden of the rest house, and then gradually he comes to know the historical past and Aryans invasion of that territory. The stories of displacement and subjugation of adivasis come very rarely in this novel. Commenting on adivasis historical past which is not suggestive enough, the narrator opines:

> Our bungalows guards are hived from Vano and enjoy a reputation for fierceness as descendants of the adivasis races that held the Aryan invasion of India at bay for centuries in these hills. Indeed, the Vano village deity is a stone image of a half women with the full breast of a fertility symbol but the torso of a coiled snake, because the adivasi believes they once nailed a great snake kingdom until the gods of the Aryans defeated them. Saved from annihilation only by a divine personification of the Narmada River, the grateful adivasis conferred on the river the gift of annulling the effects of snakebite (Mehata: 1993:33)

The novelist tries to show that adivasis are so superstitious that they believe that madness and causes of snakebites are to be cured by worshipping to the Narmada River. It can be accepted that adivasi are nature worshippers, they worship the sun, river, hills and trees but as for the concern of disease and madness, it cannot be cured only on going to the Narmada river. The novel, A River Sutra, was written in 1993, which was an era of globalisation in India and industrialisation was at its high peak in the adivasi belt. The resistance of adivasi was also tremendous, and in such turmoil, the novelist is projecting adivasis as so superstitious. It seems unconvincing. As for the adivasi concern, there is no such mythology, where snakebites person is taken to the Narmada or any river in the adivasi belt to cure such diseases. Obviously, following discussion between the adivasi ladies shows that the novelist is only glorifying, and sensationalising adivasi women's conversation. She does not seem responsible about the adivasi feminism when her narrator speaks the romantic dialogue about adivasi women,

> "The Saheb finds our face pretty today, Rano." "It must be the season, and spring rouses even old tigers." "It is true don't you see a prowl to the sahebs walk this morning." "Kama must be sharpening his arrows of blossoms and stringing his arrows of blossoms and stringing his bow with

sisters. "Take care the Saheb does not leave us to a seduction" (Mehata: 1993: 92-93)

The above discussion between adivasi women shows the stereotype mentality of the novelist to present adivasis as very ignorant. The pukka sahib attitude of the novelist comes out which takes the adivasi as granted. Adivasi women who live a very harsh life in adivasi territory become victims of the elite mentality of a sophisticated society. A novelist could present adivasi women's hard work and their struggle for survival, but the above conversation between adivasi characters is far away from real adivasi life. Adivasi characters who do not hold even a name in the novel presents sensuousness, is the only example to create hype among urban locality about adivasi women. It is stereotype literary gimmick of the novelist so that R. S. Pathak comments very seriously about the partial knowledge of urban writing towards adivasi struggle he says, "Since Indian English literature owed its inception to the "dominant minority" amongst Indians steeped in western education, values and culture, we find adivasi people, local and values infrequently treated in English novels written by Indians" (Pathak: 1999:179).

Nitin Bose is the character who is the narrator's ex-colleague's nephew attempts suicide, comes to rest house to introspect himself from the magical enchantment of adivasi women, Rima. Nitin's diary contains all the matter of his relations with that adivasi lady. The moral effect on Rima on him is presented in the diary as "Rima seduced me with adivasi songs in a language I could not understand so that I heard the only sweetness of the melodies. She told me tales of a great serpent kingdom lying inches beneath the soil. She spoke to me of charms that gave men the strength of elephant in a rut and of magic performed during the eclipse of the moon when a man soul could be captured inside the two halves of a coconut" (Mehta: 1993:126-127). The above mention description is only body celebration of the adivasi character of Rima. The mythology has profoundly used to enhance the character of the adivasi lady, Rima. A typical male attitude seems predominant when we closely study the thought process of Nitin about adivasi women. He considers Rima, responsible for his enchanting madness.

The magnetic elements in the description of Rima remind us of Bilasia of *The Strange Case of Billy Biswas*. Billy was attracted to Bilasia because of her adivasi grace, and he also presents her body praising. Similarly, Nitin is celebrating her body parts in the above discussions.

Rima's husband is a coolie, she is the tea picker, this is quite enough to guess her economic situation, but by neglecting the adivasi realism of survival issues, the novelist has only glorified and romanticised adivasi feminism, showing no reality. This is unnecessary descriptions of adivasi life. Various rituals have been performed by the adivasis in the novel *A River Sutra*, but the adivasi's rituals are not like other religions. Adivasis are often shown as superstitious, but they are nature worshipers. Nature is their religion, but a mass conversion is taking place among adivasis in major adivasi areas in India. Adivasi is dominated by the other orthodox religious groups that they are denied to choose their religious beliefs also. In this regards, Gladson Dungdung makes a hurtful comment on the conversion policies of orthodox structures in adivasis region:

> The Indian state did not recognise the religion of the Adivasis. Though many religions Hinduism, Buddhism, Sikhism, Jainism, Christianity and Islam that emerged much later in India were recognised in the official documents in the country. As a result, thousands of Adivasis accepted other religions. Enmity was created among them, and thousands of their sacred groves were destroyed in the name of development, and the uniqueness of their religion was lost. (Dungdung: 2013: 28)

The mental dilemma of Nitin Bose is very similar to Billy Biswas. Nitin feels the intense rejection of monotonous and sophisticated city life with its artificiality. He wants to take a break from urban humdrum, so he takes refuge in the tea estate of Assam. Nitin is the boss in a tea estate where adivasi Rima comes under his power. Without much inquiry, he developed his relationship with her and seduced her. Here, power relation seems dominant, Nitin is boss, and adivasi Rima is a servant. No matter to say no to her exploitation. She has to obey her boss.

Nevertheless, now Nitin finds himself crazy about Rima. He could not spend the night without her. Once she calls him from a distant dark place, and he runs after that voice madly. This shows that he has crossed the limits of his rationale or conscience. Though the intense passion, he again shows the impact of her enchantment, "Like a magician she drew me into a subterranean world of dream, her body teaching mine the passing of the season, the personal rhythm of nature, until I understood why my grandfather's book called these hills Kamapara, the kingdom of the God of love. Headless of the low branches whipping against my body, I ran after her through the jungle calling her name, my voice loud in the night" (Mehta: 1993: 133).

In the novel, when Nitin follows Rima's voice and reached there, he is possessed by her spirit. When the adivasi priest fails to cure him of the enchanting effects of Rima, he takes him to the shrine situated on the River Narmada. The adivasi prays to Goddesses Narmada to cure Nitin. Adivasi suggest him to carry an idol of Goddesses and immerse it into the river. Nitin performs the ritual according to adivasi tradition, and ultimately he gets the result that he is exempted from the possession of adivasi Rima's spirit. Rima is the central adivasi character who emerged into the novel after Nitin Bose.

Nevertheless, we find her character very mysterious, slow, silent, full of romance and more areal than earthen. Her beauty, charm and her effect on Nitin have been presented very grippingly by the novelist. This stereotype description can be justified and granted from mainstream literature, but from the adivasi's point of view, the novel does not show their problems like deforestation, displacement, exploited feminism and economic misery. Their religious functions with the fusion of superstitions have been presented promptly in the novel. As Billy Biswas finds himself very helpless from the effect of the beauty of Bilasia, Nitin finds himself helpless to get rid of the enchanting beauty of Rima. He has presented the character of Rima in a very sensuous word where the realism of adivasi women and her several predicaments seems no place. "Desire was too mild a word for what I felt at that moment. It was closer to madness. The terrible madness of a man who after great sin and much suffering finally finds himself in the presence of his god. She had that untamed beauty that comes to flower only in our primitive people" (Pathak: 1999:69).

In the literary history of the Indian subcontinent, intellectuals and writers could not give an expansion to their social ideologies on the political level. Therefore the dangers of neo-colonisation are coming before us. The novelist creates social conducts and norms. They should identify their concerns about their writings. The novelist must be aware of the possible dangers of neoliberal global policies. They are controlling fashion, tradition, sports, economic policies, employment, and education, including literary sensibilities. Therefore novelist writing on metro culture glorifies new modern trends in urban areas, but they could not depict or do not want to depict the distorted, broken and fragmented life of the Adivasi community in Bastar, Ranchi, Dantewada and Jagdalpur. The standard adivasi population of India is sandwiched between the Naxal terror and governmental, military operations. Human rights violation is on its peak in those areas. Every opportunity of adivasi life, every opportunity of education is going far away from them. If the Indian English novelist could not identify the danger of the corporate policies and post-globalisation, then their writing on adivasi life has not any relevance with human dignity and social uplifting of marginal and broken communities.

It must be admitted that though the novelist has not presented the barbaric, wild picture of adivasi characters, still they have neglected in the novel. Subaltern and marginal issues of their survival have not been presented with responsibility. Adivasi natures and customs have glorified in the novel, and the character of Rima finds no adivasi touch of struggling Adivasi life. Again under her enchantment, when Nitin befooled himself, the adivasi goddess cured him. Adivasis dances, laughter, way of living life do not show the evil touch of industrialisation and disorientation, which is a matter of research for mainstream society. Though the novelist tried to show adivasi ethos strongly, it seemed unconvincing. It must be noticed that the story revolves around the character of Nitin and the narrator. Their observations about urban and sophisticated life predominate in the novel. Therefore we get only small glimpses of adivasi life. The separation of Rima from her husband is because of their economic misery which is nowhere explored in the novel. These pathetic situations of adivasi life where they have to leave their families behind for the earning and have to migrate somewhere have not presented in the novel. We can be assured that Nitin feels life as dull and monotonous, which becomes the central theme for the novel but the havoc and struggle of adivasi life from centuries are as usual remains in silence. Mainstream writers deny their pathos. This is what we see in this novel also. Mainstream writers must look at these issues seriously. Notice the statement of R. S. Pathak regarding this romanticisation:

> Geeta Mehta has devoted some space to adivasi people, locals and values in her novel *A River Sutra*. On the whole, these disadvantaged people have often remained related to the periphery of Indian society, and it is but natural that not much attention has been paid to them and their ethos by Indian English novelists. Helen, in *The Coffer Dam*, hurries to reassure Bashiam, a adivasi you are not some kind of freak to me. We are freaks only to the caste we come from, not to each other." Nevertheless, this kind of reassurance is rare and would contain a ring of insincerity to the adivasi ear. (Pathak: 1999:179)

The adivasi character, Rima, does not find a proper presentation of adivasi feminism in the novel. Being adivasi, she does not follow the patriarchal pattern of Hindu society and remain outside of traditional society. The novel shows, she has taken her control, herself and finds comfort in several appeals. In the novel, her lover Nitin also considers her as Goddesses. Though the novelist has shown the character of Rima as possessing some supernatural power, still her glorification seems unconvincing. While using religious spiritualism and its connection with adivasi life, the novelist has glorified the adivasi theme.

Nevertheless, even after glorification, the adivasi character of Rima does not leave any impression on the theme of this novel. The novel *The River Sutra* is gripping while presenting religious myth and spiritual regeneration in modern life. The novel was written on the thresholds of globalisation in India, which looks the fancy words for us but the barrenness of modern life and spiritual lacuna in worldly life are the results of these global policies. Nitin spends his entire life as a supporter of metro life and reaches nowhere but gets madness; still, we do not have enough explanation of globalisation in the novel. The novel deals with the elite, bourgeois culture, its sophisticated manners and their various sources of recreation but the adivasi in the novel seems like a leftover. This is the attitude of mainstream writing towards the significant population of Adivasi in Indian English literary contexts.

On the other hand, adivasi life has seriously affected with such drastic policies. Their bread and butter have been snatching by corporate policies. Every opportunity of good leaving has denied for them, but the novelist does not speak a single sentence about this disorientation and deculturisation of adivasi. The adivasi life, character and circumstances are not adequately treated. The novel lacks authenticity while depicting adivasi life, culture and several problems.

Indian English fiction writers should understand this fact that literature is also a product of class conflict. The elite class which has nothing to do with the hardships of adivasi and Dalit life will never focus on marginal ground realities. They will promote the elite issue of cosmopolitanism and globalise culture. When these people write for India, they advocate new world orders, new economic power and give strength to the establishment of foreign values on Indian ground. Globalisation came in India with economic promises. The middle class of India was advocating these policies, but now their dreams have broken. The majority of middle-class ideologies of India support new global policies; therefore, when some of them become writers or novelists, they support and strengthen the theories of western dominancy. Therefore Rakesh Kumar Singh opines:

> The world of Intellectual writing is going through the phase of dependency and neo-colonisation. If writers do not challenge these policies, then we will be deprived of alternative criticism, and the neo-imperial world order will be challenged less. Today western theories are making neo-colonisation of minds of intellectuals and dominant western theories are globally acquiring acceptance. Those who advocate postmodernism, post-structuralism, multiculturalism, diaspora and make debates on these issues are indirectly diverting us from the resistance and protest literature of marginal and broken community. Indian English writing seems weaker while dealing with these complex internal situations. (Singh: 2014:38)

## Depiction of Adivasi Pathos in *The Inheritance of Loss*

Kiran Desai, published, *The Inheritance of Loss* in 2006 which deals with the period around the 1980s.Novels present the analysis of globalisation, immigration and threats of terrorism. The novel is decorated with many strong characters like retired judge Jemubhai, his granddaughter Sai, her mathematic tutor Gyan, judges cook and his son Biju. While going through the characterisation, we come to know that each of these one, shares a common experience and socio-historical tradition of alienation. It deals with the feeling of the outsider, of humiliation, negligence and cultural impotence in our land and other places also. Everyone is continuous, feeling their inheritance of loss. This is the story of postcolonial cultural hybridity of three continents where characters find themselves distorted and helpless who could not give justice to the feeling and love of their loving one. Biju's letter writing to his cook father, his memories for his mother, Retire judge and his longing for becoming a prompt European, his granddaughter Sai is in love with Gyan who is the successor of Gorkha mercenary gangs could not give justice to Sai nor his motherland. The novel makes a big comment on centuries of silence, subjugation by cultural, sociohistoric domination of western materialism. Noticing the postcolonial craves for the identity of her characters, Dipti Sarkar foregrounds:

> Almost all of Desai's their encounters with the west have stunted characters. A retired judge is one of those „ridiculous Indians as the novel puts it, "who could not rid themselves of what they had broken their

> souls to learn" and whose Anglophilia can only turn into self-hatred. These Indians are also an unwanted anachronism in postcolonial India, where long-suppressed peoples have begun to awake to their dereliction, to express their answer and despair. (Sarkar: 2012:170)

Though everyone in the novel feels a kind of loss, in the seventeen chapters of the novel, we get some startling dialogues about the adivasi community. It seems surprising that novels deal with multiculturalism, hybridity, and at the same time, we find racial, indifference between the main characters and the unnamed adivasi characters. The novel deals with the emotional board and love relationship on the one hand and on the other side adivasis are shown as barefooted as they can show. The novel presents the struggle of adivasis for survival and identity in the novel. Nevertheless, their existence in the novel, in the episode is denied. Adivasi in the novel tolerates much humiliation and much discrimination. These groups of adivasi characters are from Zanzibar, but the situation and circumstances are from India. The Indian and Pakistani characters are related in Indian context along with the characters like Biju, Saeed and Omar in this novel. Saeed, a major character in the novel, is a struggler and immigrant working in the *Tarts Bakery* in America, lives in his confusions. His shelter is not enough for himself. He could not help others for food, shelter, or any kind of help but suddenly a group of adivasis boys landed at the gate of his bakery. All faces of the adivasis look exhausted. Saeed belongs to the town of Zanzibar, and all these poor fellows are from the same town in search of employment, food and shelter. They do not have employment in their own country; they come to America and want to meet Saeed. This group of adivasi boys has the address and phone number of Saeed which they had collected from his mother. Nevertheless, when Saeed noticed them on the get of the bakery, he lost his temper. He told Biju to send them back and compels Biju, not give any hint to them about him. Possibly, Saeed has his struggle to settle in America, and he has no sources to help others, in such a situation he comes to know that adivasis are waiting for him, he comments:

> More tribes, more tribes. I wake up; go to the window and their more tribes. Every time I look at another tribe. Everybody is saying, Oh no Visas anymore, they are getting very strict, it so hard and in the meantime everybody who applies, everybody is getting a visa. Why they do this to me? That American Embassy in Dar – Hwy? Nobody would give that Dooli a visa nobody. One look and you would say OK, something wrong here but they give it to him." (Desai: 2006: 96)

Saeed is continuously blaming the American government for giving a visa to Dooli. When Saeed glanced out the window, again he blames those outsider adivasis. Saeed sheer hatred for adivasis seems exaggerated because without giving much stronger reason he is blaming them. This is the stereotype mentality of the Indian English writers while dealing with the indigenous cultures and the characters of blood and bone. In their literary vision, adivasi is nowhere. "Oh myee God!" whispering.

"Tribes, man it's the tribes please God. Tell them I don't work here. How they get this address! My mother! I told her, "No more!" please! Omar, Go! Go! Go tell them to leave". (Desai: 2006:98). While this emotional turmoil and intense hatred of Saeed are going on, outside the bakery, a group of these adivasi boys is continuously searching Saeed, for the help. Nevertheless, nobody even shows sympathy for them. They look very weak, submissive and needed help but Saeed, Omar, Biju look at them from the window of the Bakery, but they don't want to help them. It looks. Thus they had been traveling several lifetimes, scratching their heads and staring at the Queens of Tarts. Adivasi of India also lives their life in such deprivation. The indigenous community across the globe indeed faced the same challenges of survival and intense existence. When Omer says that you should not help those adivasis, previously he used to help them, but because of their increasing number he stopped to help them, now all of them know that Omer will not help us, so nobody comes to him for help. Omer's ruthlessness makes a clear picture of their hatred towards adivasi. When Omer comes out in anger to scold them, he shouts on adivasis. "Who? Saeed? No, no, whats, name?"

Sayeed? No, No one of that name. Just me, Kauafya and Biju. (Desai: 2006:96) "Nevertheless, when adivasi counters Omer that Saeed mother has given his number to us and they want to meet him. Omer reacts very strongly he warns them: No, no. You all get moving. Nobody here whom you want to see, and if you make trouble, we get into trouble so not I ask you nicely, Go" (Desai: 2006:96).

The behavior of Biju, Omer and Saeed towards adivasis, their rude behavior about the needy adivasi indicates the materialistic mentality of the generation of Globalisation where nobody cares about their habit. Adivasis, in the novel, are frustrated and talking to one another but not moving from that place. This shows their dependency on Saeed. At any cost, they are not ready to accept that Saeed is not here. Innocent tribes could not understand the delicacy of Saeed. Biju, Saeed and Omer all are the immigrants, finds no settlement in America, they do not want to treat adivasis like the way they are treating. Again Biju goes outside to go back, but they ask for the mobile number of Saeed.

Saeed knows that even though having the number, they will come back. "I know him, they will come back they will try many more times, or one will stay, and others will go. Close the door, close the window…" (Desai: 2006:97). Kiran Desai has created the adivasi characters in the novel has no place, no nationality. In the novel, other mainstream characters are clear about their sense of loss and their inheritance. Nevertheless, adivasis in the novels having no ambitions like other characters. They simply want to meet their native friend, Saeed. They want employment. They want to shelter in an alien land. Their understanding, hardship and need for psychology have not been presented by the novelist. Other characters are clear about their objectives of life, but there is no hope for adivasi characters in this novel. Novel covering a broad canvass of three continents and nationalities, having different shades of characters like Gyam, Sai, Biju, Jamubhai. The bias mentality Of the novelist about adivasis reveals when A. K. Chaturvedi, comments regarding this:

> Nobody in America ready to help the adivasis in realizing the aim for which they left their country. When the man on whom they have pinned their hopes, hates to see them, who else can be expected to come forward to extend a helping hand to them. Novelists and Saeed's attitude towards them represents the general opinion about them. (Chaturvedi: 2008:74)

All the worker in *Tarts Bakery* is not with a sympathetic attitude because they are possessed with their materialistic crave of identities. They want to settle there, earn huge money, but while keeping their dream in mind, they forgot the fundamental values of generosity of hearts. These are the effect of growing material values on the average youth of the present generation. Biju, Saeed and Omar are the representatives of the butterfly generation who wants to make their career abroad but they don't have kind-hearted feelings enough to help needy people from their local places. Omar's antipathy towards adivasi reveals from his sentence when he opines: "No, No! You all get moving. Nobody here you want to see, and if you make trouble we get into trouble so now I ask you, nicely, Go" (Desai: 2006:97). Though Saeed and Omar have their limitation, nobody can be justified their inhuman treatment which they have given to the adivasis. Their activities and conversations are anti-adivasi. The novelist has presented the adivasi character as the subordinates who could take the burden of the main characters on their shoulders. Adivasis in the novels are more worsen than the status of marginal or subaltern. Because the cook of Jemubhai is also a marginal character, but this novel gives him recognisation. His mental anguish, his hopes for his son has presented by the novelist with great positivity, but the adivasi of novels are facing the same problem of survival and identities. A novelist could not create a broader picture of internal colonialism in this novel. The novelist does not look serious about adivasi's presentation in this celebrated novel. "They closed the window and the door, and from the floor, he telephones his apartment." Hey Ahmad, do not answer the phone, man that Dooli and all those boys have come from the airport! Lock up, stay down, do not stand and do not go near the window. (Desai: 2008:97).

The attitude of Saeed, which is not matured look unsympathetic towards the other adivasis in the novel. It seems that being a adivasi and looking for employment in white land seems a crime, as Saeed and other characters are giving treatment to them. In a multicultural country like America, adivasi could not find a place, shelter for themselves, it's pathetic. This sense of alienation and humiliation is equally strong like the sense of inheritance of loss of other characters in the novel. Saeed antipathy is continuously growing then he says, "Hah, why they give them a visa/ how they buy the tickets!" They could hear the voice at the other end. Then it vanished into Swahili in a potent dun form a rich, steaming animal evacuation" (Desai: 2006: 97).

Even when the phone bell rings in the bakery, nobody wants to pick it up because they do not want to entertain anyone. They think that the adivasi outside gives the ring. After discussing a lot about the adivasi and their longing to meet Saeed, Biju Ask Kavafya to pick up the phone. They are so terrified to pick up the phone of adivasis. They comment, "The tribes! They are always sacred of the answering machine!" Nevertheless, on the insistence of Biju, Kavafya picks the phone! Poor adivasi says, "Emergency, Emergency! We are coming from the airport. Emergency, Emergency, Saeed Sa-ee-d?" (Desai: 2008:98). Saeed mercilessly put the phone down and unplugged it. Such is the condition of the poor adivasi presented by the novelist

Kiran Desai. She could create a positive picture of adivasi since she has dealt with the theme of multiculturalism and cultural assimilation.

Nevertheless, she could not give justice to adivasi boys in the novel. In this regard, adivasi in the novel only seems leftover. There is no need to introduce adivasi episodes in the novel but to show the pain of alienation in a foreign land, and she has taken adivasi characterisation without giving proper justice to the theme. Regarding the pathetic situation of adivasi, writer A. K. Chaturvedi points out:

> The Gate of the Queen of Tarts Bakery is close to them, so is the gate of fate. Biju, Saeed's other colleague, is asked not to open the get of the bakery till they depart. Ultimately they do depart from there with their broken hearts. Seed feels a great relief when he hears that they have gone. (Chaturvedi: 2008:74)

The novelist, creative writers and academic forums should ask themselves seriously what should their roles in social upliftment? What should be the subject of debates and discourses when the significant population of India belongs to adivasi, Dalit and agrarian culture is displacing and disorienting? Will they ask themselves where they are standing and where will they go as responsible, creative writers in this challenging age of post-globalisation or new colonisation? Today minorities, adivasis, laborers and agrarian communities in India are going through the phase of cultural and educational imperialism which directly or indirectly becomes powerful because of the silence of writers and negligence of policymakers. If the novelist could understand their unavoidable role in the path of human freedom, then how global neo-colonisation could be successful in making our cultural colonisation. In this case, the role of English writers and their culture of silence is responsible for making marginal classes more broken. When intellectualism corrupts, nation corrodes and neo-colonisation flourishes. After the reading of the novel, we hardly remember these adivasi characters and their predicaments in the novel. Their struggle for survival in a multicultural pot like America, the tension of immigrants, their bare existence, dumbness, and their *Waiting for Godot* like optimism for Saeed's's response leaves in the background. Adivasi in the novel, *The Inheritance of Loss* leaves in silence. Though the novel does not focus much on adivasi characters whole section of characters seems marginalised. Regarding this marginalisation, Soumen Mukharjee opines:

> *The Inheritance of Loss* is a narrative of marginal individuals, where people like the cook, by and large, represent all those less educated powerless men, who work like donkeys all their life, because they accept it as their destiny. The cook's behavior is puzzling, but the reason for his almost suicidal actions lies in his mental praxis. (Pradhan: 2013:154)

In the world of Indian English writings, much discussion is taken place on literature including representations of marginal groups and debates that have taken on theoretical issues of the upliftment of subjugated communities. However, adivasi community and their betterment are not there in such discourses. Writers of literary writing also seem bias from cultural educational and psychological imperialism because they are the victims of that global conspiracy. Therefore, the regional novel writing of Vinod Kumar, Rakesh Kumar, Sanjeev, Ramendra, Maitri Pushpa, Vandana Tete, Yashwant Manohar, Vinayak Tumrav, Ganga Sahay Meena and Kedar Prasad Meena focuses on indigenous cultures. Dalit, adivasi, female life and its distortion from colonial forces, internal exploited power machinery are the core issues of their novel writings. Such committed regional novelists are very few in numbers in India. They write in vernacular, but the responsibility of Indian English novelist is very significant. They should play their vital role in the eradication of the evil things from the society, but modern novelist writes much on metro and campus life which deals with less realism of less population. Therefore the main issues of society remain in darkness in a country like India. IPL matches, football matches, corporate Kabbadie, Mr. and Mrs. Beautiful competition and various literary festivals become the issue of the press release and in print digital media but malnutrition, foeticide, honor killings, child mortality ratio, degradation of the educational system, agrarian collapse, evils of caste discrimination pretend of a casteless society, religious orthodoxy, terrorism, Naxalism, the suicide of formers, demonisation, employment, distorted marginal groups, evils of the global community, dark aspect of cosmopolitanism and meaninglessness of multi-nationality never becomes the main themes of the writings for Indian English writers. Cultural imperialism, neo-colonisation of mind and corruption of literary sensibilities are at the root of all this disorientation. Regarding this ground reality of the Indian academic and literary world, Rakesh Kumar says:

> In the contemporary scenario, literary stalwarts, writers, readers have also influenced globalisation because it promotes competition, envy, fascism, individuality and dependency among themselves. Different groups of

> literary writings and writers have developed a kind of self-centered ideology. Breaking of social commitment and crave for hype and prize is the result of capitalism. This is an unwanted gift from Neo-empirical culture. In this way novelists, writers, journalists have become the parasites. They deceive among themselves for the job, prizes and the craving for publicity. (Rakesh K.Singh: 2014:47) (Translation)

## Sensentionalise Adivasi Feminism in *A River Sutra*

## Bare-Existence and Invisibility of Adivasi Life in *The Inheritance of Loss*

Both the novel *The River Sutra* and *The Inheritance of Loss* was written on a big canvass of the social, political and historical transformation of Indian culture. This novel covers the issue of nation and nationalism, cultural hegemony, subaltern and marginal issues, religious mythology, spiritual salvation and sense of emptiness or sense of cultural or identical loss. In both, the novel, the picture, characterisation, situations and incidents about the multicultural society have been decorated with a great study. Nevertheless, when we go through the characterisation of the novel, we hardly remember the adivasi pathos. All the credit goes to the mainstream characters leaving behind the main causes of adivasi sufferings. Adivasi's ancient inheritance, the effect of modern civilisation on adivasis natural life finds no proper representation. Adivasis in India are the wretched souls during pre-colonial to the postcolonial historical, political, social and literary sphere of nationalism in India. The novelist seems ignorant towards the real causes of adivasi sufferings. Therefore she has presented romantic pictures of the adivasi in the novel. Regarding the realistic postcolonial condition of adivasi in India, Parmod Kumar Mehata comments:

> With the advent of the so-called economic growth and industrialisation, things began to change for the worse, so far as the adivasis were concerned. Cunning people, in connivance with the state authority, came to realise that most of the forests were rich in minerals; fuel oils and many other valuables things. So plans were chalked out, and a ceaseless campaign began for numerous projects of mining, drilling and other activities in the forests. The adivasis were uprooted from their soil where they had been living for centuries. (Mehra: 2015:144)

*The Executive Story* in the novel, *The River Sutra,* shows the glorification of adivasi life. Retire civil servant's attitude towards adivasi life shows the sympathy to this disoriented class. Nitin Bose, a womaniser who abuses women, finds himself haunted with the thought of Rima and her enchanting adivasiism, shows his mentality about the women when he comments, "as a consumer's goods, simple objects, and instrument of pleasure, a priced commodity" (Mehta:1993:44). The novelist has shown that adivasi lives on the bank of the Narmada River are blind with superstitions. When Nitin is possessed with the adivasi women Rima's enchantment, Priest advise him to go to Narmada Goddesses and the adivasi takes him to River Goddesses. The whole scene, where adivasi took him to deep down in Narmada River seems unconvincing. The novelist has shown that adivasis are simple and religious, maintained their relationship with nature. Nevertheless, it must be accepted that adivasis are nature dwellers, but they are not so much superstitious that they believe disease of mind and body can be cured only by diving into a river. Nitin Bose, the corrupt womanizer, the haunted soul cures only when he comes with the mud image of the Goddesses on his head and performs the rituals of goddesses the river of Narmada.

Adivasi characters from Vano village, adivasi women, and their rituals find a superficial touch in the novel *The River Sutra.* At the same time, the adivasi Rima, her longings, her separation from her husband, her seduction, tea estate of Assam, internal suppression of adivasis lives in the background. Much focus is given on Hindu rituals, the myth of the Narmada River and the involvement of adivasis in these religious rituals. Adivasis in the novel are shown helpful and well mannered. A adivasi woman of Vano treats the narrator with respect and dignity, so his frustration of life and the gloom of old memories vanished. The manager of the tea estate of Assam, Nitin Bose cured of his madness with the help of tribe's rituals. This novel was written when Industrialisation and globalisation were taking deep roots in scheduled areas of adivasi regions, but we find nothing unpleasant about their land dispositions in the novel. Adivasi's distortion, their deculturisation and displacements have no information in the novel. The novelist has given an only partial, one-sided depiction of the life of adivasis with romanticising mythological rituals in which adivasis finds no suitable place. A. K. Chaturvedi, remarks on this reality:

> Industrialisation and deforestation are playing havoc with the life of adivasis Technological advancement and development projects that may be beneficial to the civilised world are causing irreparable loss to the adivasis who still naturally want to leave away from the madding crowd. They prefer to remain cling to their old customs, traditions, rites and

> rituals. The move to deadivasiize them is proving dangerous. (Chaturvedi: 2008:71)

Geeta Mehta's presentation of adivasis in the novels dominated with Hindu mythology. Her presentation of adivasi might not be barbaric or unrestful, but the simplicity of their life is not as presented in the novel. Adivasi's hard struggle for survival, their vanishing identities in the global world, eradication of their roots from their land, deculturisation and disorientation could be an immense panorama to describe and discourse. However, the adivasi of Vano village, their natural rituals on the banks of Narmada River, their faith in their primordial power could not save them from the waves of colonialism and neo-colonialism. So there should be a real and not ariel presentation is expected, but Geeta Mehta's description of the adivasi holds no attention in this novel. Gladson Dungdug, adivasi activist, foregrounds:

> Adivasi – Adivasi culture is not a monolithic one. Each Adivasi community has an ancient and highly sophisticated basket of beliefs, rituals and behavior patterns. Nevertheless, since the British Raj, government after government has tried to decorate it, homogenise it into the "mainstream". On the one hand, adivasi face state-sponsored crimes against them and on the other hand, the so-called educated, civil person of the mainstream society also treats them as a sub-human beast and whatnot. The very core of human rights of the Indigenous peoples is being denied, injustice and atrocities are inflicted upon them almost every day of their lives. (Dungdung: 2013: Acknowledgment)

*The Inheritance of Loss* does not show more hope for adivasi life. The characterisation seems obscure. The presence of adivasi of Zanzibar in America reminds us of only the memorable play *Waiting for Godot*. Here, adivasis wait for Saeed, who is their local in Zanzibar to whom they come for help of shelter but denied to meet them only, Saeed shows his intense anger about them. The characterisation is the soul of a novel in which the novelist shows his functioning and draws the result. C. L. Khatri opines: "Characters are the essential component of the novel as the story centers around the human being and their actions, passions and mature. The novelist has to show his character functioning within a wide variety of contexts, situations and relationships" (Khatri: 2003: 01). Characterisation of adivasis in *The Inheritance of Loss* seems that the novelist understanding of the adivasi life is not adequate. Kiran Desai's understanding of adivasi life, culture and problems is minimal. She believes adivasi life is full of happiness and carefree attitude, therefore he relates their life with peacock dancing and cuckoo singing. She considers that jungles are impenetrable, but the modem realities are different from her imagination about adivasi life. She wants to elope to the adivasi territory to save herself from the daily humdrum of city life but the way she has presented adivasi in her novel, she neither serious about adivasi life, nor she wanted to bring any change in the attitude among the mainstream reader about the adivasi life. Notice the view of Kiran Desai about adivasi life:

> As contrasted to the urban area, crumbled under the weight of poisonous humidity, traffic jams, power failures and the crowd teeming across the broken pavements: (p.110), the area populated by the adivasis seethes with activities on the part of peacocks, parakeets, cuckoos and pigeons. The jungles are impenetrable on account of shrubs, bushes and thickets. The entire area is dominated and presided by the dark forces of the jungles, and people are obliged to do a adivasi workshop to be invariable. (Desai: 2008:96)

Adivasi's life is in connection with nature and natural objects. Forest is an unavoidable part of their culture. Forest products are the source of their livelihood. Though the novelist shows their life in the city, is inappropriate. Their traditional culture is rich with love, desire, struggle and spontaneity. *The Inheritance of Loss,* could not depict adivasi's struggle for existence. They are costing their life in the name of development in India and abroad also. The novel was written in 2006, which is the period of neo-colonisation, which threatens adivasi communities across the globe. The survival problems of the adivasi are becoming critical day by day, and their existence comes on the worst level of danger. Forest dwellers come to the city for their bread and butter, and they are given dehumanised treatment. In metro cities, every morning open markets of the adivasi laborer took place, and they are taken on construction sides. Only giving a fascinating presentation of jungles, mouthful praises for adivasi rituals, and customs are not enough to protect the indigenous community of this country. The novelist should show much concerned while depicting their culture and struggle for survival writer A. K. Chaturvedi notices:

> The report of inhuman exploitation of adivasi, especially their women, by privileged classes does painful reading. It has been going on in almost all places where the Adivasis have been brought only willy-nilly in contacts with the plaint people in the name of conferring on them the fruits of development. In the process of change, much of their natural habitat has been destroyed and their traditional sources of living, i.e. the forest depleted beyond recovery. The rhythm of the adivasis, which our poets

> have sung about, is now almost a thing of past. The alienation and deculturisation of these communities resulting in a long number of them taking to the voices of modern civilisation. If this is progress, the Adivasis would have been far happier without it. (Chaturvedi: 2008: 72)

In the novel *The Inheritance of Loss,* after much waiting, the adivasis do not go; Saeed granted them to take inside of the bakery. He knows that adivasis will not return until they meet Saeed. Nevertheless, nobody cares about the adivasis in the novel. Each one of them tried to humiliate them without knowing the reason for their arrival. Adivasi presence in the novel is distorted. In the man- women relationship of other characters like Sai-Gyan, Jamusheth- Sai, Biju-Cook, Saeed-Omar, Adivasi, do not fix their place in the multi-pot of America. They are not shown as exploited, subaltern who cannot speak about the reason for their arrival, nor has the novelist given any update for that. Sometimes it seems that the novelist could omit this episode, or she could present the place of the adivasi in the multiculturalism of the western world. Saeed's mentality shows that he has excellent disrespect for their sudden arrival. He thinks they are a parasite. In this regard, Saeed's opinion is essential when he says; ultimately Saeed does not help his local native adivasis but shows his distress before Biju. The problem of employment brought Saeed to America so as the other adivasi of Zanzibar but after coming to America, these poor adivasis get the insertion of Saeed who even does not wants to see their faces. Finally, Biju tells him to keep quiet, "Come out wrong, too softly, so they did not hear, or just as they had turned away" (Desai: 2006: 99).

The exploitation of an individual or community is possible only when there is no literacy among them. We observe that the adivasi community is very backward in education. There should be mass-awareness movements for educational pedagogy of adivasis through the literature just like the Dalit Panther movement, but novelist could not give justice to the educational issues of Adivasis. In these neocolonial perspectives, globalisation gave importance to commerce and management education. Therefore money-centric courses increased somewhat the courses of humanities. Literature and social sciences are the moral backbones of any society, but they are given lesser importance because of the propaganda of corporate. *End of History* is becoming the new slogan for the global word order. In India where economic, social disparities are so deep, it's a real danger to commercialise primary education. Only elite classes will be in the mainstream, but marginal will become more margins. Decolonisation of literary modes should be a clear focus of postcolonial studies, but the literature seems silent on this most responsive subject writers, novelist seems concerned only with the benefits they get on the cost of their culture of silence. Elite classes are handling educational academic and literary fronts which are now turning towards corporates institutional values.

In the novel, *Strenge Case of Billy Biswas,* adivasis are romanticised. In *The Coffer Dam,* adivasis are victimised. *The Inheritance of Loss* Adivasi is marginalised and seems no way to get rid of the problems of employment and economic misery. In this age of globalisation, adivasis are breaking their stereotyped image of forest dwellers and demanding their rights of fair treatment from mainstream society. Nevertheless, instead of giving them power, adivasis are crushed under the powerful machinery of globalisation and neo-colonisation. Novelist Kiran Desai could deal with this adivasi marginalisation from an excellent perspective, but with her lack of knowledge about adivasi livelihood and less understanding of adivasi life, she could not create a lively picture of adivasi in her novel. A. K. Chaturvedi gives a fair solution to the mainstream writers,

> Any effort of bringing into the social opinion about adivasi is replaced by a healthy and positive attitude towards their natural way of life. As is evident from their desperate efforts highlighted by Kiran Desai, they want to join the race of advancement in the fast-paced modern world. Nevertheless, the deeply rooted prejudice of modern society will not easily let them reap the benefits of Globalisation. (Chaturvedi: 2008: 74)

The novelist must decide what is essential for them to, Ecological sustaining or corporate system? Is this the place for rich people only or ecology should be given equal importance? Animals are the same right to live on this cosmos. We have lost the traditional importance of forest and capitalism has transformed it into furniture. If referring to sustainable ecology or agrarian society is to be considered as traditionalism, then this traditionalism is much better than post-structuralism and post-globalisation. The novelist should show their ecological concern through their writings. Social, political, economic, educational and cultural subjugations of adivasis are continuously going on, but literary silence is also continuously growing up. Intellectual silence predominates when Government, corporate and internal colonisers interfere with literary creativity. The novelists in the English language are well aware of their negligence towards the main issues of adivasis, but political and social benefits make them silent. Writers, academics, journalist fraternity in America and Europe are continuously protesting against globalisation and corporatisation of the world. Noam Chomsky, Edward Said, Ajaz Ahmad, Samir Amin, James Petras, Neomi Clain, Arundhati Roy, Vandana Shiva, Howard Zinn and Dawid Harvy are some of the names who protested against the imperialism and new colonisation of the world through their political and social writings. Literary voices are also not silenced against these post-global realities in Euro-America, but literary writings of India read western researches and debates but do not want to implement them in Indian situations.

It is the fact that when there is a wide gap between intellectual interest and issues of common masses, in that society people's movement and their voices go on at the edge of marginalisation. Eurocentric capitalists are ready to loot, the economic resources of third world nations for the safety of their future planning of becoming master of a one-world nation. The middle-class theory was purposefully planned for the implementation of consumer culture, but Eurocentric capitalists never promote middle-class literature and social concerns. Capitalism, the imperialist, invests their capital in such areas where they have a guaranty of double return; therefore, adivasi areas are to be chosen to invest for FDI. Land act, customary law was distorted to make bare grounds for corporates big projects. These things are done not only in the case of natural resources but also in literary creativity also. At current kinds of literature in India are promoting the materialistic values inspiring by multinationals of western society. Mainstream Indian English novel writer focuses only on sophisticated and convenient topics of their interest. Issue of family, nationhood, marital life and young generations metropolitan life comprises the central theme of their writings but economic liberation of adivasi, freedom of adivasi women, opportunities to the adivasi youngster in the nation making policies, they have no writing agenda. Regarding these factual issues of subjugated communities and the insensitivity of Indian English writers, the comment of Rakesh Kumar Singh, is very appropriate:

> Colonialism is deep-rooted in the psyche of Indian society. It's challenging to break the knots of deeply rooted colonialism. The ideology of Gandhiji, play their first role in the decolonisation of eurocentrism and promote the native, agrarian values to defeat fat imperialism. After Gandhi, Indian society could not free itself from western values of life which resulting in Globalisation, Neoliberalisation, and privatisation. (Rakesh K.Sing 2014:119) (Translated)

In both the novels *The River Sutra* and *The Inheritance of Loss, we* can say that Indian English Fiction writers have underrated and demeaned Adivasi life because, in both novels, the novelist has not described adivasi's marginalisation. The subaltern aspect of Rima's character has been washing out. The novelist in *The River Sutra* and the adivasis in *The Inheritance of Loss* show the height of misery, poverty and negligence. Regarding the presentation of adivasis in this novel, Anand Mahanand observes:

> Indian English novelists are perhaps delighted by their very use of English, and an air of inauthenticity often affects their writings, and this could be said of the novelists considered in this chapter. The novelists discussed all are talented, and the novels themselves are aesthetically pleasing. However, from a political or ideological perspective, one can notice that they seem to repeat with the same subjects and situations which are stereotyping and severally indulged in by the Anglo-Indian novelists. (Mahanand: 2011:102)

Indian English fiction writers should forward this hypothesis that globalisation is nothing but the reestablishment of neo-colonisation and post-globalisation. It is the result of neo-colonisation. When literary fraternity does not bring light on the suppressive policies of the state ruling class, then the danger of recolonisation increases because of their silences. New American Imperialism wants to transform the Indian subcontinent as their consumer hub; therefore, they want to erase those sections of society whose living standards are not up to the mark of their sophisticated ideologies. It is resulting in the displacement of aboriginals across the world. Everywhere in North America, Latin America, Australia, New Zealand, or first nation people of Canada are getting displaced because of the economic interest of multinational in adivasis natural resources. In India, the condition is not different those these Adivasis territories are colonised by the internal as well as external colonisation. Therefore it is the responsibility of mainstream writers to educate the common masses of India to identify the real face of economic policy results of its implementation. The novelist can make aware the public and address them that suppression, corruption and nepotism can never be in favor of public welfare. These literacy classes should argue with readers that nations should not transfer into an open market for the greed of few corporates. Literature can ask the question that policymakers cannot move out of their responsibilities.

The public intellectual, academicians and creative writers should come forward to realise the responsibilities of the state and has to take the lead of mass movements against displacements, disorientation, Europeanisation and neo-colonisation of the society and should make comments through their literary writings. If our writer or novelist understands their responsibilities, then new voices of revolution and protest against unjust and discrimination will take place. Indian English fiction writings can play a crucial role in promoting and creating *Organic Intellectualism* or *Public Intellectualism* through their literary crafts. When one section of society is becoming helpless, exploited, degenerated, distorted and deprived only then could social reformers, mass leaders emerge out from such depressed classes. Indian English writers must not leave hope to strengthen the voices of the aboriginal communities.

The Post-Independence Indian Bhasha Literature is sustaining its credibilities in changing decades of globalisation. Issues of socialism, colonialism, postcolonialism, Neocolonialism, displacement, urbanisation, Adivasi, Dalit and feminism seem realistic through their literary observations, and few exceptions will be there. A novelist like Madhu Kankria, Rajendra, Rakesh Kumar, Sanjeev, Ashwini Kumar, Mahasweta Devi, Gopinath Mohanty and C. K. Janu has given the real depiction of India. The Caste system, corporate robbery, dislocation of adivasis and the discontent of the growing younger generation of India in the light of liberalisation and globalisation has brought out convincingly by these novelists. Such commitment about ground realities of subaltern classes has been neglected in Indian English fiction and fiction writers. When literary creativity lacks moral vision and self-dignity, then they become unable to hold the grip on the system. The middle class gradually forgot to protest against the commercialism of public life and becomes weaker day by day. When intellectuals and creative writers accept the fascist policies of elite classes without any condition, their role in social, political and educational empowerment becomes weaker. This weakness of cultural silence in writing promotes literary barrenness in the national culture of any country. Significant sections of Indian Society have faced the deadly effects of globalisation. However, the literary Inteligencia is unable to build a mass cultural revival, mass literary movements in favor of public interest and in against the materialistic value system of the corporate world.

Today, Intellectual corruption is growing because of the writer's interest in political and economic benefits. This culture of silence will distort communal harmony and divide the society inter narrow-minded walls. Literary marginalisation of adivasi arises because of the blend of literary sensibilities of the writer and famous market. The novelist should get some parameters of subject treatment in the literature. Otherwise adivasi life, dissertation and exploited feminism will be out of the literary flow of mainstream writing which is controlled by the corporate market. The novelist should address to writing classes to investigate the social-political and historical glimpses of multinational capitalism of the third world and aboriginal adivasi communities. English writers should take into consideration that again third-world nations should strengthen themselves for the freedom of humanism through the bloody eagle claws of multinational neo-colonisation.

India is an agrarian country. If our literature does not endorse these village cultures from their literary crafts, then it's challenging to save the adivasi, Dalit and agrarian identities against global capitalism. Novelists, writers and policymakers are not serious about how to counter the oppressive mechanism to save the environment from the clutches of the fat corporates. If the environment is damaged, then adivasiism will be damaged. Because of the global warming streams and rivers are getting draughts rapidly. Because of big dams, big roads hightail building, the massive crowd of vehicles and the number of factories, global warming is threatening to ecology. The rapid destruction of trees and the neo-colonisation of forests and village cultures indicates that in the upcoming few years corporate system will erase the identity of the village and agrarian economy with self-suicidal. This will be a national loss of Indian culture. The novelist should show serious concern about ground issues. Farmers and Adivasis played their crucial role in the eradication of colonisation in India. Now again Dalits, Adivasi, Farmers, laborers, novelists, poets and intellectuals should again play their role to challenge directly to neo-colonisation, neo-liberalisation and new feudalism and all those exploited types of machinery which are running by corporate boards. Indian English Literature should have taken serious note that with the entry of capitalism in every sector, it has distorted the foundational pillars of that society, organisations and communities. Resisting globalisation is not the core issue of only Adivasi, laborers, feminist, but it has now become the issue of national sovereignty. To save the social, economic, cultural, educational rights of marginal, the novelist must oppose the corporatisation of the nation.

The adivasi community has their livelihood on their agricultural systems. This is the backbone of the adivasi community. Today there has been a tremendous change in the Forest Act, Adivasi Sub plan, Corporate Social Responsibility and District Mineral Foundations but those facilities are not getting to the adivasi landholders or farmers. When they protest against corrupt policies, they are labeled as *Aggressive*. When they resist against displacements, they are considered as *Naxal*. Adivasis protest for their constitutional rights have been suppressing very brutally nowadays. Adivasi is the community that never believes in violence, but different ideologies mislead them for strengthening their violent ideological grounds. Their protest is suppressed intentionally. The power controller of economics does not want that adivasi should be aware of their existential issues and create mass agitation. They should not be aware of international customary law. Great care is taken for that. Creative writers can write the reason behind their aggressiveness. They have known the reasons behind the mass agitation of tribes. Those adivasis from Maharashtra, Jharkhand, Chattisgarh and Andra Pradesh who are protesting against corporate loot are the real protectors of the environment. Will Indian English novel writing avoid these traditions of protest or neglect Adivasi resistance against neoliberalism? This is the central question before today's Indian English literary forums.

CHAPTER 5

# Disillusionment and Subjugation in *The English August* and *The White Tiger*

## Treatment to Postcolonial Issues in the novels of Upmanyu Chatterjee and Arvind Adiga

Indian English fiction writings have flourished after the post-independence period. Most of the Indian English novels were dealing with post-partition, changing social-political values and the impact of colonial rule on Indian Psyche. During the 1980s a new wave of postcolonial writers came on the horizon of Indian English fiction writings who dealt with postcolonial Indian developments, bureaucracy and administrative services. How the elite mentalities of sophisticated classes of new India were longing to adopt westernised values, have also been checked by these postcolonial writers. Some of the prominent novelists who dealt with postcolonial social and psychological issues in their novel are Vikram Seth, Boman Desai, Rohinton Mistry, Upmanyu Chatterjee, Nalinaksha Bhattacharya, N. K. Singh and Anurag Bhattacharya. Upmanyu Chatterjee started writing when India was changing rapidly in the political, social and economic sphere. The urbanisation of India was in its full swing. Urbanisation and alienation were taking place in the psyche of highly educated classes of Indian society. The radical mentality was taking shape. Indian politics, fundamental rights and bureaucracy were checked through these writings. Upmanyu Chatterjee wrote some of the famous novels focusing on changing values of Indian society in postcolonial India were having high education and all comforts of life, characters in novels finds themselves in a cultural dilemma. Upmanyu Chatterjee was the first novelist who satirizes the Indian Administrative services of postcolonial India. His magnificent novels are *The English August* (1981), *The Last Barden* (1997) and *The*

*Mammaries of Welfare State* (2000) where we find the anti-hero's observation of India. The heroes of these novels find themselves in a cultural clash. They are confused between their modern upbringing and traditional values. Their urban materialistic mentality, family values in the contemporary scenario and their inner turmoil. Upmanyu Chatterjee's novel gives us an idea of how was the consequences of encounter and the fusion of traditional Indian Society and British colonial mentality. The way Chatterjee has narrated the colonial ruling and native responses through his writings; it seems that he is the byproduct of both the cultures. He has an excellent study and analysis of East and West cultures and their value system. In this regard, Minakshi Mukherjee has given an excellent opinion, "The intellectual nature of his writing becomes for such a writer a theme of profound interest. Therefore the search for one's identity is found to be a common and recurrent theme Indo Anglican fiction" (Mukharjee: 1971:66).

Through his novels, Chatterjee has shown his protagonists crave for identity. Social traditions in India are brilliantly focused on him. A postcolonial trauma of cultural hybridity and cultural assimilation runs through his novels. The frustration of the characters, inner struggle and marital conflicts are some of the points on which the novelist observes their psychological states. His characters come to know that the root problem of their alienation in western educational modes, a different attitude toward physical needs and their parental relationships. Upmanyu Chatterjee's novel, *The English August, The Last Burden* and *The Mannoses of Welfare State,* all deals with the difference between western materialism and eastern upbringings. The cultural uprootedness, cultural loss and the identity of a confused mind find the central theme of his novels like the other postcolonial novelist including, Rukim Advani, Mukul Keshvem and Nalinaksha Bhattacharya. In this regard, S. N. Sharma opines in his *Recent Revelation of Indian Fiction in English*,

> When an individual goes abroad and stays there for quite a few years quite possibly, there is a silvering and disbranching. He gets alienated from his roots in native soil. He is no longer year's chestnut, the great rooted blossomed. When he gets back home with the accretions of foreign cultures, he finds himself in distress acclimatising himself. His is the case of rootlessness, loyalty and identity. This agonising awareness of difference and sameness is the plight of the isolated individual trying to forge a delicate balance precariously. (Prasad: 1983:207)

Chatterjee has shown August Sen as the anti-hero of the novel posted as BDO in the small town of Madana, West Bengal but because of his urban and elite education, he finds life utterly boring, his other administrative colleagues are dull, and his administrative mechanical work finds him no reason of useful life. He takes refuge in drinking and drugs. This novel is a striking satire on bureaucracy and how bribery is indirectly crucial for officialdom. Sophisticated cynicism despite the efficient stage of mind has been brought out convincingly by Upmanyu Chatterjee. In the novel, he experiences selfish civil servant, opportunistic political leaders, the violent face of Naxals, wretched adivasis, and a true Gandhian Dr. Rammana, who is a worker for the leprosy patients. After seeking his refuge in drinking and drugs, Agastya takes his job seriously, taking inspiration from Ramana. Following the conversation of Augusta and his colleagues shows his disliking about his working culture, fitting with the three men, he was again assailed by a sense of the unreal. "I do not like a breaker what am I doing here. I should have even a photographer or a maker of aid films, something like that, shallow and urban" (Chatterjee: 2003:02).

When Ahmad asks him about his marital status, he answered that he got twice and instead of having twenty-four, he feels that his age is twenty-eight. Agustya boredom of working place can be noticed from his in interest while working with his colleague, and Shiv K. Kumar opines, "Augusty is an uneven hero, drifting like a pendulum and hangs in the limbo just as Dantes character, hung aloof the corner." (Augusta and His English Tradition 1988 P. 36) Chatterjee's concept of antihero presents the youth of modern India, who are sentenced to make the career to which they hang miserably only, not passionately. The novel focuses on the illusion of happiness, of English educated Indian Modern youth, who suffer from his psychic level are find themselves between have or have not. In this context critic, Akash Kapoor opines, "Augustus stay convincing, entertaining, moving and timeless. It merits an accolade that's for harder to earn than authentic. Augusty is the slacker view of modern India. He is the Hollow man head fulfill with straw" (New York Times Book Review: 1995: 11).

Chatterjee, another novel of postcolonial social realism, is *The Last Burden* (1993) where three-generation lives under one roof having different outlooks towards life. In a real sense, *The Last Burden* is the story of the unaccountability of life. Jamun, the central character whose philosophical longings finds no escape nor gives any concrete idea of his reasoning about human existence. He is shown as a drifting object between family expectations and personal longings. R.S. Pathak comments on this psychology as follow, "This is the unbearable burden of family ties as Jamun the protagonist comes to realise when he returns home, after being informed that this mother is critically ill. The better and sweet memory of the past mingles with the tensions and irritations of the present. This could have made for an absorbing drama in the theatre of the mind" (Chatterjee: 1993:70). The psychology of modern educated Indian youth has been depicted in the character of Jamun who depicts an average Indian youth, who considers that his life will be more comfortable in London or New York than in a small place in India. The relationship status in middle-class Indian families is the main focus of Chatterjee's writing. The protagonist is born into a family, which is hateful. Notice, the mindset of the protagonist,

> At fifteen and twenty-eight, Jamun recognised the disparity in what money denotes to him and Berfi rather at fifteen, and he was certain at twenty-eight, he fancied that a difference in their attitudes might exist, but also that it might not matter. He gauges money to be wily. If he has the money, he will by chewing gum or condoms or a refrigerator. If he does not, he will puzzle himself to do without. The self-discipline becomes in itself quite piquant. Nevertheless, for Burfi, deprivation is a failure, a cudgel to his self-esteem. (Chatterjee: 1993:69-70)

Chatterjee's next novel, *The Mammaries of Welfare State,* is the sequel of his first novel, *The English August*. It presents a more drastic picture of modern bureaucracy than his first novel. Chatterjee takes us on an entirely new pattern of *'Banderland of Bobudom'* and uses several ironical devices to pinch their absurdities. The novelist brilliantly delineates bureaucratic red-tape, nepotism, sheer corruption and lethargic pigheadedness. The novelist has skillfully constructed management of the corrupt politics, bureaucracy with their benefits to certain classes, the depravity of marginal, subaltern section and finally the false image of the Welfare State. *The Mammaries of the Welfare State* is a much bigger and much wider book them its precursor. Augusta Sen is older now, but as shiftless minor character drifts in and out when you least expect them in again. There is not even the excuse of a plot. Because really nothing happens except a lot of bureaucratic confusions" (The Hindu: 1 April 2001: 04). The novel shows the barrenness, opportunistic state policies and the elite families who fail to understand the meaning of life. The novel presents sordid personalities with sordid deeds. What he has started with the picture of the bureaucracy from his first novel *The English August*, he continued it with dull, insipid and unchanged life through this second installment in *The Mammaries of the Welfare State*. In this regards, Ashish Nandy, Points out:

> This self-examination, of course, was conducted not from traditions or for that matter, from culture-free or culture fair vantage grounds. In practice, it meant nothing more than waging an uncompromising battle against anything that went against the newly internalised now clinched vision of a desirable society that emerged directly out of the European English tenement (Nandy: 1997:42-43: The Future of Dissent Seminar).

Indian English fiction writer looks down the regional literature; therefore, they do not want to educate themselves with the regional themes and kinds of literature about the various perspective of local and native life of the Indian community. Writing in English is one kind of linguistic imperialism. This must not forget that English education in India was a kind of linguistic imperialism. This is the language that was forced on the Indian psyche. It could be a better medium to resist neo-colonisation in India.

Nevertheless, English writer is still in the hallucination that they are getting world recognisation by the western literary world. Writing in western style, entertaining western materialistic values is another form to revive colonial legacy. Indian English fiction writers should oppose the recolonisation of Indian minds and literary subjects. They can take inspiration from African writers like N Gugi WA Thinogo and Chinua Achebe. The Indian writers should give priority to native, aboriginal themes in their writings. They should promote indigenous culture, local issues and strengthen the voices of the agrarian society in India. Writing with western values cannot become you westerner. Despite all the literary crafts, you will be still orient in the eyes of sophisticated western canons of literature. Indian English writers should take regional themes and revive the martyrdom of freedom fighter, which should become a literary discourse in the western world also.

In the postcolonial writings of India, writers and their literary creations have not treated the theme of imperialism at the center of their writings. The colonisation of Indian cultures was the dark period in India, but still, its social, psychological, historical and cultural aspects are not adequately presented by the writers. The imitation of western life peeps from their contemporary literature.

Good literature can enhance the national life of a nation. Good literature can beat the imperial policy of Eurocentric capitalism. Adivasis in India are well aware of the internal colonialism. They know that Western Imperialism and its supporters are the real enemies of the nation and native communities. Postcolonial identities reveal in his novels. The concept of the welfare state is rechecked through their novel after the colonisation of centuries. Poverty, deprived sections, gender and nationality all find prominent presentations through their novel. This novel strengthens the concept of postcolonialism in Indian English fiction.

Arvind Adiga came on the literary platform with Booker prize-winning novel *The While Tiger* in 2008. His second novel was *Between The Assassination,* and the recent novel was the *Last Man in the Tower* in 2011. Through these novels, one can study postcolonial literature of India, which deals with the decolonisation of the minds of colonised communities. Fundamental issues like socio-economic disparities, cultural domination, ethical subjugation, identical marginalisation, political nepotism, and corrupt bureaucracy have been brought to the forefront by Arvind Adiga in postcolonial Indian English fictions. He has studied adivasi- Dalit and minority life under these policies. Most of the evils, which are the root cause of the discrimination among adivasis and Dalits are still exist in India after Independence. His first novel *The White Tiger* deals with numerous contradictions of the early free Indian villages. The novel presents the dark life and sufferings of adivasis and underclasses. The novel has taken Laxamangarh, Gaya, and Dhanbad as its prominent locations which are major adivasi-Dalit dominated territories. Dalits and adivasis are still the oppressed souls in this country. The novel presents their exploitation, problem of illiteracy, employment, zamindari practices, social taboos, rigid class discrimination, corrupt politician sick educational system, shrewd entrepreneurs, illusive media and moll cultures. He believes that all these materialistic objects contribute to exploit Dalit, adivasi and marginal society.

*The White Tiger* is the gripping story of adivasis, underclasses and their misery where life begins for food, for the rights of the land, seeking shelter at the roadside and their place in the 21st century of India. Balram also belongs to the marginal community. Here, we can consider that Balram is the mouthpiece for Dalits, adivasis, laborers and farmers because most of the part of the novel is situated in

Dhanbad (Jharkhand) which is the significant adivasi populated territory. Here Balram opines:

> So the rest of the village waited in a big group outside the shop. When the buses came, they got on packing the inside, hanging from the rolling, limbing into the roofs and went to Gaya, there they went to the station and rushed into the train, packing the inside, hanging from the railings, climbing into the roofs and went to Delhi, Calcutta and Dhanbad to find work. A month before the rain, the men come back from Dhanbad and Delhi and Calcutta, learner, darker, anger but with money in their pockets. The women were waiting for them, they hide behind the door, and as soon as men walked in, the pounced like wild cats on a slab of flesh. (Adiga: 2008:26)

The novel, *The White Tiger,* is set in U.P. and Jharkhand which are Dalit-adivasi belts of India. Obviously, after the seventy years of Independence, Dalits, mainly adivasis, are still struggling for their rights. Their struggle for survival is continuing for the last three centuries. Nevertheless, the Government is not able to give them their constitutional rights. So for the employment, adivasis are leaving their local places and wondering to North India. This is the contemporary reality of India on which Adiga has commented. The novelist has shown a rural as well as urban society which is deceased with western parameters of modernity. The east is copying the west. Therefore the problems are arising. Novel boldly attacks Indian evils like the significant ratio of illiteracy, cast discrimination, cultural deprivation, superstitions, exploited adivasis, struggling farmers, marginalise women, malnutrition infants, the rise of Naxalism, poor health service, tax-evading rackets, weakening family structures, prostitution, corporate success, and its fallouts. Everything is incorporated brilliantly, which makes the real picture of postcolonial India. Novelist Adiga has created the picture which he has shown from his little brisk sentences:

> Half backed that the whole tragedy of this country. Typhoid, cholera and election fevers are the major diseases of this country and the last one the worst". Voters discuss the election helplessly as eunuchs discussing the Kama sutra. (98) Moneybags, muscle power, police, strategic alignment of various factions and power to woo the underclass assure the victory in the political game. Balram reports I am India's most faithful voter and I still have not seen the inside of a voting booth. (Adiga: 2008: 102)

In a post-colonial world, socialist and democratic powers are standing on one side and at the other hand; Imperial powers are making ground for the genocides of marginal. The struggles between ideologies are continuous in this novel. This struggle between democratic socialism and American Imperialism will worsen in the future. The novelist must explore that Imperialism is the biggest enemy of humanity. Writing against imperialism, struggle against imperialism is to be considered as to give strength to the democracy and concept of the welfare state. If the novelist neglected the issues of identity and existence of the massive population of the country and focuses only on materialistic possessions, then he is not a severe aspirant of the literature of creative writings. Unfortunately, this doubt seems to appear in realism in the writing of Indian English writers. Sometimes it smells the conspiracy that new global policies promote postcolonial writers writing. The western parameter of literature controls Indian English writing. A novelist is itself a product of the history and social sciences and therefore critic, Anand Swaroop Varma, comments:

> A serious and responsible, the creative writer could not sustain the culture of silence and put himself away from the burning issues of mass society. Literature is the representation of the human instincts of society. Literature is the mirror of social behavior; therefore, it is the responsibility of the literature that it should strengthen the realistic social discourse or certain issues f that social realism. (Varma: 2009:142, Translated)

Adiga has developed the theme of his novel from the villages of early free India. No doubt his description of economic disparity, growing materialism, suppression of aboriginals and marginals are compelling as compare to other novelists who justified the social realism of India after independence. We can say that the novel *The White Tiger* is, in the real sense, a *Postcolonial Manifestation of Modern India.*

Adiga has made a profound comment on the writing culture about India when he has given an interview with *Guardian* claiming that, one of the most critical challenges of a novelist is to write about people who are not anything like me. This is the reality for a lot of Indian people and it's vital that it gets written about, rather than just hearing about 5% of people in my country who are doing well. Now the question arises why this happened in postcolonial Indian English Fiction. Regarding this analysis, A.K.Chaturvedi comments:

> To bring into the light the lifestyle and social status of scheduled tribes, in particular, a few Indian writers have depicted them in their writings. Although twentieth-century writers have profusely dealt with rural life, they have rarely touched upon adivasi as such in their writings. This smells to a conspiracy of silence against a large chunk of our society which is

doomed to remain marginalised and lead life in its periphery. (Chaturvedi: Prafece: VII)

Adiga's novel *The White Tiger* is a prominent voice in postcolonial India which demands a socialist manifesto to dismantle the inequalities and dissemination between Big Belies and Small Belies. The novel attacks on bureaucratic and political corruption in adivasi-dominated territories which are the darkest area of our country. In the novels, everyone, including taxpayers, entrepreneurs, and doctors, are seeking refuge from political leaders to fulfill their vested interest. The novel question the election process of India, which is feeling proud of our glorious, moral democracy, is easily manipulated. Through this process, power transfers from one to another political party, but the common man, Adivasi- Dalit's fate remain unchanged. Now in today's scenario of India political, social and educational circumstances are not in favor of the common man. The novelist has made a significant comment on homelessness rootlessness unemployment and displacement of adivasi societies that are dislocated from their land and find shelter in the muddy area of the metro. His picture of modern India visible from his next comment, "Thousands of people live on the side of the road of Delhi. They have come from the darkness too. You can smell them by their bodies, dirty faces, by the animal-like way they live under the huge bridges and overpasses, making fires and washing and taking like out of their hair while the car roar past them. These homeless people… never wait for a red light" (Adiga: 2008:120).

The novel, *The White Tiger,* makes a profound comment on the stereotype mentality which rooted in the prejudices of casteism and class consciousness in colonial and postcolonial Indian society. Here, Balram belongs to the subaltern caste becomes the mouthpiece and representative of the whole marginalised and exploited section of society including Dalits, adivasi, minorities and weaker sections along with feminism. His observation is real when he observes that the higher post in reserve for the elite class who has the supreme authority to dominate, exploit and harass to lower cast. Balram breaks this social chain and wants to go to their class, and he goes and becomes a mouthpiece of exploited, the section of Indian society. After Bhabhani Bhattacharya *He Who Rides the Tiger*, this novel *The White Tiger* appears very appealing and presenting an accurate picture of Indian society. Bhabhani Bhattacharya's novel presents the life of feminine of pre-independence India where heaps of dead bodies of people are lying on roads, but the poverty and degeneration of life as is presented in *The White Tiger* seems more convincing. It is beyond imagination that after 70 years of independence still, people of the nation are deep indulged in the issue like cast, class, hegemony and discriminations. His other novels are *Between the Assassinations* and *The Last Man in Tower* both the novel deals with postmodern political and social drama of India. Stories deals with the assassination of former Prime Minister India Gandhi and the *Last Man in the Tower* deal with humdrum, city life of Mumbai and the struggle for real estate in metro Mumbai.

The novel, *The White Tiger,* gives a historical view of India that poor, adivasi, Dalit, farmers, laborers are exploited, based on their culture, cast, occupations and economic status by the elite mainstream. The history of the world is the history of ten-thousand years of the war fought between the rich and the poor. Each side is eternally trying to hoodwink the other side. (254) This results in the incurable paralysis of one part of the society to which Balram, adivasi, Dalit belongs, and other remains sophisticated, elite with their materialistic mentality. This paralysed community is presented with extreme realism by the title as *The White Tiger.* Final message Arvind Adiga gives to the social, political and democratic system to be aware of the adivasi, Dalits and marginals rights. He longs for the social, political, economic rights of marginal and broken communities. They are still waiting for their constitutional and social rights of respect and dignity. If their suppression, exploitation and dominance continue, they will bring out the monster in themselves and become criminals. These marginalised are sympathetic towards their broken communities and for entire human races on the planet. It may be turn out to be a decent city where the human can live like human beings, and the animal can live like an animal. Regarding the regional voice of Mahashweta Devi for adivasis, Dinesh Mishra opines *In Marginalisation of Adivasis: Literature as Resistance* in the edited book, *Literature and Social Change,* opines:

> The adivasi have suffered marginally and its inevitable deprivation for a long time. Literature has been a witness to it, but not a dumb witness. Writers like Mahasweta Devi in her novels, short stories and prose writings have exposed the villainy of profit mongering industrial and mining, corporates, inconvenience with the writing classes. She is of the view that forest belongs to the forest dwellers, the adivasi communities. They must not be ousted from their land and environment, just to satisfy the ambition of some profiteers with insatiable greed. (Mishra: 2015:148)

It is expected from postcolonial Indian English fiction writers that they should oppose the neo-colonisation of the native communities. They should understand the importance of mass resistance against Imperialism. They should come out from their colonial educational background and sophisticated western patterns of literary writing and make a collective front of the world's socialist order where society, social concern, values of equality and liberty will be the main focus of writings. They should learn from the dark reminiscences of colonialism but should be very attentive to contemporary issues of writings. They should relate the Indian English literature with the postcolonial writings of Africa, America and Asia. They should strengthen the voices of adivasi aboriginal, minorities, laborers and farmers against recolonisation of the world. Indian English writers should focus on imparting the importance of social justice and communal harmony. They should promote the rural masses to be the ruler of the state and promote public centric policies. They should refuse the interference of corporate in governmental administration. In this way, Indian English fiction writers can promote resistance literature and challenge the intensity of global capitalism. In this way, our novelist can give justice to broken identities and existential issues of the Adivasi community.

The postcolonial writing in India speaks about Indian transformation after Independence. Nevertheless, global policies, corporate interference in governmental decisions, neoimperialism of Indian culture, adivasi language and literature rarely become the topic of novel writing whereas we can notice these subjects as the main topic of African and Latin American writing. Today Imperialism has maintained the governments of the many third world nation countries through their corporate agents. Imperialism uses the local military to suppress the resistance of indigenous communities. These happened in Native America, Latin America, the African continent, Asia and Australia. Regarding this, Anand Varma says:

> Imperialism is the power structure of dead capitalism. Handfuls of stock exchange shareholders of Wall Street decide the future or death of a company. They can decide what to eat and where to eat. They give birth to drought, pollution war or cultural genocide. The common man, the farmer who is away from these global policies, becomes the prior victim. The huge profit of these multinational seems only on the screen of the bank computer. In the contemporary global world, the organisation likes the International Monetary Fund and World Bank are deciding the policies and future of the mass population of Africa, Asia and Latin America. (Varma:2009:161) (Translated)

## Subjugation and Acculturisation of Adivasi in the Novel *The English August*

The exploitation of adivasi women is an old aged reality of India. Throughout the feudalism to the British period in India, because of industrialism and displacement, adivasi women were exploited by internal and external colonisers. Adivasi women have great respect in their society. A woman works with a man and takes essential decisions at home. They are a hard worker and very industrious and not like the ladies of feudal lords who only leaves at home and give birth to children. Adivasi women do not like to become a showpiece; therefore, they play their role in employment and sources of livelihood. Nevertheless, with the industrialisation, outsiders also came to the adivasi territory, and these poor adivasis searched for employment opportunities among mainstream people.

Industrialism in the adivasi area becomes the main reason for the exploitation of Adivasi women. Adivasi women were the center of attraction for the feudal lords along with their natural resources. A landlord used to take over the custody of adivasi women when the adivasi man could not pay their debt, unwillingly adivasi women becomes the victim of their rage and lust. Adivasi women could not complain against this exploitation to the police because their attitude was also unsympathetic towards the adivasi community. Adivasi women working in mines and industries were never secured from the lustful eyes of their bosses.

Along with adivasi female exploitation, displacement brought misfortune to the Adivasi community in postcolonial India. For the development of communal land was taken from many adivasi villages in the name of national progress. This land acquisition brought massive unemployment in the adivasi area. There was no employment, no land, no production. Therefore problems of migration increased in adivasi areas. Thousands of Adivasi people migrated to city areas in search of employment. This was the irreparable loss of adivasi identity and challenge to their existence. Such a pathetic, challenging subject of Adivasi migration could never become the topic for mainstream novel writing in Indian English literature. Regarding this social, political and economic marginalisation of Adivasi's, Prasad Meena opines:

> It's not at all true that adivasis were not socially politically conscious. They were united and fought against the exploitation of the British Raj. Nevertheless, their struggle and leadership were suppressed by the British

> and Mainstream. These mass revolutions were destroying ruthlessly. Sidho Kanho's *Hool* (1855) or *Ulgulan* (1900) by Birsa Munda. Eradication of social and political leadership of Adiasis was serious there from the beginning. Mainstream society never gave their support to their mass agitation of rights. Because adivasis struggle was also against of internal colonialism of mainstream. (Meena: 2016:109)

The Postcolonial writing always shows it's continuous resistance towards the typical colonial nations in the mindset of native, aboriginal inlanders. The concept of nation is presented again through the point of view of the colonised. The novelist has tried to depict the sordid life of postcolonial India from his point of view, when Augusta, an urban, western minded man posted in Madna, a small town of India, really unsettles, disturbs him, "Cigarette and pan dhabas, disreputable food stalls, both leads by fierce kerosene lamps felt as he was living someone else's life. Life in Delhi and life in Madana seems two extreme points of an unseal existence" (Chatterjee: 1988: 177). Novel deals with the exploration of adivasi life, which seems very limited in its scope because the posted area of Madna is a adivasi-dominated territory, but in the novel, we find the bare existence of adivasis. Their day to day struggle has not been presented with sufficient literary craft. Novel deals with globalisation, typical western mentality, cultural complications but adivasis are invisible in these global circumstances. Adivasi, as depicted in the novel, is shown as a struggler, poor, having deprived of the basic amenities of life. Draught stricken area, scarcity of food, exploitation of women by bureaucrats is the only meaning of adivasi life in the novel. While depicting adivasis in Jompana-Chipanthy, one of the characters opines:

> There is no cast war or anything like that in the area. It's just economics and politics. The adivasis have been ignored for decades, primarily because of them, stayed in those inaccessible hill forests. The money that was pushed into Jopanna was directed by the politician to benefit the non-adivasi population of the plains. The government should not blame for this. (Chatterjee: 1988:240)

Governmental attitude towards the upliftment of adivasis seems biased in the novel. This must be admitted that outsiders who came to adivasi villages get every facility with the fund of adivasi sub-plan. Instead of providing adequate facilities, bureaucrats tried to show the adivasis as superstitious as they do not want necessary facilities. Discussion between Bajaj and Augusta we come to know the seriousness about the drought-stricken adivasi areas of Chipamthi, we become aware of the hardship of adivasi life in postcolonial India, "Chipanthy, you must visit Chipanthy. It's a central adivasi village in a group of villages spread over a vast area. The company is terribly by drought-prone block. Everyone will be complaining to you about the scarcity of drinking water from the first day. In some villages near Chipanthi, there were rumors about two years ago, of human sacrifice. (Chatterjee: 1988: 241)Adivasis shown in the novel are struggling for the drinking water. When adivasis rapidly complaints to clean the well-being dried up, nobody pays attention to them. When the adivasi lady comes to Augusta, he rang to Deputy Engineer in this regards, but his reply seems the slap on democracy:

> The Deputy Engineer protested feebly that Chipanthy was the heart of the Naxalite area and quite dangerous, to which he retarded. (253) Chipanthy was at the base of the low hills that had once been heavy with timber. Now the trees brought less rain, and the adivasi had rained the jungle as the changing world had rain them. Generations ago they had been kings capable of foundings townships, and now they were emasculated, relying for survival on government largely. (Chatterjee: 1988: 254)

As the adivasi area of Chipanthi-Jompana has described in the novel by Upmanyu Chatterjee, but we find no ray of hope of survival for the Adivasi community in described situations in the fiction. One can notice there only red sand, scrub, scraggy trees, dead forest, a heavy noon-silence, a worm late November sun and the crack of a twig beneath their feet. When Augusty comes to Chipanthi, he saw all the adivasi faces darken, deprived and somehow alien to him. Nevertheless, the adivasi women who met Augusty now look very confident and bold. The novelist has given a very drastic picture of the drought-stricken adivasi area where adivasi women are hanging themselves with the ropes for bringing up the buckets. The buckets were full of some thin mud. There is no water in nicely but the mud only. It was shocking to think that adivasis are so oppressive and deprived of their fundamental rights of drinking water. Is this the concept of the welfare state that is ready to doom to adivasi communities? To fill up the bucket from the well, small adivasi children were bending knees and taking the buckets in the well. The scene, depicted by the novelist, really shows the shameful picture of Independent India.

> The only sounds were the echoing clang of the buckets against the wall of the well and the tired sniveling of a few children on the side. He looked at them. Putting elbow and knees from the sound walls, one child had a wound like a flower on his forehead. The women who had come to the

> office were looking at him in a kind of triumph. He looked into the well. He could not see any water, but the children were blurred wraiths forty feet below, scouring the mud of the excellent floor for water, like sinners serving some mythic punishment (Chatterjee: 1988: 255).

The novelist has not even used the characterisation of adivasis in the novel. He has not given a detail (Para) a name to the adivasi women who come to his office with a complaint. Such is the bare existence of the adivasi in the Indian English novel writings where their pathos, their basic need for food, cloth and shelter find no place but alienation diaspora, multiculturalism and cosmopolitanism life becomes the core issue of postcolonial literature. Such examples of adivasi hardships are rarely represented in our literature. When Augusty went to Chimpathy; Prakash Rao is the person who meets him. Augusty thinks that Prakash Rao is older than fifty years, but he could not be Naxalite. He is a social worker. Body celebration of adivasi women is an unavoidable gimmick of literature writing for the mainstream English writers, so without losing any opportunity, they give their romantic comment on this matter. Notice Augustus comment:

> He was now feeling happy, at having escaped the office in such a delightfully bizarre way at the thought of an afternoon spent in watching taunt female bodies struggle to extract water out of a well of mud. He tries to make his faceless lustful. When Para, (the adivasi women who come with complain) came towards them with the tea. Her thin sari outlined her full hard thighs. When she bent down to place his tea beside him, he saw the veins blue beneath the skin on the inside of her upper arm. (Chatterjee: 1988:257)

Though the Augusta come to Chimpathy to solve the problem of drought in the adivasi village, his meeting with Para arises a curiosity in him about adivasi women. By the time Sen and Rao discuss freely on the issue of Naxalism in the adivasi area. The most critical issue of adivasi is discussed by them that is rural exploitation'. Rao admits that the exploitation of adivasi women is the reality in adivasi areas. The mainstream elite class takes disbenefits from these adivasi women in dense forest zones. Their free nature is often taken granted by the outsiders. Outsiders try to take the sexual benefits of these adivasi women. Nevertheless, nobody is paying attention to the exploitation of adivasi women because most of the time, government officials are responsible and indulged in such cases. Rao has given the example of an Assistant conservative forest officer. Mohan Gandhi who molested adivasi women working as his cook, Naxalites cut down his hands as punishment. "A man called Gandhi even he abused the honour of the adivasi women who cooked for him. The men of her village were outraged. They visited Gandhi there nights ago and surprised them both. In revenge and as punishment, they cut out of his arms. It was impossible to stop them" (Chatterjee: 1988:259).

The novel, *The English Agustya,* again focuses on the conversions of the adivasi in Christianity. In the interior area of Chipanthi, German had set up a big Dutch hospital for the health facility of adivasis. The entire missionary was working for this conversion. The hospital facilities and missionaries were spending much amount to convert the oppressed, sick and tormented adivasis into Christianity. This is a big issue that could be detailed discussed in the novel, but the novelist remains silent on this burning topic.

> Lacks of rupees just to seduce a few adivasis to make the sign of the cross over some sick, illiterate and bewildered individual called Anganagla or something like that and insist on a David or John before or after his name. Maybe he sometimes thought when he passed the hospital, they had a red phone, a not line to the Vatican, and had to send in daily reports. Your highness, "Four more heathen's captured today, two unsuccessful cases were Muslim. They were very, very angry and snatched the medicines out of our hands and left." (Chatterjee: 1988: 245)

The missionaries are deculturising them through the process of conversion for the last three hundred years. Adivasi's glorious heritage of fight for right has been erasing by making the Christian upbringing. Though the novelist tried to present the exploitation of adivasi in the Madna district, he could create a longer panorama of drought-stricken areas, exploited adivasi feminism, illegal conversion and above all adivasi health issues. Nevertheless, the novel is only objective towards adivasi pain, suffering, and pathos. In the novel, Augusta Sen finds himself a victim of his educational sociocultural upbringing and nurturing. The novel presents the whole postcolonial Indian society of the last quarter of the globalised twenty-first century including Indian urban life at its different levels. August posted to Koltanga from Madana, again in a small town with a sense of meaninglessness and futility. The novel covers themes like subversion, scatology, cultural clash, lies, and oppressed adivasis, tragic conversion, drought-stricken areas. Finally, Augusta goes through the lines of Marcus Aurelius, Today I have got myself out of all my perplexities, or rather I have got the perplexities out of myself for they were not without, but within; they lay in my outlooks" (Chatterjee:1988:288).

## Disposition and Distortion of Adivasis in Arvind Adiga's *The White Tiger*

Adivasis and their schedule areas are gradually colonising again by global capitalism. Regional adivasi writing in Jharkhand, Bengal, Orisa, and Maharashtra have always given strength to the adivasi voices of resistance. Regional novels are very serious about adivasi uprisings and their martyrdom. Regarding the internal colonisation of adivasi, Kedar Prasad Meena, opines:

> The situation of Adivasis in India is very much similar to the Red Indians of America, Eskimos of Australia, and Black of South Africa. Still, the colonisation of Adivasi is continuing by the outsiders. This colonisation has changed its pattern from time to time. In between, Mughal and British also came with new colonial policies. Adivasis of India fought a long battle against them and sent them back from the adivasi territory. If the Indian mainstream were not with British colonial policies, then we could have got freedom many years before. (Meena: 2016:153, Translated).

Arvind Adiga's use of the English language in all his novels shows typical Indianness. It seems that the author is at his home with the Indian English language. *The White Tiger* is the best example of Indian English. The novel is written with extreme ease and simplicity. Regarding the decolonisation in the novel Prashant Jadhao comments:

> *The White Tiger* is the most heart touching picture of imbalanced societies in India. The novel primarily refers to the cultural and social issues of marginal tribes in the early free Indian villages. It boastfully pictures what happens to colonised people and places after colonialism has met its end. The novel slowly but steadily criticizes both the phenomenon, positive and negative developments in the places such as Laxmangarh and Dhanbad where the end of an imperial rule meant new possibilities of cultural self-determination but also a kind of chaos both the pain of developing indigenous culture and political system. (Jadhao:2014:37) (New Man International Journal of Multidisciplinary Studies 2014 104 vol. 1)

When in the different areas of pre-independence India, adivasis were fighting against the Britisher's exploited economic policies; mainstream society has neglected the freedom struggle of adivasis and not even given place to them in mainstream literature and history. The writers of literature, social observers and historians have underrated them while writing the national history. The information, we find in a literary book about adivasi is also inspired by colonial bias mentality. In free India, adivasi struggle against oppression seems less significant to mainstream society. Mainstream literary writing has rejected adivasi presence in India's national struggle. They were kept outside the margin of the civilised society or so-called literary canon establish by mainstream writers. Therefore in the Indian English fictions, we find glorification, romanticisation and dehumanisation of adivasi life. Still, there is much scope for exploration of indigenous-adivasi life with its several aspects of living and survival.

The regional novelists of India have given place for adivasi struggle during post-Independence society, but the period of any struggle has its impact. In the Independence period, adivasi's marginalisation and subjugation have more serious matter than the previous age. Mainstream India English writing could bring a new era of resistance literature while dealing with the adivasi history of self-dignity and struggle against feudalism. The novelist can show the capitalist barbarism of which adivasi becomes victims. Still, Indian writing in English can give justice to the exploration of adivasis disillusionment in contemporary India. Literature is the manifestation of human emotion and a mirror of social instincts. Social instincts of contemporary India have been brought out so convincingly by Arvind Adiga through his novels. Subaltern and marginal sections of Indian society, their connection with religious social, economic and cultural issues are the main themes of his novels. If we want to understand the postcolonial Indian society of the 21st century, we must have to understand the circumstances of the last decade of 20th century India. During this period India has accepted the mix and market economy and the era of consumerism and industrialisation, globalisation and new globalisation have started which mostly affected all marginalised societies of India especially adivasis. The Adivasis were proved the hardcore victims of LPG policy, and now in this neoliberal India, their situation is worsening. Commenting on adivasi's pathetic situation in the contemporary period, Felix Padel opines:

> A psychic death of Adivasi that non-adivasi people rarely understand. Underlying the cultural genocide is the invader's total lack of respect for adivasi people's tradition. Mainstream culture ceased a long time ago to be rooted in the soil. As land prices shoot up, collective attachment to the land that a village has worked over successive generations has no value in the incomes eyes which focus only on profits they hope to generate. (Padel: 2015:334)

This new age of LPG has brought so-called prosperity in a consumer culture which resulted in popular culture of telecom, media and mall industry which are considered brighter sides of shining India and this was the same cultural blooming, which brought some severe problems like deforestation, deculturisation, disorientation and economic disparity for marginal sections. Adiga's novels, though not comment directly about adivasi life, adivasi culture and their disintegration in the contemporary period but the problem he has shown through his novels like corruption, bribery, racial, social and economic discrimination all deal with adivasis and poorer's life. So the Balram Halwai is the mouthpiece of the predicaments of Dalit and adivasi predicaments. He is the representative of the dislocated and disoriented adivasi life. Here, we can consider Balram as a hardcore adivasi of Bihar. The situations and incidents which took place in the novel are from Laxminagar, Dhanbad, Delhi, and Bengaluru. Major scenes of the novel are taken from Dhanbad which is the adivasi territory of Jharkhand. The issue of Naxalism has also been treated in the novel which takes place in Dhanbad. He has shown the oppressive system of Jamindari, malnutrition and displacement that also deals with rural adivasi life. Balram says, "We have left our villages, but the masters still own us, body, soul and areas" (170).

The novel, *The English Augusta* is suggestive about India within India. It deals with India of Darkness and India of Light. Balram belongs to India of darkness which faces a struggle of hunger, poverty, employment and illiteracy where everybody wants to live a happy life but no opportunities are there for subjugated. Secondly, India of light is dominated by a few crony capitalists who are becoming rich at the cost of the life of India in darkness. They are murdering the subjugated communities, and those belong to India of Darkness to fulfill their desires, to strengthen their capitalistic empires. India of darkness presents low life and miserable life, which is no better than the animals like instincts just like they keep chickens in the shop. Regarding this wide social-economic disparities, Adiga opines:

> Hundreds of pale hens and brightly colored roosters, stuffed tightly into wire-mesh cages, packed as tightly as worms in a belly, pecking each other and shitting on each other, jostling for breathing space; the whole cage giving off a horrible stench the stench of terrified, feathered flesh. They see the organs of their brothers lying around them. They know they are next. Nevertheless, they do not rebel. They do not try to get out of the

coop. The very same thing is done with human beings in this country. (Adiga: 2018:174)

Though Balram could not continue his school education, he learns more from the outside world. As he entered to Delhi, as the driver of Ashok, he learns how to befool others by not only tricks but also committing crimes and justification of that wrongdoing with expert insensitivity. Ones he opines, "My life is a tale of how I was corrupted from a sweet, innocent village fool into a citified follow full of debauchery, depravity and wickedness." (197) He has authentically presented contemporary Indian society shortcoming and poverty with their cultural amnesia. Adivasis are often shown in connections with naxal issues. They are considered as naxalite, but nobody wants to justify the reason for this problem. In this novel, naxal activities are shown to the linking of poverty. Poverty generates Naxalites is a common truth. If we want to bring adivasis in mainstream want to protect their culture then we should confer them their Constitutional rights. Adiga focuses here on the oppressive consumerist culture of postcolonial Globalised India that generates social divide, economic disparity, drought-stricken villages, malnutrition in younger generations, and so many kinds of inequalities. By showing this conversation, Adiga shows the wide gap between the rich and the downtrodden. When the pornbook seller tells him that most of the books come from abroad having much cost, only for rich boy, then Balram asks:

> Balram: Amazing how much money they have, and yet they treat us like Animals
>
> Bookseller: It wants last forever, though the current situations have you heard about Naxals? They have got guns. They have got a whole army. They are getting stronger by the day. Just read the papers. The Chines bomb is coming to Burma and into Bangladesh and then into Calcutta. They go down south into Andhra Pradesh, and up into the Darkness (Adiga: 2018:208)

The novel attacks on the wide gap between rich and poor. Balram is an antihero, who learns worldly activities and cleverness and becomes creamy. He learns to manage government officers. Adiga's triumph is that social forgery was exposed for the first time by Bhabhani Bhattacharya after post-independence India and after many years, Adiga has taken his place. He left nothing to depict the global neoliberal India which is getting in sexism, racism, bigotry, casteism, violence, herd mentality, exploited feminism, conversion zamindari, adivasis farmers, and Dalit downtrodden all takes tongue from his unique novel in postcolonial literature of India. While commenting on India within India Balram opines:

> A rich man's body is like a premium cotton pillow, white and soft and blank. We are different. My father spines was a knotted rope, the kind that women use in the village to pull water from wells, the clavicle curved around his neck in high relief, like a dogs collar, cuts and nicks and scars, like little whip marks in his flesh, ran down this chest and waist, reaching down below his hipbones into his buttocks. The story of a poor man's life is written on his body, in a sharp pen (Adiga: 2008:27)

The setting of the novel took place in Dhanbad of Jharkhand, a prominent adivasi territory. Though the adivasis are the owner of their land, they are displaced from their ancestral property to which they are hanging and protecting for the last many centuries, but now they are dislocated and sentenced in distinct parts of countries as homemaid and laborers. This is the pity of the adivasis and Dalits that they are deprived of their fundamental constitutional rights in their homeland and have to move away from their native places for employment purposes. Novelists shifted from villages to cities, are mostly deals with adivasi, Dalits and marginal issues. Novels tell us that the psychology of depressing and subaltern classes, who finds no hope for the betterment of life. The novel stresses whether it is a city or village, pangs of casteism are the same for everyone and everywhere. He adopts treachery to become successful in life. The murder of Ashok by Balram is nothing but his deep-rooted grudge of underclass exploitation. Comprehensive exploitation and a big gap between higher and lower class along with the humdrum of city life are responsible for growing violence. A postcolonial observation of mobile culture, moll culture, and hectic urban life present the realities of global India are rushing to darkness. The novelist has made a hurtful comment on the growing popular culture in India where the rich are eloping with absurdities and needy peoples are depriving of their primary facilities. In this new, India there is no place for adivasi, Dalits and marginals in the multilayers and supermalls of new shining India.

Starting the journey of his life from a small village of Laxamangarh to Delhi, Balram has learned the if's and but's, haves and have nots of life. Crime, murder, negotiation, bribe management have now become an integrated part of his life. Once he was a cap driver, but now he has become a successful entrepreneur. Balram is the representative to all those marginal communities who have to nurture one thought in mind and heart of the underprivileged craving for a prosperous tomorrow. When Arvind Adiga makes the comparison between rich and poor, between capitalist and socialist, it must be noted that the process of neocolonialism is going on in its full throat in India, but still, the illusion of a developmental state is rapidly taking place. Today, the contemporary scenario tells us that only a handful of big shots are becoming millionaires leaving a vast majority of the population of the state in darkness, misery, exploitation, hunger and poverty. Notice the comment of Akhil Gupta on the neoliberalism in India:

> Development planning in India has been the hallmark of the postcolonial sovereign national state and yet has always been inflected by transnational processes and ideologies. Whereas centralised, socialist planning like that under Nehru dominated roughly the first four decades of independent India, the post-liberalisation Indian states development planning agenda is shaped by global neoliberal ideas and policies (Gupta:2012:241)

The Adivasi community of India has gone through a long period of transformations. They are the witnessed of colonial, feudal and caste system of India. The post-global scenario of Indian English writing has also not in favor of indigenous adivasi. Novelists are busy with global and cosmopolitan policies that seem dominant in Indian English literature. Aboriginals are still in their territory with their broken culture and suppressed identities. Their sources of livelihood are snatched away from them. Adivasis are migrating swiftly from small villages to metropolitan where along with employment problems; they are facing several survival issues. Regarding the issue of internal colonisation, S. Armstrong in the book *Notation of Identity in the Indian Subcontinent* which is an edited book, *Exploring Fourth World Literature*, Raja Shekar Pateti opines:

> The colonial, postcolonial and Indian histories distort and misrepresent facts of India. Adivasi indigeneity in India has failed to take into account the facts of culture, anthropology, archaeology and ethnography. Colonialism suppressed indigeneity and created colonial or casteist categories with the unholy alliance of the local dominant groups.(Pateti:2011:418)

In the contemporary scenario, adivasi women are exploited from several types of machinery on construction sites in the cities. Women are becoming a maid and tolerating the pain of separation from their homeland and their families. Adivasi man is moving to illegal employment or doing illegal work for bread and butter, having no livelihood opportunities. Postcolonial scenes of adivasi areas seem much hopeless for them, so the implementation of social political and economic policies in adivasi areas is a concern. Constitutional adivasi rights are still away from them. They are fighting, struggling for basic amenities of life. The Adivasi of India indeed has to struggle for their self-determination rights for their territorial possessions.

Adivasi politics and social mobilisation in India should positively be discuss in mainstream literature. Adivasis awareness for their rights and the action plan for their social and economic upliftment can bring positive change in their subjugated life. It is now the responsibility of mainstream Indian English writers to address the contemporary world about the distorted life of Adivasis in India. It should write the literature by placing adivasi's social, political, economic, educational and cultural rights as the center of their literary creativity. Adivasis in India belong to the race, and racial studies should be the parameter of their cultural investigations. They belong to a different race, therefore adivasi is to be considered as underprivileged, marginal and uncivilised. Novelists in India have to study them as the African and Native American is studied from the racial point of view of literature. Adivasis are outside of the four Varna systems. Social marginalisation of the adivasi brought for them political and cultural deprivations. Any kind of exploitation fears the concept of equality, justice, dignity and the brotherhood. Therefore literature that diverts from reality and promotes sensuousness cannot bring light to distorted life. Established writers cannot take much care of those entire situations to maintain where margin could not understand the reasons behind their backwardness. This cultural hegemony often works with marginals but what is happening with the mainstream literary psychology who could not depict the gloom and predicament of those peoples who are left in such pathetic conditions where they have encountered only with poverty and subjections.

The novelist should not relate to the crave of honors and prizes. If these happen with them, there will be nobody who could dare to speak against this corporate fantasy world where survival of the fittest is the rule. The novelist should promote the ideas of humanitarianism. We are human beings, and humanitarianism is our religion. Rules of forest life cannot be applicable in human society. The writer is a worrier. He is a savior because against the exploitation of mass sections of society, no capitalist, no feudal lord and no industries will raise their voice but then the novelist, poets and writers are there who can decide the way of social progress of the country and the civilisation. Writing literature is a synonym to forming culture, a culture of humanism. It is like a flowing stream. Only those novelist who has felt the gloom of their exploited cultures at the center of their writing, therefore they are respected everywhere. Cultural upbringing is an unending process. It is a continuous, flowing stream of knowledge. If it stops, it will dry up. The novelist should be aware of themselves with the new "ism" in adivasi and Dalit life. Our mainstream novelists should study the grammar of human relationships. The novelist should question the ideologies which create a difference between class and caste. They have to analyse the definition of culture. In this regard famous poet, Yashwant Manohar opines:

> Creative writers and literary genius should be susceptible, and a reasonable observer of the society in which they give their valuable timing. They should minutely study the bonds of the social relationship between humanity. How the peculiar community behaves with other social group and why is it so and what will be the result of such behavior on the social code and conduct should be study and analysis by the writers of literature. (Manohar: 2014: 09)(Translated)

## Subjugation of Adivasi in *The English August* and Deprivation of Adivasi in *The White Tiger*

*The English August* is a satire on postcolonial educated Indian youth who find life intolerable and finally failed to understand the quest for self-realisation. Just like in Arun Joshi's *The Strenge Case of Billy Biswas* where hero Billy is choked with the sophisticated manners of the westernised world, August Sen, the protagonist of this novel feels frustrated in the city and urban humdrum of life. His posting as BDO in the district of Madna makes his situation more pathetic where he finds the rural culture alien for himself. Though the theme of the Gandhian movement, political leader, the naxalites, the missionaries and suffered adivasis have taken place in his novel, the ultimate situation revolves around the sense of alienation and rootlessness of Augusta Sen. The novel touches several firmaments at a time, his contemporary discussions of adivasi life could be more enhanced if he could enlarge the draught like situations, exploitation of adivasi women, the younger adivasi boys risk level for drinking water and ultimately he could put the fair side of Prakash Rao as a social activist.

The English August strikingly attacks the colonial mentality of the Indian bureaucrats and forgery of Indian political leaders. In the novel, the Politician's attitude towards the voters represents their frustrated outlook towards democracy. They are far away from the definition of a Welfare State. Naxalite reflects that they are the savior of adivasis in a remote part of jungles. The role of Christian missionary of Dutch hospitals shows their hippocras in the name of God's service. Their forcible conversion finds little observation in the novel. The novel presents the postcolonial lacuna in the life of young English educated urban recruits who having passed through examination, posted to the rural area and took an interest in positions, several assignments on papers, hoardings and misutilisation of public property. These bureaucrats are sincerely not serious about their jobs, so they found their life unhappy, and a sense of alienation caught them. In the novel, when a adivasi woman from Jompanna, complains against the water scarcity, for the first time, August took his job seriously. His sense of efficiency took a grip on this hazardous problem of water scarcity. Upmanyu Chatterjee opines, "The whole water issue is his first outward movement. Nevertheless, not in a dramatic way, it is just the hint of looking outward even though he is longing to be self-absorbed, went in themselves can pull a person out (60). His observance of adivasi land, forest and completely silent, dried life of adivasi village makes him compelling to think above the hardship of their life. He finds nothing comfortable in that village; so far he could praise the government system. No school, no meaning of his existence. Critic Murali Prasad, comments in this regard, "Augusta appears to be close to changing his mindset after a visit to Chipanthy… moved by the plight of the helpless women… for a while he recklessly hearts." (43).

While deeply peeping into this novel, one can notice that waves of globalisation, capitalistic mentality, industrial hazards and environmental threats can be noticed in the novel The English August. Augusta finds a typical colonial setup of a missionary Dutch Hospital. While moving to Chipanthi, he feels surprising that in such a damaged, drought-stricken area, what is the use of such a big hospital but gradually he comes to know that they are undercover agents of religious conversion machinery who tried its possible to convert adivasi's people in Christianity. They are ready to give lakhs of rupees to the poor adivasi to accept the Christian religion. Augustya opines. "What had induced the Dutch to build a hospital of charity in an obscure corner of India or the German to funds an Indian curer of leapers? Nevertheless, a few weeks later, I learned, missionaries at the hospital were converting adivasis to Christianity. It is observed in this age of AIDS and the atom; some missionaries were converting the heathens to the Lord's path before healing them" (Chatterjee: 1988: 244).

The situation of the adivasis seems more pathetic when Augusty went to the village well. When he goes to well, he noticed the muteness of the village. There was no laughter, no conversation. All the youngest of the village was busy bringing water from mud. After some time, inside the well, the ropes were bringing up buckets. When he glanced through the well, he is shocked by the sight of inside the well.

That sight is the slap to the Independent nation, "Augusta peeped into the well. One by one, they all peeped and came away with a suitable expression of horror. The numbers around them had increased. Agustya spotted a thin middle-aged man in khadi; he did not fit in with these hard half-naked bodies" (Chatterjee: 1988:255). Some of the loyal and responsible officers want to do good work for society through the bureaucratic power they have. Bajaj is an officer who is the responsible one, but he did not find support from his superiors and colleagues. In modern democracy in India, officialdom seems a tedious job. Bajaj gives orders for a water tanker; he calls to the junior engineer. He shows his constant business to know the responsibility of Bajaj when he opines, "You know, Sir, their laziness hidden by jargon – and I would have agreed, because sitting in the block office at Jompanna, Chimpanthy and its problems would have seemed remote and everything would have been postponed" (Chatterjee: 1988:255).

Augusty was observing the hustle-bustle of other officers, including the adivasi youngster among a crowd of women and men. Augusty was frankly ignored with all this day to day problems of adivasi life. It seems hard to think for him that only for the sake of drinking water; adivasis of the remote area had to struggle like death. He was standing there, looking at the wounded adivasi children into the well but something was going on his mind. "He wanted to get away from the office for at least a few hours to a new world where he could see some sexy faces of women. The jeep left, blaming gracelessly over the red sand, crowded with glum and confused men. He and the adivasis watched its career into the forest. He was feeling heroic and foolish" (Chatterjee: 1988:256). Upmanyu Chatterjee has delineated the hard life of adivasis in his novel in postcolonial India where they have no severe identity. Adivasi women, men, and children are the subject of mocking for the governmental bureaucrats.

When Augusty is taking tea and looking at adivasi women Para, suddenly, he listened to the loud gasp from a woman who is at the wall because the knot of the rope suddenly undone to which a adivasi boy was hanging. He was carried gradually by the women at the edge of well. Everybody was panic at the well. "The child scrambled against the wall for a foothold, like some monstrous broken spider. After looking, his terrified face appeared above the darkness, paler than the sun. Hands help him out. He sat down on the damp sand and began to blubber. The women tried to soothe him" (Chatterjee: 1988: 258).

Throughout the picture of the adivasi life as presented by Upmanyu Chatterjee in the novel *The English August,* is not sufficient, as they live, the daily hardship of such incidents. Their basic amenities like food, water, clothes and shelter all are in danger. Their dialects and traditions are rapidly vanishing. Corporates and local landlords are snatching them every opportunity, including every hope of a happy life. This postcolonial trauma does not find a prominent and authentic place in this significant postcolonial Indian English fiction. Adiga directly comments that casteism is no longer of value in sweeping of urban, metro and modern anonymity. Novel comments that the cast is the central issue for the corruption in India. Though the novel does not use the word Adivasi Culture, native and original inhabitant, the novel tells the pathos of the aboriginal people. The story is set in Dhanbad, a adivasi-dominated territory where adivasi formers are still in the clutches of oppressive landlords. The biggest threat to indigenous communities was too lost their land, and culture along with the exploitation of their women and daughters. In this regard, C. K. Janu has commented, "The settlers have taken over lands, turned our menfolk into drunkards and desecrated adivasi women. We have to decline self-rule for our self-protection, to prevent more fatherless children from being born. An Adivasi colony is not a brothel for outsiders to come out goes the firebrand Janu lists a catalog of crimes that are committed against the adivasi community by non-adivasis" (Janu,2002).

The Subjugated life of underclasses which is shown in the novel by Arvind Adiga is the replica of casteism in India. The author has made a hurtful comment on caste conscious mentality of Indian people who do not allow any, adivasi or week man into the big molls of the city. In the Indian context, adivasis are so marginalised that even after their long struggle of the last four hundred years starting from Baba Tilka Manzi, Tilka Mazi to Birsa Munda and from him to Gandadhur, they fought bravely for their *Jal, Jungle and Jamin. However,* still, they are uprooted, bare existed, and invisible from the English literary panorama of India. After Independence, we barely find their literature written in English, but we will get repeated themes of poverty, partition, marital issues and alienation of the elite class mentality of the mainstream society of India. It could happen because of the caste conscious mentality of novelist and their ignorance about the recolonisation of third world nations and including native communities. About the systematic killing and adivasi deprivation, Gladson Dungdung in his famous book, *Mission Saranda: War for Natural Resources,* foregrounds:

> The Corporate model of development which the Indian state has been promoting for decades is not only dominating the Adivasis, and it has also become the cause of the destruction of forest and biodiversity. Adivasis are asking the question to these development policies that what kind of development is this, where there is no place for them and even for their god. How can someone sell their land, water, hills and minerals without their consent? (Dungdung: 2015:233)

In India, everything, everything including literature, society, politics, economic and environmental issue are checked and rechecked in the light of cast. Though Adiga did not mention here the adivasi life, suffering in the novel, but most of the characters, settings, and situations remind us of adivasi suffering in this nation. Regarding the unavoidable issue of the cast in India to which marginalisation and subjugation of adivasi and Dalit are hanged. He makes a very bold comment:

> On the fifteenth of August, 1947, the day the British left the cages had been let open, and the animals had attacked and ripped each other part and jungle law replaced zoo law. Those that were the most ferocious, the hungriest, had eaten everyone else up and ground big bellies that were all that counted now, the size of your belly…That why he had fallen to the mud, to the level of rikshaw-puller. That's why I was cheated out of my destiny to be fat and creamy skinned and smiling. (Adiga: 2008:63-64).To sum up, in the old days there were one thousand caste and destinies in India. During these days, there are just to cast, men with big bellies and

the men with small belies. Moreover, only two destinies eat or eaten up. (Adiga: 2008:54)

Adiga says that the stories of rottenness, exploitations and corruption are always read by interest. *The White Tiger*, comments, in India wealthy cheats poor people, low cheats rich people but going one more step now in a globalised scenario low cheats poorer and richer cheat rich. He has commented on the aristocratic mentality of the postcolonial globalise psyche. "What blindness you people are capable of. Here, you are sitting in class buildings and talking on the phone night after night to Americans who are thousands of miles away, but you don't have the faintest idea what's happening to the man who's driving your car" (Adiga: 2008 257). Balram's character is the making of a hero and anti-hero of postcolonial Indian English literature. His story is about rags to riches, where he started as a driver and ends as an entrepreneur longing worldly qualities to management. He learns to the management of government officers, management of social trends and the management of caste-ridden Indian psychology. He wants to merge everything. He was a criminal in a sense but deep-rooted grudge about a century's suppression of the downtrodden; he wants to revive the whole marginal communities in India. He was a man of several traits, various strengths which born once in a generation. He concedes himself that omnipotent person who wants to cover the whole world in his hands. His comment is varied rebellious, though it is suggestive:

In any jangle, what is rarest of animals the greater that comes along only once in a generation I thought about it and said: "*The White Tiger?*"

That's what you are in this jungle. (Adiga: 2008: 35)

Balram's observation of Indian society, history, and politics is just having significant realism. He comments on the class-struggle, conscious caste mentality of Indian society which is going on for the last thousand years. He knows that this is unending phenomena until the white tigers like him get up and roar at those who are the propagator, who is the symbol of the oppressor. He wants to eradicate those all who promoted caste discrimination, therefore, be opines; The history of the world is the history of the ten thousand-year war of brains between the rich and the poor each side is eternally trying to hoodwink the other side. (Adiga: 2008: 217)*The White Tiger,* a superb postcolonial response to globalise world. It gives a message to the stereotype masters of Indian literary canon that the rights of the poor, marginal, adivasi and Dalit should not be snatched away. They should have been given the treatment of dignity. Adivasi Dalits are the original inhabitant of the indigenous tradition of this land. Therefore there should be no discrimination against them in the name of social strata or under the name of civilised or uncivilised cultures. He proposes that one should be given importance and honour based on his hard work. Balram finally declares that he with his omnipotent ambitions, shrewdness and cunnings, responses to the future of this country, India.

> I am tomorrow. In terms of final education, I may be somewhat lacking. I never finished school, to put it bluntly, who cares! I have not read many books, but I have read all the ones that count. I know by heart the work of the four most outstanding poets of all time Rumi, Iqbal, Mirza Ghalib and a fourth fellow whose name I forgot I am a self-taught entrepreneur. (Adiga: 2008: 06)

Through this magnificent postcolonial narrative, Adiga opens the eyes of global, shining and digital India with the warning that this is the demand of time to break the narrow wall of caste and creed. This is a contemporary novel of absolute criminality and moral ambiguity. If this is not controlled, the nation must cost a hefty prize resulting in the sheer hatred and violence. This novel is a strong message to the policymaker, and the so-called owner of this country to open their eyes does not pretend to be sleeping because the marginalised are going to raise their voices and take their revenge, their vengeance of centuries. Remembering the elegant lines of the greatest Urdu poet Faiz Mohammad Faiz, I conclude if these poor beasts ever lift their heads, humanity would, then, forget all deeds of rebellion if they decide; they can own the universe, even chew down the bones of their cruel masters." (The Dogs: Sun Sucha)

Postcolonial Indian English writers should check the power struggle and ideological struggle of the different sections of society. They should understand that particular established dominant forces have made literature or creative writing as a tool for maintaining their power structure and tries to spread mental slavery on marginal sections. This is metanarrative that novelists have no caste, no religion and no race but in the Indian scenario caste and race play their dominant role in the literary area while dealing and doing justice with social strata. A novelist should create his masterpiece in social, political, or economic chaos or the situation of disparities. If he wants to deal with marginalisation, subjection and deprivation of the mass section of society, he must be free from ideological bias and chose the issues of ground reality. They must follow lineage that if you are confused, go-to people. They want to be impartial themselves from political, capital and cultural pressure of particular ideologies. Postcolonial Indian English novelists must ask one question to themselves that how a good novel or literary masterpiece could be written who justifies the inequality or moral degeneration of civilisation. If a professional becomes corrupt, it will bring dishonesty upon his profession, but social writers and literary personages corrupt its brings dishonor to society and civilisation. In this regard, J. P. Sarte opines. "A blacksmith can be affected by fascism in his life as a man, but not necessarily in his craft, a writer will be affected in both and ever more in his craft than in his life (Sarte: 1980: 16)

Literature decides the progress of the social life of a nation. In the age of globalisation, neoliberal policies are dominant in the literary world. Code, conduct and rules of social living are dominated by the handful of multinationals owners of the world. Under their rage, the marginal sections of aboriginal communities are crushed violently. *'Global God'* of Corporates is trying hard to maintain their reputation as undefeated. History is evidence of the struggle between the powerless and powerful. The novelist should choose their tents whether they want to work for a handful of dominant peoples or wants to join themselves with large sections of the subjugated society which is left remain marginalised in this era of economic imperialism. Regarding the conversion policy Virginis Xaxa opines in his book *Tribes, Conversion And Sangh Parivar* in the edited book *Prosetylisation in India-The Process of Hinduisation in Adivasi Societies* gives an opinion:

> Next, to Hinduism, it is Christianity; there one can see the phenomenon at the conversion of the tribes to Christianity is spread over the length and breadth of the country. The conversion of the tribes to Christianity, unlike those of the non-adivasi population, began during the colonial rule and continues to some scale even today. Hence considerable concern and anxiety have been shown over the matter in a certain social and political circle. This concern over conversion is the real concern, but it is camouflaged under the garb of the means emplaced on which Christianity can easily be attacked. (Kumar: 2009:26)

The novelist should promote the values of democratic socialism where the voice of the oppressed could be taken to the center-periphery. Literature is the ideological product of the class struggle. In this sense, literature is a practical laboratory where the novelist must make serious efforts to promote social democratic values. A man cannot develop himself without social norms. A writer rises from this society. Social reality is the birthplace of any literature from any society. The reflection of the significant population should be explored in the literature. Indian English novelists can uncover broken faces of exploited Adivasi who are broken, torched for the last many decades. Literature is the product of class struggle, so the dominant classes manage their authorities of literary creativity at any point in the development of human civilisations. This reality is running on for the last many decades in Indian ground and the many third world countries.

CHAPTER 6

# Unearthing the Unexplored: An Overview of Regional Indian Adivasi Novels from Bengali, Oriya, Marathi and Jharkhandi Literature

## Literary Representation of Adivasi in Indian Regional Literature

Indian English fiction writing shows the development of Indian literature which dives deep into the colonial past of India along with the detailed observation of the history of deviation of social strata and its psychological effects on common masses of India. Social realism was checked through the early independence period of English writing. In Indian English fiction writing, partition trauma was glorified, celebrated as the main theme and the Gandhian age is also described by most of the prominent novelist like Raja Rao, Chaman Nahal, and Khushwant Singh. The women novelists took the initiative after the independent period, and Kamala Markandeya, Ruth P. Jabhawala, Shashi Deshpande, Geeta Hariharan, Anita Nair and Namita Gokhale have shown the rebellious feminism though their postcolonial sensibilities. If we want to write historical, social and cultural literature of India, we do not have escapism from the history of adivasi victimisation and several adivasi harassments of centuries in India. Adivasis marginalisation is the dark reality of India, but hardly any Indian English writer seems serious about this theme and there, realistic literary presentation. Indian English fiction writing shows their connectivity with the particular subject which are the issues of the largest population of this nation. The majority of the novelist writes for the interest of the Indian reader, but such literature can never be a part of social revolution or gradual social transformation for the welfare state. In this regards, famous writer and novelist Sharankumar Limbale in his famous book *Towards an Aesthetic of Dalit Literature: Histories, Controversies and Consideration,* opines:

> There has never been a revolution in the world for the sake of pleasure and beauty. Many governments have been overturned for equality, freedom and justice. This is history. The literature that glorifies pleasure gives a central place to the pleasure of seeking aesthete. The literature that promotes equality, freedom and justice is revolutionary, and it emphasises the centrality of human beings and society. If pleasure-giving literature arouses joy and sympathy in people, revolutionary literature awakens the consciousness of self-respect. (Limbale: 2004: 16)

In Maharashtra, we have massive data literature under the title *Adivasi Vimarsh* which observes the adivasi history for the last 300 years. Adivasi's revolts, existences and upbringing during colonialism, their struggle for survival in postcolonial India have presented very acutely in Marathi literature. Many prominent Marathi writers realistically present their stories of vanishing identities, erasing dialects of adivasis. Marathi writers like Bhujang Meshram wrote poetry volume, *Abhujmal* depicting the adivasi hardship of survival. Dr.Vinayak Tumram is another big name in Marathi adivasi writings which is still giving justice to adivasi pathos through his writings. His books like *Adivasi Sahitya-Disha Ani Darshan, Rangarbhatil Jakhma* and *Gondwana Petle Ahe.* Sunil Kumare is a prominent adivasi prose writer who wrote *Jangle Jivhar, Kingari (Poems)*, Lataru Kavadu Madavi is a good interpreter who deals with the theme of the indigenous issue of Indian Adivasis. All these adivasi writers have given rebellious voices to century's subjugation of adivasis in this country. Tukaramji Warkhade is one of the prominent names in Marathi critical writing who wrote *Vaicharik Parivartnaccha Masuda, Adivasichya Astitvache Prashn, Lingo Ka Mithak and Bharat Ke Vastvik Bhumalak*. Some of the prominent academicians like Dr. Tukaram Rongate wrote Adivasi *Sahitya – Ek Chintan*, Dr. Vinod Kumre work *Adivasi Sahityatil Pravah-EK Abhyas* and Dr. Pramod Munghate wrote *Adivasi Sahitya Pravah.* This literature shows that *Adivasi Discourse* is strengthening day by day. These Bhasha literatures about adivasi life are very different from the writings and perceptions of Indian English Fiction writings.

The Regional literature of Jharkhand is the treasure of adivasi identities with several issues including exploitation, disposition and deculturisation. Some of the prominent novelists of Jharkhand are Ashwini Kumar Pankaj who wrote the novel, *Mati Mati Arkati.* Mahua Manzi wrote the novel *Maram Gomke Nilkanth Hu., Vinod*

*Kumar writes red Zone*. Vandana Tete wrote, a critical volume, *Adivasi Sahitya Parampara and Prayojan*, Abhishek Kumar's, *Jharkhand Andhere Se Sakshatkar* deals with the critical evaluation of regional adivasi novels of Jharkhand.

Novelist Reanendra wrote the novel *Global Gaon Ke Devta* Rakesh Kumar Singh's *Pathar Pe Kohara*, Sanjeev's *Paav Tale ki Doob*, *Dhar*, Vinod Kumar *Samar Shesh Hai*, Rakesh Kumar Singh's *Jo Itihas Me Nahi Hai* are some of the gems in regional adivasi novel writings.

When we study this considerable body of Adivasi literature in regional languages with the treatment of all the theories of literature including Colonialism, Postcolonialism, deconstruction, metanarrative, Marxism, Neocolonisation and Post-globalisation but on the other hand mainstream Indian English fiction writing does not show such a vast maturity of "ism" and its literary presentation through their novels. Indian English fiction writers find them out with ease when they use the word *Subaltern,* but they never think of adivasi women from this perspective, nor they have presented the community of Indian adivasi from the subaltern point of view. However, the most striking and surprising reality is that the Adivasi-Abongional are the most wretched soul, most destructed cultures in contemporary independent India. We remind the title of Gayatri Chakraverty Spivak when he asks *Can subaltern Speak*, as the adivasi is the victim of neo-colonisation and post-globalisation.

In Indian social hierarchy, we notice that the ruling class is center in every sphere of national life, including political terms, economic policies and social circumstances. They have every authority that they make a dance to the ruling class on their tunes because the ruled class has no voice in power structure or oppressive state apparatus. In this regard to the subaltern concept, Dipesh Chakraverty opines, "Subalternity, the composite culture of resistance to and acceptance of domination and hierarchy is characteristic of class relations in our society, where the veneer of bourgeois equality barely marks the violent, feudal nature of much of our systems of power and authority" (Chakraverty: 1985:375). Adivasi life, culture, identity and geographical particularities could never be a part of Mainstream Indian English literature. A historical novelist like Manohar Malgonkar deals with colonial Indian societies without considering adivasi life. He praised and abuses the both about the princely state of pre-independence India in the novels like *The Princess, The Distant Drum, The Bend in the Ganges* and *The Devils Wind* but he could hardly give justice to the Bhil adivasi in his novel. Political victimisation of adivasi could not present with sufficient detail. If Postcolonialism rewrites the nation with nationality, but in this concept of nation adivasi seems nowhere.

Postcolonial mainstream woman writers of India speaks about the marital or extramarital women relations, struggling identities of upper cast women in male-dominated patriarchy but women longing, her physical desire and rebels about stereotype traditional Indian mentality becomes the most distinct part of literary conferences but the seduction of adivasi girl Rima in *The River Sutra* or body celebration of Bilasia in *The Strange Case of Billy Biswas*, the lustful attitude of Augusta towards adivasi women Para in *The English August* could never become the topic of their literary discourse on subaltern feminism. Mainstream Indian novelists should judge and rejudge the place of adivasi women, her matriarchy in a male-dominated society and her exploitation during colonialism, postcolonialism and the contemporary period of new colonisation. The relationship of adivasi women to her husband, their family problems could also be an essential topic of third world feminism. In this regard, Gayatri Chakravorty Spivak explores the concept of subaltern women when she opines:

> Between patriarchy and imperialism, subject- constitution and object-formation, the figure of the women disappearance not into a pristine nothingness but into a violent shuttling which is the displaced figuration of "The Third world Women" caught between tradition and modernisation... There is no space from which the sexed subaltern subject can speak. (Spivak 306-07)

Indian English fiction writers barely treated the land disposition of adivasi. In the novel *The Princes* when the Indian Government wants to build a big dam in Bulwara which is a significant adivasi territory in the state of Begwad, adivasi apposed them, because the government was not giving them compensation to migrate from their land. Adivasi was promised for a better life, but the political victimisation of adivasi is an essential topic of discourse during their pre-colonial and postcolonial existence in adivasi territory. In the current scenario, adivasi are forcibly driven out from their native soil without any promises of rehabilitation and any certainty of compensations. The landlords in the adivasi area are grabbing their lands and turning it into a dumping zone by intoxicating them. C. K. Janu has a make a serious comment on this contemporary exploitation of adivasi, "They would get him drunk on arrack. Only then would be prepared to enter the forest and cut down trees. When one drinks arrack continuously, a stage comes when one cannot live without it. That is how the overseers make money corrupting their bodies and mind" (Janu: 2004:44).

In Indian English fiction, postcolonial responses deal with the rewriting of history, sociology and political upheavals but the issue like displacement of adivasis hardly takes any place. Kamala Markandeya's *The Coffer Dam* deals with the theme of displacement where the team of British Engineers with their families comes to a adivasi village, they displace adivasi hut and build their tents there. The western outlook towards adivasi is only as of the junglee. While depicting adivasi as romantic, superstitious, ignorant and uncivilised, the mainstream novelist has presented them from the matriarchic point of view. Female is given much respect in the adivasi family, but the modern, urban, elite English writers look uninterested in depicting this civilised and splendid side of adivasi. As the adivasi comes in contact with sophisticated city life, the exploitation of their women increased. Explaining this point C. K. Janu comments:

> What happens among our women is not what happens in civil society. In our case, unity in everything originates from our women. They have something in common that shelters us from meaninglessly adopting the ways of civil society. They have enough resilience in them to stand for what they feel is right even though they may have to suffer a lot for it. It is among our women that our traditions and the ways we dress live on even now. All our struggles have been struggles to establish the ownership rights of the real owners of this land for the right to live on it. (Sengupta: 2015:26)

Postcolonial Indian English novels have given voices to suppressed sections of society. The novel as mentioned above deals with poverty, hunger, famine, exploitation colonial and neocolonial traits but we hardly find that they have given voice to adivasi in their novel but on the other side C. K. Janu, a adivasi activist is well known for her adivasi fight for their land and forest. It seems that the issue of adivasi is not taken seriously by our Indian English fiction writers. Indian English fiction writing seems far away from adivasi reality, but regional novel writing is persuasive about their pathos. Disorientation of Adivasis, marginalisation of Adivasis has been depicted authentically by Raja Shekhar Pateti in his volume, *Exploring Fourth World Literature* when he writes:

> The struggle for land spearheaded by C. K. Janu was not merely a struggle for land by the landless. It was the resistance against dispassion. The

> Adivasis were trying to reclaim land on which they have existed over the millennia. The law passed during the colonial period and subsequently affected a kind of erasure of their existence and declared the land on which they live as "forest" out by giving that nomenclature appropriated it for a specific purpose and excluded them from it. (Patteti: 1998:279)

Another regional novel, *Kocharethi deals* with the disposition of adivasi from their land. The exploited machinery of landlords has shown with its ugly reality through this novel. This novel is another example that shows a better understanding of adivasi life than the mainstream Indian English fiction writers.In the introduction of this novel, Catherine Thankamna opines:

> The novel maps the Adivasis changing perceptions of land and its ownership. Its account that traces the possession and disposition of land, the innocence of a people who did not even have a motion that land was property and that they could be alienated from it. To the Adivasis, the first inhabitants, there was no question of acquiring individual rights over the land. The land was not separable from their sense of collective identity; they were one with it and celebrated this union on all rites of passage. (Narayan: 2011: Blurb)

Disposition and land grabbing of Adivasis are not the current issues; this is a process that is running down from the period of colonialism. The landlords were the wretched peoples who used to grab the adivasi land with or without their permission. By taking benefits of adivasi illiteracy or by taking benefit of their helplessness, they were used to grab the land. Gopinath Mohanty, another novelist from Orissa, has presented the striking picture of disposed of Adivasis in his most celebrated novel *Paraja*. Novels sympathetically deal with adivasi ethos, their customs, and struggle for survival. Mohanty's other novel *Ancestor* again deals with adivasi ancestry. Many beliefs, traditions, customs, with their primordial powers have been kept in this novel. Regarding the theme of the novel Bikram Das opines:

> The novel *Paraja* is much more than sociological or anthropological documentation. Sukru Jani is not merely the primitive tribesman ensnared by the predictor money lender from the city he is also a quintessential man, waging heroic but futile war against the holistic universe. The choice of the adivasi canvass, whether by accident or design, becomes singularly appropriate to Mohanty's theme; the primeval consciousness of his adivasi protagonists reflects perfectly the situation of the archetypal human being their stark joys, and interwoven anguish embodies the complexity of the human condition. (Mohanty: 1997:06)

Mahasweta Devi was a legend in the regional adivasi literature writings. In a true sense, she had taken the responsibilities to give the voices to the marginalised adivasi who were suppressed over the centuries. She translated novel *Chotti Munda and His Arrow* was the pathbreaking novel in the field of local translation. For the first time Birsa Munda, the legendary martyr and adivasi icon of whole Adivasis in India was known through her magnificent novel. During the colonial ruling, the adivasi territory was interrupted by the Britisher's tax policies and the unjust treatment of the landlords. The present novel shows the realism of the adivasi struggle. Britisher's have implemented their various economic policies on the forest of adivasis with the helping machinery of local landlords. The novel is the best example of the struggle of the adivasis against the oppressive moneylenders and colonisers. Adivasis were in continuous fighting with local landlords and the mighty British Empire, right from the colonisation of India. Hundreds of adivasi revolts took place in colonial India but hardly that revolts became the subjects of literary, social and political discourses in India. Mainstream Indian elite society and Indian English working classes never tried to introduce that warfare to the world. Mahasweta Devi wrote this novel which was the manifesto of the adivasi tradition of revolts. This is the story of Munda archer Chotti, a symbol of resistance of adivasi ancestor. Regarding the theme of this novel, we remind Gayatri Spivak's statement about the subaltern study. In Mahasweta Devi's translated Imaginary work *Maps,* she blames to mainstream literary canon for its negligence towards adivasi exploitation. Pterodactyl wants to show what has been doing not the entire adivasi world on India. We did not try to know it. Each tribe is like a continent. Nevertheless, we never tried to know them. Never tried to respect them. This is truth of every adivasi. Furthermore, we destroyed them." (Mahasweta Devi: 1995: 56).

The novel *Chotti Munda and His Arrow* is suggestive on various accounts. Her arrows are the symbol of their society, the culture that is threatened by an outsider. It is a symbol of their ancestral faith, pride, and honour. This novel shows the continuation of the adivasi movement of land, forest and water. The leadership of Chotti, who is the evidence and observer of the suffering of decolonisation from the perspective of aboriginal tribes. Her struggle was against those who came and tried to rob, their culture and erase their identity. The novel is an excellent example of double colonisation of the internal colonisation of Adivasis in India. Adivasi wants to free themselves from colonial rule, but at the sometimes they wanted to be free from internal colonisation of dikus and landlords:

> The August movement did not even touch the life of Chotti's community. It was as if that was the Diku's struggle for liberation. Dikus never thought of the Adivasis as an Indian. They did not draw them into the liberation struggle. In war and independence, the life Chotti and his cohorts remained unchanged. They stand at a distance and watch it all. (Devi: 2003: 122)

*Chotti Munda and His Arrow, present* different shade of adivasi life. Bonded labour was the most threatening problem for the adivasis from independence. Double treachery of landlords, politicians and government is satirized by the critic G.A. Ghanshyam in his critical responses, *The Voices of the Other- Post-Independence Indian English Fiction,* he explores:

> There was a change from all around. Some of which they saw in the form of industrialisation which benefited only the dikus. There was no difference or change in the way others treated the Adivasis people or any improvement in their ways of living. They could not understand the double-dealing of the Indian administrator who gave them freedom from bonded labour on paper, yet would not let them be free. (Ghanshyam: 2013:122)

Mahasweta Devi's other comprehensive and realistic novel is *Arenyer Adhikar* (1977) shows adivasi icon Birsa Munda and his Ulgulan Movement for the emancipation of adivasi territory as its central theme. *Ulgulan* was the simultaneous revolt against the social, economic and political exploitation of adivasi by British power and local landlords. The novel is narrated by an ancient Munda to tell the story of the movement of adivasi revolt to the youngster adivasi Munda. Anand Mahanand has commented on Mahasweta Devi's narration power in the following words:

> Mahasweta Devi exposes the exploitation of adivasi and its mental and physical effects on adivasi. She shows the crookedness, exploitativeness and callousness of the British Government and the ruthless nature of nonaboriginal landlords and petty officials. She does not present a romantic or exaggerated picture of adivasi but the poverty-stricken and insecure life of adivasi people for whose rice remained an external dream. (Mahanand: 2011:170)

The character of Birsa Munda is inspiring in the novel, which arose awareness among other adivasi about the exploited machinery of the British Government. He is the commander of the revolt. To win the faith of his people, he calls himself as God, but in reality, he knows the solution of adivasi problems is not in religious dogmas still to create enthusiasm in others he says himself "Bhagwan". The regional novel is rich with the literary representation of Munda Revolt, Koal Revolt, Santhal Hul, Sardari Revolt and many regional novels in Hindi were written with regional adivasi writers. Writing for adivasi rights is like a legacy, was a dignity of the regional writer but postcolonial Indian English writers, mainly Indian English novelist who neglected their adivasi past and sought refuge in romanticisation. They could not create a larger life of adivasi culture and revolts through English literature. In this regards, Anand Mahanand points out:

> Unlike writers who were stimulated by adivasi exotica and choose to romanticise idealised adivasi societies, Mahashweta Devi does not present a romanticised picture of adivasi. Instead, she portrays the poverty-stricken and insecure lives of the adivasi people for whom rice remained an external dream, where life meant wandering from one village to another due to ongoing eviction by "dikus" for whom land reclaimed the forest was the basis of adivasi life. (Mahanand: 2011: 171)

Indian English novelists have shown the adivasi as bare-footed in the novels who are the native son of the soil. Through their broad literary canvass, the mainstream has demeaned the adivasi suffering where Billy Biswas looks to adivasi life as free from all worldly activities, Bilasia, the adivasi girl as goddesses, the old Dhunia as more mature adivasi chief of the village. He praises everything about adivasi life in the novel, but the drought-like situation, the problem of hunger and the miserable situation of adivasi comes to know us from the local adivasi chief Dhunia. Marginalisation is not a new phenomenon, so as it in literature. S. N. Choudhary has made a profound comment in the introduction of the book *Social Movements in Adivasi India* where he opines, "Thousands of tribes have been displaced from their native place without any proper rehabilitation. It is neither just humanistic from a adivasi point of view. Due to the absence of voice against displacement and silence on various issues, including exploitation, industrial houses prefer to install their project in adivasi areas" (Choudhary: 2010:05). The colonisation of India has four hundred years of history, but the political, social, economic marginalisation of adivasi is older than that. Thousands of Indian English novels on the theme of post-independent India, postcolonial India, Global India as depicted in the novels of Arvind Adiga, Palash Malhotra, Salman Rushdie, Vikram Seth and Shashi Tharoor have published on the middle-class life of India. However, several marginalisations of adivasis could not become part of their literary sensibility. It seems strange, writer who had worldly knowledge about imperial exploitation and its crushing power over marginal cultures seems unaware of adivasi victimisation, exploitation, corporate loots and hardcore marginalisation. While writing about the colonial impact on the Indian psyche, novels must take adivasi culture, subjugation and deprivation into consideration. In this regard, Virginias Xaxa, comments in *State, Society and Tribes:*

> The reclamation of the forest for land cultivation, expansion of roads and railways, exploitation of minerals resources form a key economic activity during the colonial period. These policies led to the large scale destruction of natural resources and yet the problems and hardships suffered by the adivasi were not felt acutely unit the post-independence period. Either the exact impact of the policy was not realised or the policy, despite expropriating the rights of the adivasi people gives some freeway to them. By employing such processes, thousands of square kilometers of adivasi land were brought under the forest department. (Xaxa: 2008:108)

The history of Indian English fiction which took place nearly 1860 with the prose writing of Raja Ram Mohan Roy and the first English novel is to be considered is *Raj Mohan's wife*, means novel writing on Indian themes started during 1870, which was the peak period for adivasi revolts for theirs. International Adivasi *Ulgulan* of Birsa Munda started during 1890 which shook the colonial policies of the British Empire. Today Native American Tribes also consider Birsa Munda as an icon for adivasi dignity. Birsa Munda is in the heart of Native Americans. However, while writing colonial history, a massive part of adivasi's freedom fight against internal colonialism and British colonialism was excluded by the historians as well as from the literary platform of Indian English writers. About the historical background of adivasi which could be the most inspiring episode of writing for all Indian, Gladson Dungdung, in his celebrated volume *Whose Country Is This Anyway,* foregrounds:

> In Ancient times, the Adivasis had ownership rights on natural resources, and they judicially used these resources for their survival. Consequently, the Adivasis were living with autonomy, peace and prosperity. The situation changed after the Aryan invasion and became worse during the British Rul. On the one hand, the Aryans destroyed the Adivasi civilisation, denied their indigenous identity and did not accept them as fellow human beings and on the other the British imposed violence on the Adivasis by grabbing their land, territory and resources and even named a few of them as criminal tribes. (Dungdung: 2013:16)

Literature is the manifestation of one's emotions. It gives expression to pathos, sensibilities and exploitation of suppressed marginal who are broken, discontented from their culture. Indian English novelist like Kamala Markandeya, Ruth P. Jabhawala, Shashi Deshpande, Chaman Nahal and Arun Joshi brought the themes like the sense of alienation, monotonous urbanity, broken village culture, exploited feminism and degenerated identities in their senses of the historical revival of Indian English writing but social exclusion, subjugation, colonial suppression, poverty and deprivation of adivasi could not take place in their novel writing. It seems because of the writer's eliteness and westernises outlook towards the social culture of India, and they could not depict the adivasi culture of this land. Regarding the fragmented identities of adivasi, M. Hamid Ansari comments in his *Marginalisation of Adivasi in India,* in the edited book *Social Exclusion and Adverse Inclusion* opines:

> Across the nation, gigantic industrial, power, irrigation and mining projects representing the current development paradigm have caused Adivasi protest against land acquisition and displacement. Aligning our development needs with Adivasi rights and enhancing their FDI is the need of the hour. This is also essential to prevent the violent manifestation of discontent and unrest in our adivasi areas emanating from exclusion and alienation. (Xaxa: 2012:22)

The identity of Adivasi in India is assuming merely as the "Huge Labor Industry". Literature should be the voice to the marginal exploited section, but in the case of adivasis in India, the mainstream seldom speaks about them in literature. Characters in Indian English literature like Augustya, Billy, Clinton Helen, Maharaja Hiroji, Abhayraj, Nitin Bose and many others are all elite and belongs to do families well. They represent the upper strata of city life and daily humdrum of city life, but the adivasi character leaves in darkness. Rima's husband, a adivasi man is a porter on a railway station, seems only one line identity in the novel, but the writer could raise this point of bonded labour or labour industry hub of adivasi across India. Nevertheless, the main characters in the novel seek refuge in hedonism, aestheticism and body celebration of adivasi women. Bonded labour is the most spreading problem of adivasi but remains absent in Indian English literature. Regarding these labour industry of adivasi, Christian Strumpwell in his *The Making and Unmaking of an Adivasi Working Class in Western Orissa,* speaks in the edited book, *Savage Attack,* opines:

> By then the construction of plants, mills and townships was already in full swing. The first significant work was to proper the ground, cut trees, blast rocks, dig, excavation, erect power poles and rail tracks. This was done by a large army of the labourer who did not require any industrial skill. These labourers were Adivasis from the Sundergarh itself. Within a year, the ground was prepared, and the initial workforce of largely Adivasi and Oriya unskilled daily waged labourers was reduced from approximately 46000 to 300000. (Sterling: 1963:23)

## Regional Bengali Literature-With Special Reference of Mahashweta Devi and Her Adivasi Consciousness:

Postcolonial literature is a broad branch of cultural and literary study, which reexamines the suppression, marginalisation and distortion of colonised countries and cultures. We find strong postcolonial voices of resistance in the writing of Africa, Native America. However, in the case of India, we find that the postcolonial writing becomes the monopoly of the educated classes of India whose primary concern was westernised outlook towards nativity. These Indian English writers are very much interested in the diaspora element, travel writing and continental shifting. The theme of migration, multi citizenship and cosmopolitanism is the most critical issue for them than the writing about the disoriented and subjugated communities of India. After Independence, many novelists, having mastery of literacy skills and sufficient knowledge of the English language, tried to depict rural predicaments, feminine issues, agrarian families and crushing village cultures because of growing industrialisation. Nevertheless, from the 1980s, we can observe that the themes of imaginary communities, a globalised world and neocolonial policies were so dominant on Indian English writers that they have given priority to describe an elite world of sophisticated manners and not the world of adivasi darkness and indigenous subjugations. Writing about India from a foreign land and foreign publication is becoming a fashion now a day. However, in all this process, the marginal communities, Adivasi-Adivasis are feeling the pain of invisibility, alienation and negligence in the main literary canon of the country. Gently criticizing these mentalities, Anand Mahanand writes:

> Adivasi people in different parts of India have fascinated many writers through the ages. Many writers have written about different adivasi communities in India. The novels of Rudyard Kipling, Verrier Elvin, Arun Joshi, Gopinath Mohanty and Mahasweta Devi are worth mentioning. In these writings, adivasis are romanticised, glorified as noble

savages or depicted as lesser gods who need urgent attention. (Chandra: 2007:43).

In India West Bengal, Orissa, Jharkhand, Chhattisgarh, Madhya Pradesh, Telangana, Karnataka and Kerala including Maharashtra and Gujarat, are the significant territories of the adivasi community. They have the legacy of thousands of years in that particular region. The regional writers of this region have focused on their life and their predicament during colonial and postcolonial India. In contemporary regional literature of India, we find many novelists who have shown adivasi life, their exploitation, and land disposition from a realistic point of view. Famous Bengali regional novelist and short story writer Mahasweta Devi is the literary stalwart in the area of regional adivasi writing. Her shorts stories and novels bring the social forgery, painted a mask of the civilised world, the sad face of capitalism and criticize the urban mentality and snobbish outlook of elite classes in their treatment towards the ancient inhabitant-adivasi of this land.

Mahasweta Devi has written a vast literature on adivasi and marginal communities. Some of her famous novels Sal Girar Dake (In the Name of Birthday, Arnyer Adhikar (Rights on the Forest)" and Chotti Munda Ebang Tar Tir (Choti Munda and His Arrow) are the truthful portrayal of adivasi life and their history from many centuries. But apart from her tremendous novel writing, she has written a significant world of stories, among which After Kurukshetra: Three Stories is translated by Arjun Katyal, "The American Champa Tree" translated by Nirmal Kanti Bhattacharya, Bait – Four stories translated by Sumanta Bannerjee, Bitter Soil By Ipshita Chanda, Dhowli translated as Women, Outcast, Peasants and Rebels: A Selection of Bengali Short Stories By Kalpana Bardhan, In the name of Mother: Four Stories translated by Radha Chakravarty, Outcast Four Stories translated by Sharmishta Gupta, Old Women translated by Gayatri Spivak, Droupadi translated by Gayatri Spivak, Mandira Sengupta and Ramtha translate the Queen of Jhansi: The Selected Work of Mahasweta Devi translated by Pinaki Bhattacharya. The translated or regional literary work is the door of the real representation of the broken community through which every mainstream novelist must once peep in.

The world of short stories of Mahasweta Devi is much wider about the subaltern, subjected life of adivasi Dalit, minorities and female section of the society. Much of her short stories deal with adivasi life and the exploitation of adivasi women. Her fictional world and world of storytelling exposes the dehumanising treatment towards the adivasi and Dalit community. She considered herself not as feminist though she has brought the grief of Adivasi- Dalit women through her plays and short stories she considers herself as humanist and viewed the whole circumstances from a humanistic point of view. Regarding the broad themes of her short stories and novels, critic G. Gulam Tariq comments in his research article *The world of Marginalised in Mahasweta Devi's play -Mother of 1084*:

> Mahasweta Devi's predominant concern is the adivasi backwaters, the exploitation of Adivasis by the landed rich or the urban administrative machinery callously perpetuating a legacy of complicity with the colonisers, bonded labour and prostitution, the plight of women who are breadwinners and victims of male sexual violence, dependent widows, ill-treated wives and unwanted daughters whose bodies can fetch a prize are adequately represented. (Edt. Sen: 2008:08)

Adivasi of India has a glorious past of revolt against British Imperialism. Massive history of valor, bravery and courage of adivasi heroes like Tilka Manzi, Birsa Munda, Sidho-Kanho have always been ignored by mainstream novelists, but for the first time, Mahasweta Devi has presented the adivasi worriers in her novel *In the Name of Birthday* was written in 1984. It deals with British penetration into the adivasi land of Chotanagpur and spreading the barter systems, railway and postal system by eradicating the forest. Tilka Manzi raises the revolt against the same policy of the British. Paharis and Santhals fought bravely against the British army. Tilka Manzi was the leader in the battle. They defeated the British army and then Captain Brook, played the trick of "Divide and Rule" and given patronage to Paharies by recruiting them in Battalion.

Nevertheless, Paharies came to know their duplicity and again started the revolt. Noticing the brave hearts of adivasi, Mahanand Comments, "However the Paharis realises their folly and fought with British. The British have superior Weapons. They win the battle but with many difficulties. Mr. Brooke, Philips, Cleveland are killed. Among the adivasis, Tilka Manzi and Mansa are killed. However, these deaths bring unity and determination among the adivasis" (Mahanand: 2011: 169).

Mahasweta Devi's most celebrated novel about adivasi life is *Arnyer Adhikar* (The Rights of The Forest) is the manifesto of Birsa Munda's struggle for land, forest and river. He does not want that

British power and alien diku's ruled the adivasi territory. He wants to fight them and recover all the ancient heritage of their ancestor.

Indirectly Mahasweta Devi has presented the Birsa Munda and his Ulgulan (Comprehensive Uprising from 1895 to 1900). Before the writing of this novel, Birsa Munda and other adivasi revolt were entirely ignored by the mainstream novelist, but Birsa's movement was fought against both the British and local landlords. He was demanding complete freedom of adivasis on their territories. K. S. Sigh's opinion about Birsa's movement is very suggestive. "He spoke of a new millennium for his distress people of freedom and salvation, status and power, opportunity and fulfillment in the new world in place of the old one which lay shattered within a few decades of colonialism" (Singh: 1972:01). Dhani is the main narrator of the novel *Aranyer Adhikar* who tells the young Mundas, the story of their ancestor. Mahasweta Devi has minutely captured the psyche of Birsa Munda, his rebellion, various changes in the thought processes of Munda. She has captured Birsa's state of mind in the following words:

> Today's Mundari would be tomorrows Christian again Mundari and Christian, But whatever your name was Suguna, Komta, Bharami, Dhani, Daud, Mothy, Yahan or Abraham tomorrow in your blood the lord Singabonga will always hold sway. Birsa knew that it was a great sin even to think a life different from the Mundari life lived by lakhs of Mundas. Nevertheless, Birsa had committed that great sin. Somewhere in his blood protest and indignation had gathered day by day. (Mahanand: 2011: 173)

Mahasweta Devi has introduced the movement of Birsa on a different scale of political, agrarian and religious parameters. In style and idiom, the use of Mundari language is a superb one. When we compare Mahasweta's outlook towards adivasi life, Indian English writer seems for away from adivasi revolt, the Birsa movement and the martyrdom of Tilka Manzi. Regarding her presentation of adivasi in this novel, critic Anand Mahanand foregrounds:

> "The novel, as a form is unparalleled in documenting human lives. Adivasi societies, however, as classified and documented by writers can be represented more vividly in fiction and hence, they become more accessible through novels like *Arnyer Adhikar*. In this regard, *Arnyer Adhikar* and her other works have played a significant role in documenting authentic aboriginal lives." (Mahanand: 2011:178)

This must be admitted that Mahashweta Devi was writing in the same decade where Indian English writing and writers were taking an interest in the global world and its humdrum. They were busy proving themselves more advance and cosmopolitan in modern world. They were far away from the marginal and subaltern group and significant subjugated population of India. A regional writer like Mahasweta Devi was much closer to the ground reality of downtrodden communities. Regarding her ageless writing, Dinesh Misra in his research article, *Marginalisation of Adivasis: Literature as Resistance* Comments, "When Mahasweta Devi wrote Aranyer Adhikar, She recreated the Character of Birsa Munda, who lead the adivasi revolt. In her narrative, history folklore and fiction are all mixed up, to create a state of emotional high. This affects the reader's coincidence. It highlights the spirit and passion of the time. She does not indulge in sentimental romanticisation" (Misra: 2015: 148).

*Chotti Munda and His Arrow* is the remembrance of the adivasi revolt of Birsa Munda with changing the passage of time even after independence. Mahasweta Devi notices that the exploitation of adivasi has much increased than the earlier period. Chotti Munda raises his voice on the ground of Birsa Munda against all the criminal practices of the adivasi region. Mahasweta Devi confesses that though there were no adivasi writers who wrote about their revolt and struggle their life flows like a river from their ancient folklore and riddles. The story of this novel covers the passage of seventy years after the Birsa Munda and his rebellion. It explores the exploitation and adivasi resistance from the last part of colonial rule to the first part of Indian Independence and its dramatic rule. Notice what the Mahasweta Devi has written in the Blurb of this novel. "The novel is remarkable on a vital issue that raises questions about the place of the adivasi on the map of the national identity, land rights and human rights, the museumisation of "ethnic" culture and the justification of violent resistance as the last resorts of desperate people, among others" (Devi:2002: Blurb).

The novel, *Chotti Munda and His Arrow* deals with the pain of duel colonisation of adivasi community and their continuous struggle with internal colonisation. Novels cover the Congress fights of liberation from British rule, but adivasi were also fighting against European power and exploiters. Mahasweta Devi's comment is very suggestive. "The August Movement did not even touch the life of Chotti's community. It was Diku's struggle for liberation Diku's never thought of the Adivasis as Indian. In war and independence of Chotti and his cohorts remained unchanged. They stand at a distance and watch it all" (Mahasweta: 2002:122). The novel covers several aspects of bondage labour, administrative bribery, and female exploitation in modern India where industrialisation took place in the adivasi region without their permission, in fact forcibly eradicating them from their ancient locality. Therefore Chotti took his Arrows and arched out and gives a raising voice to other Mundas to protect their legacy. Novel comment on the illusory freedom or emancipation of adivasi in India after 1947. This novel which is written during the contemporary age is very much similar to the situation of globalised India and multiple harassments of adivasi community in this neoliberal panorama. Commenting on the symbol of arrow critic, Arijita Pradhan in her *Legacy of Loss and Resistance in Mahasweta Devi's Chotti Munda and His Arrow* comments:

> .... Chotti and his community realised that both these traditional skills and his arrows are enclosed with cultural power that will propel him the position of a leader, not only of the Mundas but also of the other Adivasis. Chotti's arrow is credited with the community's most successful revenge missions in the face of political corruption and injustice which pervades post-independence India. (Ghanshyam: 2013:127)

Mahasweta Devi has tried to give justice to the adivasi exploitation through her novels, but her short stories collection is as strong as in rebellious attitude like her novel writings. Her long short stories like *The Hunt, The Doupadi* and *Pterodactyl* are like a short novel combining different issues of adivasi feminisms, women's marginalisation and the struggle between adivasi historical past and capitalistic greeds. *Pterodactyl* is a story in the *Imaginary Map* deals with the mountain-dwelling adivasi of Madhya Pradesh who are losing their cultural identity. Puran Sahay goes to Pirtha a adivasi region to study drought-like situations and famine and come to know the misery and exploited situation of adivasi from the capitalist and mainstream. The cave painting found at Pirtha shows that how much outsiders rob them. When SDO observes their painting, he comes the know the agony of adivasi people in the following words. "I did not see the pictures five years ago. I had not gone looking for pictures, then anyway pictures of drunkenness of communal dancing with drams, painted by people... that awful hard, Puranji. Can one measure the distance from the sun by releasing a kite?" (Devi: 1995:106). *Pterodactyl* is the picture of half man and half bird in the form of the spirit of adivasis ancestor. It is a symbol of adivasi against the exploitation. This story focuses on the exploitation of adivasi by outsiders, corporate machinery. About the comprehensive of this long stay critic Dinesh Misra comments:

> Pterodactyl is the crux of the adivasi experience. It associates the struggle of that whole adivasi community against exploitation and oppression with a new myth. It tells the reader about the all-devouring and voracious capitalist onslaughts and the age-old equitable cultural and social traditions where readers travel through human tragedy from the spiritual to the physical. It tells us not only about the present, but the future is also laid bare before our eyes. (Mehra: 2015:147).

*Draupadi* is a very suggestive story about adivasi feminism by Mahasweta Devi. Draupadi is a naxal and captured by Senanayak for interrogation. Draupadi's is brutally raped in custody and abandoned in feminine pain. For the first time, such type of exploited adivasi feminism is presented in Indian literature. Regarding this whole scene of brutality and horror is thrillingly represented by Mahasweta Devi in the following words:

> Trying to more, she feels her arms and legs still tied to four posts. Something sticky under her ass and waist. Her blood. In case she says "water" she catches her lower lips in her teeth. She senses that her vagina is bleeding. How many came to make her? Then Draupadi is brought to the tent and thrown on the straw. Her piece of cloth is thrown over on her body. (Mahasweta Devi: 1987:401)

This exploitation of adivasi worries in false charges should be given a place in literary discourse, but we do not find such representation in mainstream literature where the adivasi female is only presented with romanticisation. When Senanayake looks at her naked body, he feels fear for the first time. Draupadi does not use the cloth now and ask the Senanayak "Are you a Man" because you can tear my clothes but cannot put me my clothes. She dares to challenge the system. She asks a question to the judiciary, which is not honest and justful for common masses. Finally, Rajni Dwivedi presents the climax of the story in *Archetypical Deconstruction in Mahasweta Devi's Draupadi* in the following words:

> Quite surprising Draupadi pushes Senanayak with her two mangled breasts, and for the first time, Senanayake is afraid to stand before an unarmed target afraid. It is ironic to know that Senanayake, who at the beginning of the story gave the order to make up Doupadi, finds himself badly afraid at the sight of Doupadi's crude female sexuality. This is how Draupadi, the Subaltern and most exploited adivasi women represent her women. (Dwivedi: 2014:243)

After much of the realistic writing, Mahashweta Devi confesses that mainstream and their money-centric mentality has created a threat to whole civilisation and it goes beyond irreparable loss. She wants the adivasi world should be given respect and recognition. It should be explored more through literature because they are the ancient inhabitant of this land. She was an activist and a writer par excellence who lived adivasi life and wrote about adivasi life. She was familiar with adivasi dialect, phrases, ceremonies, music and used it in her writing. The most important thing is that she was very much aware of the constitutional adivasi rights, several adivasi schemes, programmers, projects for adivasi upliftment from local to the global perspective. Therefore we noticed, hardly she left anything about adivasi life to introduced and depict on real ground base. Her fictions are full of authentic touch relatively mainstream Indian English fiction. She was in a real sense, a *"Adivasi Mahasweta Devi"*.

### Regional Oriya Literature – With Reference of Gopinath Mohanty and Depiction of Adivasi Life from His Selected Fiction

Along with Mahasweta Devi, famous Oriya writer, Gopinath Mohanty has written vastly on the adivasi and downtrodden people of India, through the Oriya language. Gopinath Mohanty is the Sahitya Academy winner novelist of India who wrote more than fifteen novels and short stories collection. Some of his celebrated and critically acclaimed novels on adivasi life are *Ancestors (Dadi Budha) 1944, Paraja 1945, The son of the Immortal (Amrut Santan) 1947 and Siba Bhai 1955.* Gopinath Mohanty has used the adivasi culture, their customs, rituals to show the adivasi way of living. He has focused the exploitative rural policies working against the dehumanisation of the adivasi community. His novel *The Ancestor* reminds us of the novel of Chinua Achebe's *Things Fall Apart* where Ibo tribes are at the center of the novel. In contrast, kondhs tribes are at the center place in *The Ancestor* The image of Dadi Budha (Ancestor) is to be considered as the deity and pious by the kondh adivasis of Lulla village but because of the outsiders, their culture started crushing and conversion took place among the kondhs. Missionary prays for them to cure adivasis, but basic amenities of needs are much important for them, they ignore this fact. He criticized the missionary attitude in the following words, "The formless heavenly god carried the burden of all our sins-that fine. He would bear the burden on his shoulders. However one led one's life, all sins could be wiped off in his blood someday or other" (Mohanty: 1944:32).

*The Ancestor* is the story of the upheaval of Lulla village and the study of the adivasi characters like Thenga Jani (a adivasi youth) and his loving relationship with a Christian girl (Santosh Kumari).Thenga is betrothed to the girl of his adivasi community naming Saria Daan. Gopinath Mohanty movingly presents a love triangle, ego of elders and broken customs of the adivasi community. Thenga marries to Santosh Kumari and comes to the city. He makes rebel to his community, but he comes in contact with humdrum and selfish city life. Conversion of the adivasi into Christianity and loss of adivasi inheritance, their lacking faith in their ancient primordial power and ancestor Dadi Budha becomes the prominent theme in the novel. The sermon preaching and other religious activities were continuously practices in the village. About their activities, Mohanty comments:

> In the scorching heat, the missionaries in black coats moved from one village to another, preaching the message of Christianity. They sweated profusely, and their feet were blistered. Wherever they come across someone, they would preach to him the message of their religion. Have faith in God, the almighty who sent his son to wipe out the evil from the earth. Have faith in him alone. (Mohanty: 1941:32)

Mohanty has poignantly criticized the religious dogmas, practices that were performed in adivasi Lulla village. Missionary ignores the fundamental problems of adivasi and focuses on religious matters. It seems they are indulged in the process of deculturisation of adivasis. Problems of survival, disorientation is presented in a gripping way in the novel. Mohanty admits that the entry of outsiders and missionaries into the adivasi area would make an irreparable loss to adivasi customs. Many new practices like *thana, the court* is responsible primarily for creating an attraction among adivasi towards elite culture, having a loss of faith in their ancient rituals. Through this novel, Mohanty has presented a adivasi world of love, courtesy, ritual, acculturation, subjugation, revenge and marginalisation. *Paraja* is to be considered as the classic of the modern regional adivasi literature translated in 1945. It tells an epic stay of a happy family, and its decline before the moneylender and capitalistic policy becomes the representative example of the whole Paraja tribe of Orissa. Regarding this epical drama, Yashodha Misra, opines, "In Paraja both the exploited and the exploiter emerge as human characters, in the end, it remains a stay of a people; of exploitation and how man tackles it for his existence" (Misra: 1992: Vol.16, P.01).

The novel *Paraja* in many literary parameters seems per excellence. It feels like the everyman story. It riches the regional literature by incorporating rural situation, character, practices, and psychology. The climax of the love relationship between Jili-Bagla, Mandia – Kajadi, the exploited feminism of Jili, helplessness and sense of irreparable loss of Sukru Jani is the representative example in modern moneymaking world policies. Everyone in Sukru Jani's family goes through the hardships of life. Suku's son Mandia, Tikra, his daughters Bili and Jili, landlord, Bisoi is the responsible character in the novel. Practices of courtship and marriage, religion and rituals, bonded labour, Paraja and law, Paraja and justice have been grippingly incorporated in the novel. When the forest guard fines Sukru in the charges of cutting the tree, he takes the debt from moneylender Bisoi and Mandia become the goti' (Bonded labour) of landlord Bisoi. Regarding the problems of bonded labour critic kumkum Dayar comments, "The practice of goti among the parajas implies a fixed arrangement by which a man has to work instead of an arrangement instead of making cash payment for benefits received" (2003:148). Mandia, Tikra, Sukru all becomes the goti of Sahukar.

The custom of the bride prize among Paraja adivasi community is presented in the novel. Bagala a non-adivasi rejects Jilli because she is lower in status, so Jilli becomes the mistress of old Sahukar Ramchandra Bisoi. Mandia loves Kajodi but does not have sufficient money to pay as a bride prize. Therefore here love and lovers fail. The climax of *Paraja* is pathetic and the issue of bonded labour for adivasi society is realy very deadly and humiliating. Adivasi rights on their ancestor forest, governmental laws are primarily responsible for the uprootedness of adivasi. Jilli, having the capacity of bride-prize also becomes the victim of exploitation by Bisoi. Finally, in frustration Mandia, Sukru kills the Bisoi, pain and suffering of Jill remains silent. She is the most exploited figure in the novel. Commenting on the climax of the novel, Niazi Hazam, opines, "Mohanty has represented his characters as victims of the process with both internal and external manifestations. Their limited access to resources for sustenance and the ever closing snares of money lenders and landlords lead to their tragedy. Had they greater access to resources and opportunity, things would not have gone wrong the way they do" (Hazam: 2014:06).

*Amrut Santhan,* which was translated as *The Son of the Immortal* tells the study of Dongria Kondhs. The family relation of the Dongria

Kondh tribe, alienation from their land, poverty, money and greed of outsiders finds the central theme in the novel. The novel also shows the philosophical musing of adivasi beliefs. The novelist has highlighted kondhs meetings to solve the problems and women's participation in such a meeting. Mohanty has made a statement about the domination of Kondh by outsider in the following words, "Kondhs makes a field clearing the forest. Civilisation follows him, followed by the moneylender and the white-collared officials. They find the land to be good and make it their own. Kondhs moves away and up the hills. Up there too there is the forest and there is Kondh. Once the land is cleared, Kondh is once again chased at to other places" (Mohanty: 1947: 60, translated by Mahanand).

We can notice that the writing of Gopinath Mohanty about adivasi life is realistic and different than the mainstream writers. He has spent his life, among adivasi regions among the adivasi community. Therefore adivasi customs, problems and exploited machinery all show its presence through his novels. He focuses on the disappearing adivasi traditional values in the materialistic stream of modernisation. Mohanty has written the other novels like *Siba Bhai and Apahancha* (The Unreached). *Siba Bhai* deals with the spreading of ideals of Gandhi and Vinoba Bhave among adivasi. *Bhoodan* (Land Donation Movement) is describing in the *Siba Bhai.* The novel presents the different aspects of adivasi in this novel that adivasi are the followers of the virtues like equality, brotherhood and communal harmony. Mohanty has shown the impact of Gandhian ideal on adivasi communities. Anand Mahanand Notices, "It is to be noted that it is mainly the outsiders who come and decide what is good for the adivasis. It is important to see what the adivasis themselves look for. A mark of Mohanty's interiority in adivasi matters is his intimate sense of adivasi specificity and reality. He mentions even small streams, waterfalls, small villages like Maniguda, Chandrapur, *etc.* in his fiction. This demonstrates his fidelity to place the location and gives his fiction specificity" (Mahanand: 2011: 139).

## Selected Regional Adivasi Novel Writings from South India

S. Shivrama Karnath is a famous Kannad writer from Karnataka and contemporary of Gopinath Mohanty. His most celebrated novel is *The Headman of the Hill* (1949) and translated in 1951 and was made into the film in Kannad with the title *Malaya Makalu.* This is the story of the headman and his grandson Karia of Kudia tribes of Western Ghats of South Kanara. They are the worshiper of Malaysia, their ancestor. Both used to live on the hill, but when Bhatt, an entrepreneur comes for the business purpose, he uses divide and rule policy among adivasis. After the headman's death, Karia is legally inherent as headman, but Bhatt for his economic benefit chooses Tukra who is loyal to him as headman. Kariya proves himself brave among other adivasis and becomes the headman again, but by the time Bhatta becomes superior on the hill. He is lustful towards adivasi women. He wants to seduce adivasi Kempi, Bhatta tries to intertwine in the religious matter of adivasi but Thimma opposes him. Major Braganza is the character who wants to spread the missionary work among adivasi.

Novel *Headman of the Hill* shows the colonial approach of Braganza and Bhatta towards Kudia tribe. Because of their entry in adivasi land, Kudia tribes get disturbance. Bhatt ultimately reduces Kempi and wants to seduce Giddi, Thimma's wife. Therefore Bhatta is beaten by Thimma. The loss of Kudia is irreparable because of the coming of the outsiders. Anand Mahanand has opines:

> Bhatta and Braganza are stereotypical outsider characters. They are the embodiment of the colonizer. Their entry into the village results in complete cultural havoc in the adivasi community. Thimma and Giddi leave the village after Bhatt's fertile attempt to molest Giddi. Thimma knows down, Bhatta. Karia joins them later. Here the adivasi has to go out because of the outsiders and adivasi society suffers from the resulting disequilibrium. (Mahanand: 2011:162)

C. K. Janu is a famous adivasi activist. Who wrote the book *Mother Forest, The Unfinished Story of C. K. Janu?* N. Ravi Shankar translates it. *Mother Forest* speaks about the importance of forest in adivasi life. Janu has fought a significant movement for the rights of the adivasi on the forest in the Waynad region of Kerala. Janu claims that nobody knows the forest, adivasi customs, and rituals better than us. She asserts, "When we walk through the forest, she could make out the birds from the sounds they made and easily locate the direction. Ameni could catch the spoor of an elephant quite quickly. They knew everything about the forest. She could quickly sense the coming rain or the summer cold" (Janu: 2004:22).C. K. Janu creates awareness among adivasi women against their exploitation from the outsiders. She appeals to all the adivasi women to unite for their rights. Without mobilisation, we could not achieve our goods; therefore, she claims that changes can be possible only with the participation of adivasi women in the movement for their rights. Amit Sengupta has narrated Janu's view about the empowerment of adivasi women:

> What happens among our women is not what happens in civil society. In our case, unity in everything originates from our women. They have something in common that shelters us from meaninglessly adopting the ways of civil society. It is among our women that our tradition and the way we dress live on even now. There is a resolve that is hardened by the wind and the rain of the forest and the face of other difficulties. All our struggles have been struggles to establish the ownership rights of the real owners of this land for the right to live on it. (Sengupta: 2015:26)

Just like C. K. Janu, Narayan is a regional adivasi writer who wrote *Kocharethi* and other five novels and two short story collections. Narayan has explored the adivasi community Malayayar. Their certain culture, communion with nature, the position of women and land disposition policy of adivasi. Novel shows that Araya adivasi community gives equal respect to the women. Their place in the community is respected. Marriage is a traditional custom. When Kochuraman proposes Kunjipennu for marriage, she does not give a response directly; she has respect for her adivasi rituals. Apart from the shy behavior of Kunjipennu, she is rebellious towards the extreme patriarchic view and male gaze who wants to seduce women only for their pleasure. When Narayanan wants to seduce her, she gives an extreme reaction. Her words show the courage of adivasi feminism, "Glancing at him through the corner of her eyes. She spots out the betel and says, no I am not willing. So just go away quickly. That hope will turn sour. See this sickle? You won't touch me while I am alive… An Areyar girl would not hesitate to attack the man who tried to molest her; she would even slit her own throat to thwart him" (Narayan: 2012:11).

The agricultural aspects of adivasi life have been treated by Narayan very poignantly. In the novel, Kunjipennu emerged as the mother figure that is equally strong to risk her family from external threats. Educational issues of adivasi have also risen by Narayan in the novel. Only education can bring change to the Arayar tribe. Therefore the mother should be conscientious about the education of their children. Novels show Adivasi's understanding of the changing policies towards the land. Novel deals with the position and alienation from their land. The novel focuses that the land of Adivasis could not separate from their communal harmony. They are uniting with it and celebrate their joy and sorrow with it. The process of industrialisation and modernisation brings the change in the life of Malayarar tribes. Novels show the tension between tradition and modernity. J.S. Jayasree comments on the introduction, which shows the gist of the novel:

> The profound anguish over alienation from land and nature that these words echo may appear mute before the public, political discourse aimed at establishing the rights over land. It has been recognised that land reforms have failed in a state that was widely seen as progressive. Narayan's way of responding to the crisis of confidence that all of us have to confront not by active participation in political movements but by asserting through his literary works his solidarity with causes and people who are involved. (Kochareth: 2012: VVXXVIII)

Hansada Sownendra Shekhar has won the Sahity Academy Yuva Purskar for his book *The Adivasi Will Not Dance* in 2015. It is a passionate and comprehensive book of stories that shows the life of Adivasis in Jharkhand. The stories of this book take the Adivasi reader to a new path of progressive literature, showing the tormented life and hardships of indigenous Adivasis against the ugly face of capitalism and urbanity. Characters are fresh and free from the stereotype presentation of Santhal Adivasis. This writing is a path giving to political writing in India. Stories like *Eating with The Enemy, The Adivasi will not Dance, November is the Month of Migration* show the tormented, disposed and marginalised life of the Santhal Adivasi community. The book was banned for the erotic representation of Santali girl character's intimacy with non-adivasi police, but the writer has tried to show the adivasi world, as he has observed around him. The migration of Santali Adivasis from Jharkhand to Bengal and the misery in their life has been shown in *November is the Month of Migration.* Talamai, a adivasi girl is waiting for a train where a policemen offer a bread pakoda in exchange for his physical hunger, she endures the encounter. She eats the pakodas.Writer has shown his creative imagination to show the degradation of adivasi values but adivasis are not the community who sell the dignity and chastity to others for the sake of bread. The story stresses the relationship between the powerful and powerless.

Mangal Murmu, in *Adivasi Will Not Dance,* is a sixty years old artist in an evictee group who refuses to dance in a governmental program. Murrnu asks and scolds to governmental officials that you are displacing us from our Santhal land and wants to dance before governmental authorities. Isn't your VIP was noticing our displacement? Hansada's book *Adivasi Will Not Dance* is one powerful narrative of violence against Adivasis. The exploitation through the mining and other corporate companies, the duplicity of the politician, and whimsical behavior of missionary and hollowness of middle-class sympathies are coming out with flow in this novel. Hansada's comment on the mainstream mentality of the capitalistic group that they speak of Adivasis being treated as a heritage to which perform for tourists to show the rich diversity of India but are meant to forever stay as museum pieces, unable to access good education and health. Sita Rathnamala wrote the autobiography *Beyond the Jungle* in 1968. This is the story of the adivasi girl probably first writing from any adivasi written originally and published by Blackwood in 1968. She was born and brought up in the hilly region at Nilgiri hills. She is very much keen to go beyond the jungle and explore the world, but her life journey taught her that beyond this jungle, another jungle of concrete is more ferocious, cruel and ruthless. She is rejected by a man whom she loved because he is upper cast and she is wilder adivasi. This autobiography shows the cruelty of the caste system and the discrimination faced by the Indian tribe. Regional Bengali and Oriya writing are vibrant with adivasi identity. Adivasi grief, suffering, tormented life, pangs of distortions of culture seems authentically from these writing rather than Indian English fiction writing.

## Regional Adivasi Progressive Literature of Maharashtra

Marathi literature of Maharashtra is rich with the representation of adivasi life and its exploration. This must be admitted, after Jharkhand, adivasi in Maharashtra, is much aware of their historical past, heritage, custom, ritual and about literary creativity. Several literary seminars, adivasi literary conferences have been continuously taken in Maharashtra. Most of the adivasi writers, novelists of the adivasi community in Maharashtra write in the Marathi language. In Maharashtra *Gondi, Bhili, Varali, Madia, Kolami, Mavachi, Paradhi* and *Konkana* are the basic adivasi language, but hardly literature comes through these dialects. In Santali language of Jharkhand, every year, more than five hundred adivasi publication comes out. Marathi literature started around 1960-70 and a huge number of novels, autobiography poetry volume and criticism have taken shape. We are focusing on the novel-writing of Maharashtra. About the adivasi discourse in Maharashtra, Dnyaneshwar Valhekar opines:

> Because of the spreading education after independence, the adivasi community got the awareness of their identity, self-dignity, which created a generation of adivasi writers. This new generation has brought the

> adivasi life of the hilly region, struggle of survival, hardship of modernisation into the Marathi literary discourse. This was new literature for established literary canon. Within a short span, Adivasi literary discourse has got the identity. Apart from exaggerated, romanticised exploration of adivasi life, much focus is given on historical, colonial and modern life of adivasi in the contemporary scenario. This was the goal of Adivasi Discourse. (Valhekar: 2009:02)(Translated)

Some of the prominent adivasi Marathi writers who are widening the horizon of adivasi literature are Waharu Sonawane, Ushakiran Atram, Dr. Vinayak Tumram, Adv. L. K. Madavi, Madhav Sarkunde, Tukaram Warkhade, Kusum Alam, Tukaram Rongate, Najubai Gavit, and Maheshwari Gavit. Venkatesh Atram Bhujang Meshram. These stalwarts are the pioneers of the critical study of adivasi Marathi discourse. Here we are discussing some of the prominent adivasi Marathi novel dealing with major adivasi issues like, marginalisation, disposition, and subjugation and challenging adivasi life with its numerous realities.

A prominent adivasi activist and writer Durgabai Bhagwat have written the novel *Mahandichy Tirawar (On the Edge of River Mahanadi)*. It deals with the primordial beliefs, superstition, mythology, tradition, ghotul and the overall culture of Madia Gonds of Bastar from Madhya Pradesh. This novel was written in 1953, but her observation about the adivasi life in Central India is praiseworthy. Novel deals with anthropological records of Adivasi life.

*Hakumi (A Adivasi Musical Instrument)* is written by senior journalist Suresh Dwadshiwar whose main character is Kanna Madavi, the first adivasi MBBS Doctor of Gond community of Gandhchiroli Maharashtra. Adivasi feminism which is influenced by an alien culture and adivasi panchayat system becomes the central theme of the novel. The issue of Naxalism has also shown its presence throughout the novel. Novel deals with cultural transformation among Adivasi communities on the threshold of industrialisation.

Vishwas Patil who wrote the celebrated Marathi novel *Panipath* also deals with adivasi life in the novel *Zadazadati* (Search Warrant) in 1991. It deals with several incidents of exploitation of Adivasis who becomes the victim of displacement because of the Dam construction. In the novel, Mahadeo Koli adivasi, Thakar and Katkari Adivasi have shown as disposed of. Deprivation of decent income, price of land, the feat of forest authority, lack of medical facilities becomes the central theme of this novel. Novel deals with the core issues of displacement and current industrial policies which brought havoc on the marginal Adivasi community.

Madhukar Wakode has delineated the suffering and severed deprivation of Korku adivasi in his famous Marathi novel *Zelzapat (Predicament)* in 1988. Korkus festival, dances, mythology, exploitation from the moneylender, the concept of the tiger project, economic and language disparity, unity of adivasi exploitation, missionaries and sexual exploitation of Korku adivasi women takes the central place in the novel. This novel covers numerous issues of cultural and identical transformation of Adivasi life. Ugly faces of moneylenders are shown throughout the novel.

*"Eka Naxalvadyacha Janm" (The Birth of a Naxalite)* (1992) is written by Vilas Manohar and *"Encounter"* (1998) is written by Adv. Eknath Salve. In the first one, the novelist has tried to search the basic of the adivasi man and his involvement in such activity. On the suspect of being Naxal, now the cruel treatment is given by police to adivasi is pathetically presented by Eknath Salve in *Encounter*. The novel focuses on the circumstances of Naxalism. The novel shows the pathos and poverty of adivasi life and exploitation from police authorities over innocent adivasis which ultimately results in gun violence.

Dinanath Manohar has written a major adivasi historical novel covering the significant colonial period of British dominance over India and adivasis uprising against them in his famous novel *Manvantar (Introspection)* in 1999. Novel deals with the political victimisation of the adivasi communities like Bhil, Ramoshi and Mahadeo Koli. Eurocentric view, Western materialism and its impact on Indian adivasi, caste system, land acquisition and corporate policies, becomes the most prominent subject of the novel.

Najubai Gavit is a famous adivasi activist who wrote a realistic novel *Trushna* (Thrust) in 1995. The novel takes deep dive into the ancient cultural heritage of MavchiBhil Adivasi, their dowry barter system, internal casteism, several instincts, poverty and hunger of Bhil Adivasi. She has presented adivasi life with sharp detail by Najubai. She has tried her best to make familiar to the mainstream society towards the inner world of adivasi and their invisible presence in the mainstream. Prof. Madhav Sarkunde has written the novel *Wada* (The Palace) in 1996 peeps into the life of Andh adivasi community of Maharashtra. Most of the novel is written in the adivasi Andh dialect. He belongs to that tribe. Therefore pain, suffering; casteism which he experienced from the established social norms becomes the central issue in the novel.

"Wada" becomes the symbol of the exploitation of low adivasi, female, labour, Prof. Sekunde is an extremely talented academician knowing Black literature.

Babarao Madavi has written *Taho* (Weeping) in 1998 which deals with the character of Bheema, an educated Gond Youth who creates awareness among other adivasis against the exploitation, loot, bonded labour of the upper caste and encourages them to fight against such dominant mentality. *Wadgin (Old Age)* is the famous novel of V. B. Karnik written on the Warli community of Thane. The novel shows the pathetic, distorted economic misery, bonded labour, brutal exploitation of Warli young girl by moneylenders, including the several Warli customs, rituals. The novelist makes the question that though the adivasi life seems barren, bare-exist and hardly seems the hope of their betterment but it is the duty of the mainstream that they should uplift this writing and strengthen their voices against all the odds of exploitation.

The novel *Jait Re Jait* is written by Gopal Dandekar on the adivasi life of Thakar community which was later brought into Marathi movie 1965 was highly successful. Katkari lives in the lap at Sahyadri hills of Maharashtra. Different problems of Thakar Community, superstition, marriage – ceremony, several wandering, hunting, drumming has been presented so convincingly by Dandekar. Rani Durgawati has been written on a broad canvas of the Gond Empire of Madhya Pradesh in 1975. Gond King Dalpatshah, Queen, Durgawati, their love for each other, their love for their kingdom and sacrifice has been presented with great acuteness.

*Eklavya* is the epical novel, written by Sharad Dalvi in 1988. We know Eklaya is the adivasi Bhil character of Maharashtra, but we hardly know his history. For the first time, Sharad Dalvi has collected the historical documents and presented the biographical detail of subaltern Eklavya in his novel. From the birth of Eklavya to his sacrifice in the battle of Mahabharata has been delineated into the novel. *Havasu (The Pardhan Man)* is the first Marathi novel written on Pardhan adivasi community.

Pardhan is also known as Patadi, Pani, panaka, and sub-branch of Gond Pradhan, Rajnegi. They are large in number in central India and Maharashtra, but this is the first novel written in these communities. A adivasi hero "*Havasu*" comes before us as a representative of the struggling life of the pradhan community. His struggling life, family attachment, emotional turmoil has been presented so convincingly by the novelist Pandurang Kambale in 2015. About the novel novelist Pandurang Kambale opines:

> Havasu is a representative of the pradhan community which suffered from generations. Though he is illiterate, he has self-dignity; hardworking wants his son to be educated. He is "Havasu Pendam". His wondering for employment, economic misery, up-down in family issues, flop governmental policies, his patience, the selfishness of familiars all have been brought in one volume very convincingly. (Kambale: 2015:12, Translated)

*Bhiva Farari* of Najubai Gavit is the sequel of "*Trushna*". Bhiva is an imaginary character that reminds us of revolutionary Bhagoji Nayak. She has presented the modern contemporary adivasi generation who is diverting from their ancient heritage of courage by specific forces. Novel deals with the Bhil community of DhuleNandurbar. Their folk literature, religious beliefs, hunting becomes the introductory part of the novel. Nevertheless, later moves seriously towards Britisher's exploitative policies towards adivasi. The novelist has ultimately brought adivasi agitation against those repressive policies, the ancient history of Adivasis, prejudices of the community.

The overview of Marathi Adivasi's literary discourse will not complete if we will not take the autobiographical narrative written by the following novelist. *Famous adivasi activist Godavari Parulekar wrote Jevha Manus Jaga Hoto (when the Man Awaken)* in 1970, Anutai Wagh has written *Kosbadchya Tekadivarun.* This narrative of Parulekar shows the struggle of the life of Warli adivasi. Parulekar has justified bonded labor, extreme exploitation of women, the subjugation of economical matter. How the movement of constitutional adivasi rights flourished among Warli adivasi and how they dare to speak against exploitative machinery becomes the core topic of this autobiographical narrative.

Najubai Gavit's *Ador* deals with her struggle for adivasi rights. Ador indicates the sowing the bees infield before the rain. Medha Patkar, a significant figure of the *Narmada Bachao Movement,* has given an introduction to the book. Babarao Madavi's work *Akant (The Storm)* deals with nostalgic memories of adivasi life. He seems like a family man. Adivasi conferences, morchas, demonstrations, political speeches by leaders, government systems and continuous shifting from one place to another forms the theme of this autobiographical narrative. Prof. Maheshwari Gavit from Ahmadnagar has written the critical book *Adivasi Sahityvichhar* in which she has discussed the idea of literary representation of Adivasi through the non-adivasi writer. Nature and scope of Adivasi literature, cultural socialism in the Adivasi writings, the aestheticism of Adivasi life and above all she has discussed the place of this new Adivasi discourse in the contemporary mainstream literary forum. Notice her view on contemporary Adivasi literature:

> In Indian social structure, Adivasi has been considered as a marginal and subjugated object. We find much misery, poverty, submissiveness among Adivasis who still in the majority in the remote, hilly and forest areas. Even after independence, they are not capable of getting food, shelter, clothes. On one side shining digital, the scientific world is taking shape rapidly, but on the other hand, the majority of adivasi is struggling for basic amenities of life. History says that moneylender, corporate, high cast and exploitative mentality imposed their hegemonised culture on them. They are a broken community yet. (Gavit: 2009:50, Translated)

One of the prominent critic, writer and former adivasi planning officer Mr. Tukaramji Warkhade has written overly philosophical books which are a lighthouse for the adivasi movements in Maharashtra and India. He has written the books like *Adivasinchya Astitwache Prashn* in 2017, *Bharat Ke Vastvik Bhumalak* in 2017 and *Birsa Munda Ki Samudayik Chintandhara (2021), Gondi Dharmdarshan Ki Avdharana (2021), Vaicharaik Pragatishil Parivartan ka Masouda (2021).* His writings comprise the major adivasi issues and suggest the solution to it. He believes that significant adivasi movement should take place to sustain constitutional adivasi writes. Prof. Sanjay Lohakare wrote the famous poetry volume *Adivasi Lilavacha Prajasttak Desh.* These writing are thought-provoking about the contemporary situation of adivasi in India. Therefore, Bhujang Meshram asks for the Adivasi's political and literary movement from itself by adivasi writings, where a sizeable social pedagogy can be created among twelve cores Adivasis. He gives a perfect message to all adivasi organisations, movement to work honestly, going beyond the chip purpose of rewards and prestigious posts and economic benefits. He opines:

> Though adivasi are facing problems like disposition, acculturation, subjugation, and environmental threat and degrading policies, the solution is the political participation and political pedagogy of the adivasi

> communities. Without being strong politically, our problem and their solutions cannot be drawn. We don't want to make politics only for the political benefits, but we want to regenerate the self-respect movement of Birsa Munda, Narayan Singh Uikey are want to reconstruct a strong and unite Adivasi community on the National level. For this lofty purpose, snobbishness and polishing should be avoided, and educated classes, writers, activists should share the stage for one cause. (Meshram: 2014:36, Translated).

Marathi Adivasi's discourse is strengthening day by day. The new writer is taking the responsibility to explore the unexplored area of adivasi writing. No doubt the understanding of Adivasis life will mature gradually, and that will take shape in upcoming days. Dr. Vinayak Tumram is very much optimistic about the role of a new writer and reading class that only literary writing of Adivasi can aware of the impending danger on the adivasi community. He shows in optimism in his critical volume *Adivasi Sahitya: Disha Ani Darshan (Adivasi Literature: Philosophy and Direction)* as follows, "Adivasi discourse is searching its rich heritage. It was searching for their ancient roots and tried to explore a new horizon of adivasi culture. Nevertheless, still, there are not literary adivasi movement has taken place which can create a true social pedagogy, of emotional turmoil among common adivasi masses. Nevertheless, certainly, it will happen" (Tumram: 2012:11).

## Adivasis in Hindi Literary Discourse – With Special Reference of Novel Writing in Jharkhand

*Adivasi Vimarsh* in Hindi is in its full swing. Adivasi Vimarsh is strengthening by both adivasi and non-adivasi a writer who writes in Hindi. Literature which is written in Hindi from Jharkhand is vibrant with Adivasi contents. A large number of literary conferences are organised in Ranchi, Jharkhand now a day. *Jharkhandi Sahitya Sanskriti Akhada* is doing marvelous work to promote the Adivasi discourse throughout the nation, including outside of the nation also. In India, we find thousands of adivasi organisation of which works form social, political, constitutional and cultural way but still the fundamental problem of adivasi land, forest, hill, and natural resources are going on.

Jharkhand was reshaped as a new state on 15 November 2000. It became solely as a separate state, but after Eighteen years, problems are not solved but become complicated, and the same circumstances happened with Chhattisgarh. Natural resources are taken from adivasi land across the may part of the nation, but local adivasi are not getting the benefit of those things. Today nearly 90% per cent adivasi population lives under below the poverty line and more than seventy-five percent of adivasi women in Jharkhand and Chhattisgarh are infected with the disease of anemia. Death mortality, infant mortality, sexual abusing and many problems are increasing in these major adivasi territories of India still we find a courageous attitude to live on for the rights of living and fighting for constitutional adivasi rights. Here we will overview some of the novel written in Hindi about the Adivasi life which will strengthen our understanding of post-independence and contemporary adivasi life.

Sanjeev is a famous Hindi writer who promotes sociological thoughts through literature. His novel *Dhar* (1998) deals with the bonded labor where adivasi labour has to do reg. Go through challenging tasks into coal mines. The novel shows the rebel of mines labourers against corporate policy and governmental exploitation of adivasi labour in the adivasi region. Vinod Kumar has written their novels on the Jharkhand movement. His novel *Samar Shesh Hai* deals with the exploitation of Adivasis through the moneylender. Shibu Soren and his *Dhankatani Movement take* the central theme of the novel. His novel *Mission Jharkhand* (2006) deals with the political aspect of the adivasi area where adivasi becomes the political victim and outsiders overruled them. *Red Zone (*2015) deals with the displacement of the Adivasis through the process of so-called modernisation. The bias role of media has also helped this exploitation. Adivasis are not glorified in this novel, but the novelist has given much focus on contemporary reality.

Rakesh Kumar Singh wrote two novels *Jaha Khilate Hai Rakt Palash* (2003), and *Pathar Par Kohara* (2003) deals with the Adivasi culture, its distortions, the impact of the intruder and economic deprivation becomes the critical theme of the novels. Ranedra is the primary name in Hindi literature whose two novels *Global Gaon ke Devata* (2007) and *Gayab Hota Desh* (2014) presents the contemporary study of adivasi life of Jharkhand. Rumjhum Asur is the central character in *Global Gaon ke Devata* who exposes the distortions and acculturation of Asur adivasi community. *Gayab Hota Desh* presents the massive displacement resulting in unjust, poverty, and hunger among adivasi territory of Jharkhand. This novel enriches the Hindi literature. Rakesh Kumar Singh has written the novel *Jo Itihas Me Nahi Hai (2005)* deals with the struggle for independence where history and its pages are blank about the revolt of adivasis. Adivasi icon and their sacrifices have been neglected by mainstream historical writing of India, and this novel exposes this partiality. Sanjeev has written the novel *Pav Tale ki Dub (2005)* which deals with the storm of multinational companies in Jharkhand. It presents the extreme pollution, modernisation where adivasi identities have lost the entire heritage. Notice the statement of the hero of the novel, Sudeep:

> You know Jharkhand is ample storage of natural resources, new multinationals are taking place. Nevertheless, look at the unjust and exploitation that adivasi are displaced from their land, and they are not given the compensation even. They have lost culture, land and money is going to official and bureaucrats. Nevertheless, where are these displaced Adivasis? What happened to them, the government has nothing to do with it. Where are these "Dokari", "Makara" adivasi villages, possibly they filed with multinational "Phoonk"? They might destroy in this corporate storm. (Sanjeev: 2005:28, Translated)

*Jaha Khilte Hai Rakt Palash (2003)* is a remarkable novel by Rakesh Kumar bringing the adverse effect of industrialisation in adivasi Jharkhand. Forest zones are exploiting, natural resources are snatching, chastity of women is snatching, and jungle of concrete is taking shape everywhere in adivasi's belts. Notice the comment of Rakesh Kumar:

> Corporate are purchasing enough land, why should not, there is plenty of treasure beneath the land, iron, coal, bauxite, dolomite, gypsum and many more. Big storage of oil, petrol is taking rest underground. Now there will be no crop and agricultural projects, only well of oil and diesel. Look thirsty brother does not drink water, drink oil, and drink petrol. Let it go to foreign, and this oil will run battleships and fighter planes, enough bombing will be there on the weak and small nation. Red drinks will be everywhere. Now, brother let's eat coal, chew it. (Rakesh Kumar: 2003:147)

Mahua Manzi *writes Maram Gomke Nilkanth Hua (2012)* deals with the radiation of uranium mines on the local adivasi who works there as labour without giving necessary protection. It affects their health resulting from the newly born babies with several signs of abnormality. Atomic, garbage also put to the dumping zone of adivasi forest and near to adivasi villages. Jadugoda became the dumping zone for the whole nation. This radiation kills adivasi later, but this hunger will take their life soon. If Morang Goda was a non-adivasi territory, then it could be a nuclear west dumping station." At what extent Adivasis will tolerate such dehumanisation will nobody comes to help them, to raise voice for them" (Manzi: 2012:178). *Mati*

*Mati Arkati* is a very famous novel deals with the adivasi labour of Oraon, Munda, Santhal and Khadia adivasi community who were taken as coolie or labour to Singapore, Mauritius, Fiji, Guyana, Carrabian and in Latin American countries nearly 150 years ago. The novel traces their existence and the Eurocentric outlook of west towards the Adivasis of India. The novel covers a major aspect of caste systems bonded labour, homesickness and the broken identity of indigenous people of Jharkhand. Veer Bharat Talwar has written a big critical volume on social, political, educational, religious aspects of Adivasis of Jharkhand naming *Jharkhand ke Adivasion ke Beech Ek Activist Ke Notes* where he opines that forgetting their right on land, forest and river, adivasi should create an international awareness forum of Indigenous people. He has commented on the elite mentality of educated adivasi youth, who looks down towards their culture, language and struggle as outdated and inferior. In such circumstances, he asks the question to the Jharkhandi Adivasi:

> Nevertheless, the question is why Adivasis are leaving behind their identity. Why are educated students erasing their identity, hiding their origin with disgrace? Why they feel so shame about their language, culture and community? The answer is this so-called educated elite outsider intruder looks down on adivasi culture as inferior. They still consider adivasi as wild savage. They make a comparison between hegemonies culture and the rural culture tradition, forest rituals of Adivasis and claims it as a subject of mocking. Through their discussion, gesture, they manifest their disgust towards Adivasi culture and claim themselves that our culture is sophisticated, having higher values of the human being. (Talwar: 2012: 223, Translated)

The Adivasi discourse, which is now becoming a separate identity in the literary panorama of India is to be considered as very constructive and aesthetic. Primarily it is not the literature of rebellion or tension, but it is the literature of communal harmony. Mainstream literature has not yet given the reorganisation of these major adivasi discourses. They are biased about this real expression of Adivasi society. Famous Jharkhand writer and literary stalwart Vandana Tete, has written some of the excellent books about Adivasidom like *Adivasi Sahitya-Parampara Aur Prayojan, Purkha Ladakh and Jharkhand Ek Anthin Sangashagatha.* In her book *Adivasi Sahitya – Parampara our Prayojan,* she has explained the outlook and overview of Adivasi literature in the following words:

> In my opinion, Adivasi literature in India is related to the period of colonialism, and its impact on adivasi life becomes the main theme of adivasi discourse. Nevertheless, we cannot make Adivasi literature so

> limited to its encounter with colonialism. Adivasi literature rejects those full colonial modes which are responsible for the ultimate doom. Adivasi discourse tries to save, protect the whole universe. This literature contemplates about whole nature, and a man is one among them. In the mainstream literature, man is the center of literature, but in Adivasi discourses, not only man but the whole universe with its objects are at the center. (Tete: 2013:88, Translated)

Ramnika Gupta is the literary giant of adivasi sensibility. She is adivasi and Adivasi per excellence through her academic commitments towards adivasi life... In her famous book *Adivasi Literature – An Emerging Consciousness.* She has narrated to the adivasi writers about the danger of globalisation which will soon corrode the soul of regional literature. Through her edited writing, she has shown the contemporary exploitation of Adivasis and how new voices are resisting them. Her writing shows that today's Adivasi generation is resisting the hegemonic norms because this system is destructing their life channels and source of inspiration for their communal harmony. This money-making culture is forcing them to displace from their ancestor land. In this regards, she opines:

> The jungle has calm and quiet for centuries, but it was never dead. Whenever unjust took place, it fought. The jungle has no language, no voice but no matter, but it has thoughts and mutual understanding. It has great conscience of justice and unjust, it has the perception of freedom, therefore its challenge to British imperialism first. It is still fighting to take the risk to eradicate but still singing its rebellious and courageous song of freedom. (Gupta: 2013:85)

The contemporary Hindi Adivasi Literary discourse focuses more on the issue of displacement, mining, loot, and industrialisation. Adivasi resistance should not be the obstacle to this moneymaking process; therefore adivasis have given very threatening treatments. In military operations like Green Hunt and Salva Judum, many innocent Adivasi women and men are killed which have no counting till today. If the mainstream educated literary forum will not show grave concern with these issues then who will speak and write about these most dangerous subjects. At one side,

*"Shining India", "Digital India"*, is becoming rich with their corporate policies and on another side, the major population of the adivasi area is living their daily life in minimum resources. In this regard, Vinod Kumar says, "In this modern age, it is not possible for one country to colonised other one for a long time, therefore make the colonisation of a particular part of the same country and exploit it as much as possible and fulfill their hunger of power and money

and saves himself. Jharkhand and other adivasi places are such an example of internal colonial territory. (Kumar Vinod: 296:2005)

In this chapter, we studied the regional adivasi – Adivasi discourse from various parts of India. We can claims that as compare to mainstream Indian English fiction, novel writing from Bengali, Oriya, Marathi, and Hindi is much focused on the adivasi issue of identity crises and subjugation. Nobody can be denied that adivasi community, their existence is not a part of romanticisation, and over glorification, it should be studied and present on ground base reality as we found in regional adivasi literature. Adivasi is going through the process of silent killing and marching towards the unnoticed genocide process, then what are the solution to end such exploitative policies. The hero of the novel *Khule Gagan Ke Sitare* (Shining Stars of the Open Sky) Indra Says:

> We must never forget those cruel – barbaric pages of the history of so-called glorious human civilisation, where many Native American tribes and African Adivasis were becoming the subject of mass genocide by putting and injecting poisonous insects in their clothes. Africa was most of the youngster Adivasis with a huge mob pushed into dark ships and in the chain, were sentenced to America as slaves. If we do not want to repeat those pages of dark human history, we have only one solution – we must change the whole system where ego – worshipping, and animal instincts will find no place forever. (Kankaria: 2007:93, Translated)

Finally, I could conclude this chapter of regional adivasi literature of India with the famous quotation of Adivasi writer Vandana Tete who dedicated it to the revolutionary struggle of Birsa Munda, where Birsa is addressing to his upcoming generation to be in action for mass revolution for the better humankind:

> I am leaving to give you my words, don't throw it here or there but preserve it in your courtyard. My saying and dignity will never die, Ulgulan and its revolutionary words can never be erased; in fact, it will I grow like little grass with or after rain. Never lose your hope in humanity and don't depress that I left you alone. My Sacrifice, my ideology will always provide you with constant energy to fight against unjust, inequality and all kinds of exploitation. (Inspiration-Birsa Munda. Words-Vandana Tete, Translated).

# Conclusion

## Decultarisation, Disorientation and Political Strategies against the Adivasi: A Missing Chapter in Contemporary Mainstream Indian Fiction Writing:

Indian English fiction writers have made their particular assertions about adivasis which are incomplete, therefore; we do not find much reality in their novels. In the novels like *The Strange Case of Billy Biswas, The Princess, The River Sutra* and *The English August,* we find the unauthentic representation of the adivasi life. In every novel, adivasi life and characters are shown dependable on mainstream heroes for help.

Novelist's adivasi women and man, surrender to mainstream sophisticated social arrangements. In most of the novels, they consider the non-adivasi person as god and savior for them who is an outsider of their adivasi territory. This is a kind of internal orientalism. The political victimisation of the adivasi is the colonial phenomenon. Mainstream writers assume that the adivasis are uncivilised and no need for cultivation hence adivasis are the community for political victimisation. Mainstream kinds of literature have never depicted their victimisation on ground realities and never given a place in mainstream canonical literature.

In postcolonial Indian English literature, society and its importance were dominated by particular communities and their established values. The hierarchy of Indian society played a vital role in literature writing in English. Therefore, freedom struggle, diaspora, imagined communities, marital-extramarital issues, the concept of single women, independent women, single father, single mother, cola generations and butterfly generations often become the central themes of postcolonial Indian English novel writings. In the postcolonial Indian English literary scenario, most of the time announcement is done for *'Death of novel'* but the novel-writing flourished again in recent decades. A huge number of novels are written on the above themes but it lacks the presence of the Adivasi community, their exploitation by bureaucracy and corporate policies. We do not find the subjects like the intrusion of corporates along with state interference in adivasi schedule areas in the Indian English novels. In these senses, Adivasi in India is nowhere in this postcolonial Indian English novel writing.

In the novel, *The Princes* and in *The English August,* politicians, ruling parties, bureaucrats and officialdoms find complete failure to win the heart of the adivasi. It happens in the novel because the concepts of adivasi development or the necessities of the local adivasi were not taken in granted according to their natural way of living life and thinking of the adivasi community for their self upliftment. In the novel, *The Princess,* adivasi are loyal to Maharaja Heroji, gave tax to their *Munimji*, honored them but when Congress wants their land for the development project of a major dam, they oppose the Congress. Adivasis do not understand the language of negotiation and marketing strategies in the novel. They lack political pedagogy. Again Augustya in *The English August* came to know that adivasis are not materialistic. They only demand their basic rights of drinking water, food, school and health facilities. In this novel, governmental policies in adivasi areas are so lethargic that adivasis could not take the benefit of these policies. Adivasi communities in India are double disposed and triple colonised by the mainstream society and from the British imperialism. Postcolonial Indian English novelists must accept and explore this truth that when one community reads the pain, pathos and hardships of other communities, it has some significance and worth value. Today in the Indian literary world, one can notice that postcolonial novels are written in the favor of the state, power and the caste hierarchy. The political nepotism manages the postcolonial literary flow in India. A political ideology decides to give or not to give voice to minorities and adivasis. Therefore, Shambhunath opines:

> Cosmopolitanism and Globalisation have widened the terrible gap between social, political behavior and ideologies. Therefore in contemporary novels feminism, Dalit consciousness, native responses, surviving environments, threats to Adivasi life, dispossession, military repression, metro verse agrarian, religious secularism, religious orthodoxy, and several fragmented peoples movements from local places are becoming the dominant themes of literary writings. (Shambhunath: 2016: 236, Translated)

Adivasis as depicted in the selected Indian English novels, *The Coffer Dam, The River Sutra, The Strange Case of Billy Biswas,* have a common treatment in themselves. They remained unseen, unheard, silent and invisible. Even hundreds of research papers might be published on these novels but no effort was taken to give the adivasi community as its central place in the mainstream literature. No doubt, these novels are one of the rich heritages of postcolonial Indian English literature but it lacks the marginal representation and hardships of adivasi life. These novelists are unique in their aesthetic sense, style and techniques but seem weaker in its moved vision and virtues of subjugated and broken classes. These novels show two societies, one with ample sources of living opportunities and the other one show fewer opportunities for survival. It clearly shows economic, social, cultural separations in Indian society, particularly marginal classes. A wide gap has been shown between the areal life of mainstream characters and the earthly struggle of adivasi characters. Surprisingly, the novelist has not even shown sympathy for the cultural deprivation of adivasis. Most of the selected novel ends only with philosophical musing and ending the life of its hero's provocative thoughts about urban alienation but less discourse is taken place about inequalities in social strata. It seems that adivasi life for them in the novel is only hype oriented or only for the introduction of an imaginary or illusive savage world and nothing else than that.

The Indian English fiction writers have not taken care of when they write about, Postcolonial and Postglobal India. Along with globalisation, there must be humanitarian aspects in their novel writing. India is the country of villages. Our national concerns originate from villages, of course, metro cultures have different importance. The process of novel writings never stands in the same place. For creating new humanitarian consciousness, novelists have to break the narrow wall of elite mentality and traditional orthodoxy. There is a risk at breaking stereotype walls of caste, class and religion but it is also true that writing literature particularly about ancient communities is not a matter of luxury and romanticisation. Justice to the masses should be the reality of literary writings. Indian English Literature is now becoming global. The story, event, pathos, predicaments of a particular community mentioned in the literature, does not remain longer to them only but it becomes national-international issues. The ways, Indian English writers have projected the description of adivasi characters, their ways of looking at life seem unconvincing. In the novels like *The Strange Case of Billy Biswas, The English August and The River Sutra,* novelists have presented them as backward and dependent as they can show them. However, globalisation has destructed adivasi culture and their territory as compared to other communities. In Upamanyu Chatterjee's *The English August,* the problem of adivasi leadership has slightly described where a adivasi lady, Para goes to the district office with the complaint of the scarcity of drinking water in the adivasi village. Rao is another character in the novel to whom Augustya considers Naxal but he is the leader of the village and much aware of the changing policies of government against the common masses and helps other adivasis to understand these contemporary changes. Prof. Ramanna, a hardcore Gandhian also tries to give a nonviolent vision to adivasi people in Chipanthi village in Madana district. Chatterjee could elaborate on this problem of leadership for the upliftment of adivasis and can give a new vision to other novelists and writers to understand the basic problems of the adivasi community. The scarcity of leadership in the political, social and cultural arena is a reality in adivasi society.

Arvind Adiga, in his novel *The White Tiger,* conveys that most of the laborers, farmer and poor man goes to Delhi, Bangalore with full of a crowd in the trains. Though he directly does not comment on *adivasi migration* but the scene in the novel efficient enough to convey the problem of unemployment in adivasi regions like Jharkhand, Chhattisgarh and Orissa. Adivasi migration from their local land to which they are the real owner, moving to other places is a big issue for literature writings but yet to be literaturised. In the case of adivasis, when someone dislocates them from their territory, they became homeless, unidentical human beings. Adiga's novel comments very faintly about this unavoidable problem which is largely avoided by many Indian English novelists. If the government could offer them their ancestral right, then the problems of decultarisation among adivasi could not take a serious turn but even after seventy years of Independence, adivasi are disoriented from their Cultural Socialism because of the negligence of the Governmental authorities.

If the gradual doses of westernisation, materialism, cosmopolitanism and globalisation are given through education, one cannot easily understand the cultural and identical transformations of one's country, one's culture and one's individual. This had happened exactly with the literary classes or writing classes of India and the rest of the world. The promoters of Indian postcolonial writings have educated themselves from western universities. They study big western theories but never link them with native issues of internal colonialism. These intellectual classes could not understand the real face and hidden make up of global liberalism. Imperialism is again neocolonising the world. On the surface level, it seems idealistic but internally it breaks native adivasi culture by displacing them from their resources and indigenous roots. They promote multiculturalism to hide the identities and questions of marginal classes. It is the responsibility or the Indian English fiction writers to contemplate on Foucault, Chomsky and Edward Said and must resist the neo-colonisation of the world particularly, of the marginal and broken communities.

## Colonial Struggle-Revolt of Adivasis against Corporate Policies and It's Invisibility in Modern Global Fictions of Indian English Literature:

The treatment of the adivasi in Postcolonial Indian English fiction lacks in many grounds. Adivasi historical revolts, encroachments of British rule into adivasi territories, grabbing lands of the adivasis, exploitation of adivasi women, cruel landlords, deforestation and degradation of adivasi environmental values do not find realistic representation in Indian English fictions. In Gita Mehta's *The River Sutra*, adivasi are shown as the worshipper of Narmada River and performing some ritual on the bank of River Narmada, but adivasi religious concerns are not so much the limited and full of superstitions. They consider land, forest and water as a godly gift to them. These natural objects are itself Godlike for them but when British power and landlords took the illegal entry in their territories, they protested against them and became the epitome of valor and martyrdom in the history.

The Adivasi communities have a glorious tradition of revolts and mass movements to save their identities. An epical journey of the freedom struggles have fought by adivasi on this land, but pages of historical novels of India are blank towards these mass revolutions. The recurrent theme of partition, urban alienation, moll generation, cola generation and butterfly generation becomes the prominent theme for Indian English writers. Their hanging in two words became their core themes of literature writings. A massive history of bloodshed of adivasis remained invisible because of the mainstream writer's hedonistic attitude towards life inspiring by physical materialism. This loss of adivasi sacrifices on this land could never be repaired, it's irreparable but small attempts of literary writings can explore the adivasi sacrifices before the world. Indian English fiction writers must give justice to the cultural and psychological deprivations of the marginal, Dalits and Adivasis in the Indian scenario. In the regional Bhasha literature, through the pen of regional writers, adivasi problems of land deprivation were realistically portrayed in the novel like *Mother Forest* and *Kocharethi*. This core issue of land acquisition does not show a single sentence in the Indian English novel. Major warfare of adivasi during the colonial period remained untouched by mainstream English literature. It shows the neo-colonisation of Indian English fiction writings.

This is a new type of colonisation to which our novelists, policymakers do not want to speak or analyse because corporate tycoons give them economic benefits for maintaining literary silences. This is a culture of silence maintained by intellengia and victims are marginal adivasis, Dalits and labor classes. Because of this corporate globalisation, the common adivasi man came on the edge of becoming new slaves of the capitalistic world order. Though, on the surface, it appears that because of cosmopolitism and globalisation, the world is becoming more liberal, comprehensive and multicultural but in reality, the discussions and debates of intellectual writers upon neoliberalism, militarisation and post-globalisation of the world are pushing to third world nations to neo-colonisation which our policymakers and politicians are unable to understand or probably pretends of not to be understood. This mode of cultural amnesia is taking place in the case of literary writing also, particularly in the case of Indian English fiction. We take much pleasure in reading about *Harry Potter Hobbit*, *Moors Last Singh* or *In An Antique Land* but we are not aware of the marginal issues in Premchand's *Godan* and Renu's *Maila Anchal,* Maitry Pushpa's *Alma kabutari*, Mahasweta Devi's *Jungle ke Davedar* or Ranendra's *Global Gao ke Davta.* Mental recolonisation of an educated mind is taking us for a way to from Indian ground realities but we cannot live so ignorant about this aerial representation of life or these mental aesthetic hallucinations, purposely spread by the profit mongering mentalities. The novelist must understand these realities that without local, they cannot be global.

History, anthropology, culture and civilisations are the backbones of the literature of any nation and in any period. Africans, American and Australian aboriginal novel writings flourished because of their colonial exploitation and to give expression to the native responses of resistance to those imperial powers. Today Australian, African, Canadian aboriginal, Native works of literature are widely reading in the whole world. On the other hand, Adivasis of India, who proved the victim of several colonial policies at different stages of ancient, medieval, modern global Indian history, does not find rebellious roaring in Indian English literature, particularly in fiction. This clearly shows that the ignorance of selective Indian English fictionist about the disadvantages of colonial rule on India. Today, Indian English Literature is largely a postcolonial response to the mainstream European literary canons which were once the ruler on the colonies and the native cultures. The suppressed identities, slavery, economic, political and cultural marginalisation became the theme of postcolonial literature. After Indian Independence, writers started to scrutinise the colonial impact on Indian social, political and cultural arena, which becomes the theme of postcolonial literature in India. Malnutrition, hunger, poverty, partition women suppression and political trauma became the themes for Indian novelists. But these subjects were never developed by them in connection with adivasi communities. The Adivasi community which was colonised in its every sphere could not take shape in mainstream novels. Adivasi life is often discussed with naxal issues. They are shown as mercenary, violent, anti-national and anti-progressive in most of the literary or social discourses in India. We must check the realities of these issues because, after Independence, the mass genocide of adivasi has been taking place in the name of naxal evacuation. The violence of any kind can never be justified but literature should investigate the mass killings of Adivasi under the false labeling of naxalism. This subject of novel writing can explore the realities of adivasi heartland before the world.

Most of the regional novels of India are dealing with serious issues but Indian English mainstream literature could not give justice to the representation of Adivasis. In Chatterjee's novel *The English August,* he has shown a character of Reddy, considered as naxal head of that area, who demands the adivasi rights and to stop the forcible land acquisition of the adivasi by corporates. His characterisation shows that he is not happy, the way bureaucracy is dealing with adivasi issues, with adivasi women, so his men cut the hand of the Mohan Gandhi, who seduced a adivasi woman. Naxalism and their violence can never be justified anyway, but its spreading in the adivasi territory can be a major subject of novel writing. Even, Upmanyu Chatterjee has not given the details of these issues in his novel. The novel doesn't answer why the selective youth of indigenous communities are taking guns in their hands, in their motherland for getting their rights of education, employment and opportunities for the living of a dignified life. Adivasi is a communal word, where hundreds of tribes comprise a whole family. These tribes have their naturalistic behaviors, rituals and customs which are sometimes mocked by the highly sophisticated westernised culture of Indian social strata since Independence. Most of the time, adivasi rituals and nature love is romanticised and glorified by these elite Indian English writers as we have seen in the case of Kamala Markandeya and Arun Joshi's novels. They have romanticised and tried to show larger than life pictures of the adivasi. Adivasi anthropology is our treasure of the past but this treasure of the Adivasi community is uprooted from its heritage through the implementation of certain policies by the capitalist in the name of bringing them into mainstream society.

In the novel, *The Coffer Dam,* British Engineers team comes to the southern part of India to build a big dam, this is an example of how corporate works in adivasi areas. The corporate projects, mineral project, big water reservoir, big forest reservoir and field firing ranges were built in adivasi major territories after independence and for this purpose, the original inhabitants of the land were displaced from their villages. The same incident happens with the adivasi village of *The Coffer Dam* but Clinton and his British Engineer team appeared unsympathetic towards them. After such a long gap of centuries, again corporate policies are destructing the agrarian adivasi economy in adivasi regions of India. Arvind Adiga has also touched on this fact that mining and other corporate projects are providing benefits only to those who are having a sophisticated culture but the natives and marginal hardly get any benefits from it. For setting the corporate in the profitable territory, adivasi are displaced is the history of the past and this is the history of present India also. Kamala Markandeya has slightly touched these issues of the dam and displacement culture in adivasi India but she could present it more realistically.

The Indian officialdom as depicted by Upamanyu Chatterjee in his novel, *The English August is* the reality of modern Indian bureaucracy. The bureaucracy of India seems lethargic when the matter comes to provide basic amenities to the adivasi. When August Sen, an Indian Administrative Officer, finds the distorted life of adivasi in the village named Chipanthy, he feels miserable. He notices sheer corruption and nepotism works in a adivasi area where adivasi are far away from the mainstream society. Augustya finds the opportunity to come out from his boring office and colleagues, so he wants to go to Chipanthy, but he also is not serious about adivasis problem as the Ramanna and Rao and the local non-adivasi are. Red tappism, nepotism, corrupt political policies, dropout economic policies are very exact reasons for the backward, poor-unhealthy life and facilities in adivasi areas. Adivasi-adivasi culture is not a violent culture. Their cultural practices are indigenous. Their dance, folk songs, stories of ancestors and nature-worshipping are extremely inspiring but the mainstream looked them as savage, barbaric and uncivilised. Their agrarian Panchyat system was intercepted by the industrial policies. Adivasi has their cultural system which we find in their oral songs, is neglected by Indian English literature. Because of modernity, they are losing their culture but when they protest for sustaining their ancestral and constitutional rights, they are labeled as Naxals. *The Princess, English August and The White Tiger,* shows the adivasi engagement with naxal movement. Though adivasis have not much benefitted from these issues, till today.

Postcolonialism in India can be the view from a different perspective. It is considered that Indian society was crushed under British policies during and after colonialism. It is to be expected that postcolonial literature should critic the colonial Eurocentric mentally. As in Africa, native responses were very strong in the writings of N Gugi Wa Thiong, Chinua Achebe and Chimamanda Achebe. In American literature, Alice Walker and Ralf Ellison wrote from a postcolonial point of view giving justice to local issues but In Indian English writings, adivasis were colonised by British, feudal lords and cast bias mentalities of the people, still, adivasi representation is weaker in their novel. This triple colonisation of adivasi could have enough scope for the exploration for all Indian English novel writers but these soldiers of the pen seem sharp less in the literary representation of adivasi. Those novelists who challenge to all kind of hegemonies are the real sympathiser of humanity. These novelists present burning realism through their creative masterpieces. Telling the social norms is not the only duty of a novelist but creating social awareness and social consciousness against the exploited machinery and unjustified policies is the real work of a novelist. Literature springs from social realities; therefore, realities of the society should be explored by the novelist. It seems that adivasi was never the part of mainstream society, therefore, they are invisible in mainstream literature. The hegemony of the handful was the reality of Indian English writing before and after independence.

## Displacement of Adivasis for Natural Resources and Culture of silence Maintained by Indian English Literary Intellectuals

Because of the growing global policies of a handful of multinationals, issues like cultural identities and existentialism of dispossessed communities became very grave. Man becomes self-centered. His connections with ground realities are broken. The concept of the welfare state becomes a myth in the postcolonial era. But not only in the postcolonial period the marginal groups of India are facing this untouchability but also for the last many centuries they are going through these phases of dehumanisation. Therefore they were not part of mainstream literature. Theirs crave for identity, their aspirations and creativities were denied by social hegemony. The hegemonic literature could not give voice to the broken identities of the Adivasi community.

We are criticising postcolonialism and postmodernism for not representing Adivasi in their literature but these realities in India go through the hegemonic strata of Indian society for the lost many centuries. Mainstream literature was not socially responsible literature but largely dealing with the elite class of society. For the last many centuries adivasi wants to speak up for their displacement, subjugation and disillusionments but their voices were unheard by mainstream literary stalwarts. Mainstream literature is full of dominancy where mass society unable to find their true reflections. These educated middle class of Indian society educated themselves by colonial education and became the blind products of globalisation. They are the huge admirers of materialistic prosperities. Therefore adivasi, their existence and identity never became the important subjects of their writings. Now man-women relationship, marital, extramarital relationship, migration generations and multi citizenships, comprises the themes of their writings. Their novels seem full of hype and body celebrations but malnutrition adivasi young generation, the battle of adivasis for drinking water in remote adivasi areas, defectives food policies and insufficient employment policies were never in their gaze while writing the fictions. Such psychology of the writers seems not ready to accept that there are other ethnic groups to which we have to give representation through literary creativity. Their scope of vision is very limited. You cannot claim of mastery of farming only by standing in the once fields, the same manner, visiting adivasi areas, doing some case studies cannot make you the master of the literature of adivasi life.

*The Strange Case of Billy Biswas 1973, The English August 1988* and *Geeta Mehta's The River Sutra 1993* deals with forest life, rituals, customs of adivasi life. Though adivasi life was glorified by these novelists, they have shown the forest as the source of inspiration and the main objectives of their culture. This was the same period of urbanisation and industrialisation in adivasi areas. Many industrial projects like Steel plant, Water reservoir and Buffer Zones took place after 1955 in the present adivasi territory like Jharkhand, Chhattisgarh and Orissa of India. These projects are to be considered as the temples of the industrial progress of India, which would transform the adivasi life giving them many benefits. In reality, this development and its benefits were never given to the Adivasis. Forest policies were strictly implemented by the administration and adivasi were restricted to enter the forests. The big forest zones, covering nearly lacks of acre have been sold to big corporate magnets, with nothing doing with adivasis constitutional rights in their territorial possession. Indian English novelists could present these forest issues sympathetically, just like presented by C. K. Janu in her *Mother Forest* but Indian English Novelist lacks this creativity.

Adivasi community is struggler par excellence. They are struggling against most dangerous situations for the last many centuries; therefore, they are still surviving in this nation. Adivasis do not know the submissiveness and surrender to a tough situation. Their history is the history of martyrdom. They know that the mass revolutions for indigenous communities are taking place across the globe, therefore they hope for the best. The novelist should feel this dignity of hope of adivasi community and should present their picture with a realistic point of view. Literary writers of India should establish a big platform for indigenous writings. Then the postcolonial literature of India will be worth posting. Today corporate families are creating dominance in adivasi's forest area. Many adivasi movements are doing good work of creating awareness about the constitutional rights of adivasis but mainstream English literature is calm and uninterested in them. When the colonisation of India took place, resistance was also taking place. It was the resistance of Adivasi but it could not be treated as resistance. Racism is attached to colonisation in India. The colonisers used this tool of racism and made the mental and physical genocide of aboriginals. The colonisation of India was British capitalism in India. During postcolonialism in India, the presence of civilising capitalism and its inhuman barbarity openly comes out. These global policies seem very sophisticated and cultured in their own countries but in the colonial territories, it becomes the ruthless exploitative machinery. It happened in India in the case of the Adivasis. Toady global economic policies are threatening adivasi communities but postcolonial Indian English novels do not speak about it. Regarding these cultures of silence, Shymcharan Dube opines, "Today's intellectual class is diverting from native issues they are going for away from common man's realism. They focused on foreign languages and published their work in those languages. To publish their literary work from foreign is to be considered as prestige for them. Writers writing in regional languages are to be considered as secondary intellectuals. Crave for western parameters of literary writing and western values of materialism are increasing in today's modern writer in India" (Dube, Translated).

Today, the depriving life of the adivasi is the result of political unwillingness. After Independence, governments have changed, numerous policies have been made for adivasis but social and cultural alienation is the reality of Adivasi in India. Naxalism, corruption, lack of political will and negligence towards regional dialects as mediums of education are the prime reasons for their backwardness. Still, the territories like Dantewada, Bastar, Abhujamad, Sarguja, Telangana, Maharashtra, Gadhachiroli, Palamu, Dumka, Bihar, Manbhum, Singhbhum, west Bengal, Orisa Andhra Pradesh and Dandkarnya are yet to be free from naxal issues. Issues of employment and economic empowerment are the solution to counter the naxal violence in adivasi regions. We have very few novels in Hindi and English deal with the realities of "Red Zone" and its circumstances on the physical and mental life of Adivasis. In the novel *The English August*,

Christian Missionaries are converting the adivasis. They are ready to pay him a lot of money for this conversion. Augustya comments, those missionaries are taking the benefits of adivasi poverty by converting them into Christianity. The issues of adivasi conversion in Hinduism are also a very serious matter. This must be taken into consideration that, Madhya Pradesh, Orissa, Chhattisgarh, Jharkhand and Andhra Pradesh are the major adivasi territories where conversions of adivasis are going on at rapid speed. A big funding agency is working for them, as the Augustya observed that the links of conversion of adivasi in Chipanthy are secured to Vatican City. All the reporting of the converted candidates daily goes to Vatican City. Though, on the surface level, it looks very normal but cultural dominancy of a particular religion often works upon the conversion of adivasis.

Adivasis are the citizens of this nation; therefore their upliftment should be a national subject of debates and literary writings. These adivasi areas are multifaceted with exploitation, suppression, injustice, disparities and military repressions. The repression of Adivasi in schedule areas of India reminds us of the genocide of Latin American adivasis and the slavery of African adivasis. This literature is full of expression of exploitation of indigenous communities which now became an international theme for Fifth World of Indigenous Literature. But these waves of the fifth world of indigeneity could not reach to our postcolonial Indian English novel writing. Still, in Canada, the first nation peoples are struggling for their indigenous rights. Australian aboriginal still looks down British as the intruder and colonisers. The white people conceders that they have taken the responsibilities to civilise these native communities and brought them in the mainstream world but on another side, Aboriginal thinks that colonisers have snatched their natural resources and distorted their cultured traits. They have cut down natives from their indigenous roots in the name of modernisation. Regarding this ideological fight, Ramsharan Joshi narrates:

> After two centuries of subjugation, a First Nation person of Canada looks down on whites as outsiders. Both the communities white government and Indigenous look to each other with doubtful eyes. An aboriginal community thinks that colonisers have distracted our way of living a natural life. They have distracted us from our nature and spirituality. They have converted us in the religion which has nothing to do with our cultural, identical roots" (Joshi: 2015:125) (Translated)

Adivasi is not the followers of the Varna-system. They are an indigenous community of this nation but by bringing them into the Varna system, their existing international identities are tried to destroy. Of course, this is a very major and serious issue but Indian English fiction writers have never treated this subject seriously in their novels. Because of the rapid conversion in adivasi societies many adivasi-aboriginal communities are leg behind from their ancestral cultures. The new generation of adivasi youth wants to hide their identity as a part of the adivasi community. This is happening because of the internal colonialism has taken place in India by dominant religious groups. A novelist could give justice to this internal colonialism of Dalit and Adivasi community in their fictions but yet there is not such literary awareness and commitment in Indian English fictions and fictionists.

## Internal Colonisation, Internal Orientalism, Adivasi Genocide and Literary Marginalisation of Adivasi

While reading the Indian English novels, it can be assumed that the characterisation and depiction of adivasis in selected Indian English fictions are not appropriate. The novelist could not give justice to the struggle for survival of the adivasi community in India. Adivasi characters in the selected novels are marginalised and subjugated, find no place to remain in the memory of the readers. All the novels are mainly focused on the urban, elite background of the main characters, eastern and western culture clash. According to the point of view of central characters like Billy Biswas, Clinton-Helen, Abhayraj and Augustya Sen, adivasis are ambitionless and they have nothing to do with the rapidly changing sociopolitical milieu. They are far away from cultural evaluations and adivasi's psychological cultivation is an impossible task. Though the novels slightly touch the theme of displacement, subjugation and marginalisation of adivasis, finally entire sympathies are taken by main characters as we found in *The Strange Case Of Billy Biswas, The Princess* and *The English August.* Now the question arises why this happened in postcolonial Indian English novels.

Indigenous communities are not secure in the waves of modern utilitarian capitalist society where only profit mongering mentalities matters. These modern capitalist mentalities are looting the natural resources in the adivasi land. Adivasis of Latin America proved the victims of this corporate robbery in the nation like Brazil, Peru,

Chile, Columbia, Argentina and Vietnam. In India, regional writers like Mahasweta Devi, C. K. Janu, Shivrama Karanth, Narayan, Gopinath Mohanty, and Ramdayal Munda depicted the pain and pathos of adivasi life and corporate loot in adivasi regions but in postcolonial Indian English literature, lack this spirit of real representation. Today adivasi in India is going through the process of cultural and identical genocide. Genocide means killing of people of a particular clan, tribe both physically and culturally and this dehumanisation of adivasi is taking place with the marginal in India. Adivasi in India are the forest dwellers from the centuries. Forest is their source of living, inspiration and everything but by hook or crook, this heritage is forcibly taken by them leaving them in a dark future. The adivasi of India is claiming that they will accept the death penalty because they cannot live without the company of forest, river and natural objects which are the part of their family. Regarding this mass cultural genocide of adivasi, our mainstream Indian English writer does not seem to speak but hundreds of novels have been written on partition holocaust and exploited feminism. This cultural genocide of adivasi is going on through the colonial period is now regenerated in neoliberal India, but the postcolonial sensibilities and the danger of neocolonial prophecy seems in dark silence.

The novels dealing with Adivasi life in Indian English Literature are based upon romanticism, glorification, materialism, sophisticated futile values of urbanity to which the central characters hanged and demolished, but soothing adivasi culture, their nature-worshipping, exploited circumstances that bring poverty to them are nowhere in Indian English fiction writings, their respect for their communal life and many other reasons of their backwardness seems nowhere in the mainstream Postcolonial Indian English Novels. The novels written in India during the 1970 are dealt with the urban humdrum and growing materialism which was the result of industrialisation. Corporate policies were obliviously responsible for its callous city atmosphere for this degeneration. The adivasi territories also become the victim of synchronising postcolonial Indian history. Adivasis in India are the victims of the double disposition and internal orientalism. While writing postcolonial literature our mainstream has never written about these multicolonisations. They were seeking refuge with nostalgic elements in the metaphysical world when several cases of adivasi distortions and mental genocides were taking place during colonialism and in the postcolonial period of India.

In the contemporary scenario, major adivasi territories of India are disturbed. Social, constitutional, cultural and economic struggle is taking place in Indian adivasi territories. The government is placing a massive military in these areas. Defense helicopter is wandering in hilly and dense jungles of the Adivasi area. The adivasis of India have given self-determination rights in the Indian Constitution but with the growing presence of industrial policies, governments have opened up the adivasi reserved area for foreign direct investment and other business purposes. Mining, Bauxite, cement and iron projects have taken massive shape in these adivasi territories but adivasi displacement, employment opportunities are the most threatening problem in India. With the acceptance of mix economic policies of 1991, the monster of LPG awakens on adivasi land. Hegemonic industrial houses in India and multinational corporate houses across the globe have arrived with their number of MOU in the Adivasi area. Both of them leave no stone unturned to rob adivasi life, culture and indigenous heritage. In India, nearly eighty types of minerals and other natural resources are to be found in adivasi areas which have a huge cost, beyond imagination in the international market. Neoliberal governmental policies and global capitalistic battalions are attacking these natural resources resulting in the displacement of native Adivasis from their shelters.

Today indigenous communities like Gonds, Kondhs, Baiga, Halba, and Bhil are marginalising in India. Adivasi disposed of their native land after Independence is still waiting for the rehabilitation and compensation – money. In Bastar, iron factories were set up and the rivers got polluted. There is no employment, no educational and health facilities for adivasi youth so they chose the option of the struggle for basic amenities. Today, adivasis themselves seem like outsiders in their heartland in the adivasi area like Narayanpur, Dantewada, Kanker, Jugdalpur and Gadchiroli. Adivasi people work as Sweeper, the layman in the big homes and shops in these areas. In an Independent nation, adivasi constitutional rights are marginalised and adivasi are deprived of their forest rights. This chaos was taking place on Indian ground because for the modern state, there is no sign of a adivasi community in their agenda of development. In this way, they are left to remain doom in their territory. Regarding adivasi representation in the mainstream, Ramsharan Joshi says:

> Parameters of development should be useful only when the adivasi upbringing should be the center of government. Otherwise, these

> territories will always be unstable with revolts. The government should think large heartedly that before the concept of the nation took place, adivasi were the owner of this forest, land and hills. Adivasis were the sustainer of natural resources. British have exploited these adivasi communities in very brutal manners. The government should study which laws were responsible for adivasi destruction. Today adivasis are in the phase of internal colonialism. Now there should be an end to this neo-colonisation. (Joshi 2015: 137)

The contemporary realities of Adivasis in India will be the treasure of subjects for the mainstream Indian English writers for literary writings. However, they have depicted adivasi as marginalised, uncivilised, superstitious and far away from civilisation. Just like Joseph Conrad says, *White Man's Burden,* to see the light of civilisation to Africa and Asia, just the same way, Indian English writer performed their role and they are handling these burdens for the last many years. Now they have to accept the challenges of the depiction of the realities of displacement, oppressive governmental policies, nepotism, corruption and cultural genocide of Adivasi along with adivasi's deculturisation and disorientation. The nature and scope of the novel of Third world countries were different in comparison of Second World's socialistic ideologies and First World's capitalistic ideologies because the history and culture of the third world were different from the other two worlds. The exploitation of the third world made the ground for the industrial revolution in England. Social, economic and cultural diversities of the Third World were the exact opposite of Britain. Therefore subjects of literature for Third world writers were different. Slavery, imperialism and feudalism were the challenging subjects for native writers. Freedom at any cost was their prime target. When we study the novels of Chinua Achebe, N Gugi WA Thingo, Sembene Osman, Gabriel Garcia Marquez, or Elejo Carpenter, their writing challenges the colonialism and arouses a nationalistic feeling among oppressed classes of colonised countries. Indian English novelists have also dealt with nationalistic feelings but the oppressed classes could not peep through their writings. It seems that the political, cultural and ideological importance and unavoidability of novels for resisting imperialism could not be carried out properly by Indian English writers as it was sustained by African and Latin American novelists. Valuation of realism in social and political concern should be the first parameter for postcolonial writers but realism seems obscure in Indian English writing. In postcolonial Indian English novels, we find a lack of historical-cultural realities. The novel can be the best tool for strengthening the indigenous voices which crushed under colonialism and global imperialism.

Today the major area of North East, Jharkhand is going through the process of conversions. Adivasi conversion in different religions means the cultural and identical genocide of their clan. During the colonisation of Africa, English, Portugal, and French languages were dominated in literary scenes. Still, these foreign languages are holding their importance on African culture, literature and administrations. Therefore African novelists like N. Gugi WA Thingo started writing in the local Giyaku language. Africa has many native adivasi languages like Ibo, Yoruba, Giyaku, Jhulu and Hausa. African novels are the caravans of African history. Today African novelists are struggling against the internal colonisation of fascist governmental policies. Africa is still the biggest colony for American multinationals. Sembene Osman, a famous African novelist says in an interview that in Africa, the novelist should stand at the center of the society but it is also important that he should depict social realism and keep an objective distance from it. I participate in social progress and dialogs along with the sharing experiences. I play my role in the public struggle and know that what change we want to bring in national life. I started writing when our country was colonised. Now those colonial policies are in the hands of colored colonisers of our race and became more mysterious and harmful. We thought that Africa will do progress after Independence but after deport of whites, their agents who are black, implemented the same policy. This governmental lobby is the agent of global imperialism. We have to criticize them for their wrongdoing. We have to create courage in our people to raised voice against such oppressive machinery.

The African writers started writing in their dialect to answer the empirical forces that adivasi identity, indigenous heritage because and ancestral knowledge of Africa could be better represented by their dialect. In postcolonial African literature, novels are written in their dialect. They believe that open veins of Africa and multicolonisation could be brought on World literary panorama only through African languages. African novelist, Obbey Wall accepted that only African dialect can arise an African consciousness among Africans. N Gugi WA Thiong considers the European depiction of Africa as forgery and duplicacy. N Gugi has started to write in Giyaku language. He is struggling to established adivasi African languages in literature.

Commenting on the self-dignity of Africans, N Gugi Wa Thiong opines: "My writing in the Giyaku language is the representation of African resistance against the European colonisation. In schools and colleges of Universities of Kenya, Adivasi dialects are considered as secondary. They are conceder as backward and primitive. I do not want to this happen that the Kenyan youth generation should consider the Kenyan language as inferior which represents Kenyan life, culture and their struggle against imperialism." (Panday: 2016:103, Translated)

The Present title of the research *Characterisation and Depiction of Adivasi in Postcolonial Indian English Fiction* is very important from several points of view. After the independence era, nobody studied the adivasi life in Indian English fiction having marginalised, subjugated and neglected points of view. Indian English fiction writers tried their level best to depict the character and adivasi life but they seem weaker and unauthentic. The main reason behind this is their urban and elite background and the elite manner they are following while writing about subaltern classes they could not feel that gloom and pathos of the struggle of survival and crave for identity. Selected Indian English fiction Writer presented adivasi life from their comfort zone, but double colonisation, double disposition and dual exploitation which is the contemporary reality of the adivasi of India could not come convincingly through the writing of these mainstream writers. Therefore critic A.K. Chaturvedi gives a message of Dr. Radhakrishanan to the mainstream writers of India that they should enhance their understanding of adivasi custom, rituals and their way of looking at life.

Ngugi's statement suggests that problems of the independent countries are the recolonisation from their power and state. Therefore we should be in a role to decolonise the mind of common people of suppressed cultures. The African literature, culture and dialects are related to the socio-culture-historical decolonisation by the African population. Postcolonial African literature is not confused about their identity. They claim for their indigeneity and ancestry through their literature by resisting to the imperialism of one's body and mind. African novels have set up the parameter of postcolonialism and decolonisation. This seems very weak in postcolonial Indian English novel writing. Latin American literature flourished after the 1950s. Novelist from Brazil George Amado, Joss Maria, Argadous from Peru, Carlos Fuet from Mexico, and Rao

Bestowed from Peraugwe have decolonised the European norms of imperial writing and presented the exploitation of Latin America in a very realistic manner. *Open veins of Latin America* were written in 1967 by Eduardo Galliano which presents five centuries of subjugations and brutal exploitations of indigenous communities in Bolivia, Peru, Brazil and Columbia. In the beginning, Latin American writing was influenced by British writing but at the beginning of the $20^{th}$ century, indigenous roots started to find their identity in literature.

The responsibility of a novelist is not only to explore the peasant life of Africa or to depict the life of Red Indians in Mexico but their large responsibility is this that they should depict the sovereignty of the people of the nation. British colonisers tried to vanish the memories of Latin America. They distorted the original picture of indigenous communities of Latin America and tried to westernise the local culture, literature, education and history. Therefore much of the writings during the $20^{th}$ century in Latin America come through the Spanish language. Latin American novel writing during the 1960-70's deals with the resistance to western imperial power and claims for self-identity. Latin American novelists have tried its best to decolonise their culture, literature through the clutches of master agents of imperialism. American global capital policies are still wanted to highjack the national life of Latin American countries, still, Latin American novelist is writing for the decolonisation of indigenous cultures and literature.

Through the novel which we have taken for the research, we proved our hypotheses that Indian English fiction writing lacks authenticity while depicting the social and cultural alienation of adivasi. *The Strange Case of Billy Biswas* focuses more on the self-centered monologue of the main character Billy Biswas, so the struggle and hardship of the adivasi community remain silent. The promising novel of Manohar Malgonkar's *The Princess* shows its success in many spheres of the disintegration of India but he could not give justice to the displacement of adivasi Bhil through the mouthpiece of his main hero 'Abhayraj'. Adivasi in *The Princess* brutally becomes the victim of the political holocaust of Indian freedom struggle. Kamala Markandeya has touched on a very good theme of adivasi displacement and the clash of civilisation between the orient and the European in her novel *The Coffer Dam.* While delineating East-West encounter and lovemaking dialogue between Helen and adivasi Bashiam, the main adivasi problem of acculturation and disposition, racial injustice towards adivasi remains in darkness. The novel *The Coffer Dam* focuses on the cultural dominance of alien in native land but nativity and aboriginalities are mercilessly encountered to a deadly flood. This novel written in 1969, presents the contemporary reality of adivasi belts but in a very limited scope.

Adivasi is shown very superstitious in the novel *The River Sutra*. The novel was written in 1993 which was the peak period of globalisation in India where adivasi territory is much victimized under the global policies of industrialisation but the novelist has shown them adopting Hinduism rituals and customs and sinking in the Narmada River to cure the diseases. She could not present the disorientation and disposition of adivasi. Everything about adivasi life, including rebellious character, Rima is glorified and romanticised. In the novel, adivasi life and characterisation are as only leftover and supplementary to the main story of the novel. Adivasi heritage, their struggle for existence, their faith in primordial power finds very silent in the postcolonial Indian English fiction *The River Sutra*. Postcolonial Latin American literature flourished with literary techniques like mythology, fantasy, magic realism and black magic. They used these techniques to show the realism of the modern contemporary world. The novelist uses the utopian imaginary world and becomes the master of that story. Magic realism gives space to the character to express as the novelist wants to wish. In many countries of Latin America, military governments are ruling. Subversion of novelist poet, policymakers and social activist is a very common issue. Publication houses are also under inspections. The novelist is not allowed to describe the degeneration of the national life of other countries through their writings. We are living in the age of media dominance. The novelist must convert these societies in concern for humanism. They should save the world by becoming robotics.

Latin American masses have gone through the period of fascism where the government always tried to create elusive situations about reality. Autocrats always promote illusory ideas before the masses where the reality of incident, situation come out very rarely to the masses. They manipulate the memory, conscience and experiences of the common masses. They use political gimmicks to hallucinate the large masses Latin American novelist has used symbolism, imagery and magic realism to bring out such situations before the masses. These tools and techniques of literary writings are still to take place in Indian English writings. Postcolonial Latin American novelist has broken the stereotype norms of novel writing and exposed the barbarity and dehumanisation of corporates in Latin America. They were loyal towards the freedom of Latin American nations. They promoted the mass movement of liberation, brotherhood, social justice and gender quality. They also got the result of their literary awareness. But the postcolonial Indian literary reality could not achieve their aim of bringing social justice and gender equality in complex Indian social structure.

When we study the history of the world civilisation for the last five hundred years, one can be confirmed that these huge spans of so many years are not evidence of progress but it can be remembered for the brutal exploitation and digging of mother earth and snatching natural resources. These centuries are evidence of exploitative machinery against the ruthless distortions of humanity and ecology. These five hundred years of progress of civilisation of the world is actually to depict the greed of the handful greedy people's personal craves to have become richest in the world. Latin America, Australian aboriginal, Native America and Indian adivasi territories were brutally crushed under the policies of global capitalism. Indian English novel writing became versatile after the 1990s. India accepted the global and neoliberal policies of development. Foreign multinational came to the adivasi territory of India with big multi projects. Decolonisation of adivasi territory took place through the policies of corporate. The social, political and cultural life of Adivasi came in danger. They are deprived of their education and health. Indian English writing is unsympathetic about the displacement of adivasi. Amit Bhaduri says:

> "State has focused on land acquisition for the mining, Industry and SEZ. Jharkhand, Bihar, Chhattisgarh and Orissa are adivasi-dominated and full of natural resources. Adivasi comprises 8% population but the displacement ratio of adivasi is 40%. State sponsor's violence is there is the adivasi territory. PESA implemented adivasi territory is forcibly taken from them. Through terrorising the local adivasi, their land full of iron and resources is given to industrialists. Land, full of bauxite and diamonds of Orissa has the same stories. (Surana: 2009: 227)

Finally, this research should be studied in a very optimistic manner. Though it is a harsh criticism of Indian English fiction writing but aesthetic values in their novel are worth praising. Though the Indian English fiction writers lack authenticity while presenting adivasi disorientation and social marginalisation but this positive research will open new approaches for the study of the novel dealing with adivasi life in Indian English. Upcoming new English fiction writers will be acquainted with adivasi problems like subjugation, exploitation, political and cultural alienation of adivasi community which will provide them new parameters of the social study of adivasis realism as we found in the regional writings of Mahasweta Devi and Gopinath Mohanty. This research will be an advance and pathfinder of criticism available in contemporary burning adivasi issues in the era of globalisation and neo-liberalisation which is not properly justified before in novels written in Indian English. This research will be a lighthouse not only for adivasis but for all the marginalised and deprived sections of the societies across the globe that are going through the process of cultural, political and economic hegemonies and numerous disparities. This research will provide a humanitarian lens to all mankind to strengthen the voice of social justice, gender equality communal harmony and universal brotherhood. We can hope that this research analysis will provoke and inspire other adivasi and non-adivasi writers to stimulate further work related to descriptions of adivasis in the future literary panorama.

I would like to conclude the research with the immortal lines of Waharu Sonawane's poem, Stage and expect that his adivasi pain of being neglected and marginalised by the mainstream will be recovering in the upcoming days through the new literary sensibilities which will be benefitted through this research work.

> We never went on stage
> Nor were we called
> A gesturing finger
> Showed us our proper places.
> There we sat,
> And received Praise.
> And they stood on stage
> Telling us about our own Pain.
> Our pains remain ours
> It never becomes theirs
> Our doubts we whispered
> They listened
> Hummed and hawed
> They twisted our ears and warned us
> Apologise or else. (Devy: 2016:192)

## Contemporary Relevance Of Birsa Munda-The Pride Of Nation

Revolutionary Birsa Munda and his *Ulgulan* revolution between 1890-1900 is having unavoidable importance in the history and the social transformation of India. Birsa Munda fought against all unjust along with numerous ways of exploitation of British power in pre-independence India. Birsa's contemporary relevance is very important when most of the adivasi territories are again going to victimize through the process of recolonisation through the hands of few corporate magnets and foreign multinationals. The constitutional values and ethics of adivasi rights are in dark fate in contemporary scenarios therefore the struggle of Birsa Munda for the Land, Water and Forest should be review in the contemporary democratic framework of India. Birsa Munda's revolution was not a violent one but it was pedagogical for all those broken communities who were at the last stage of social inclusion. Birsa Munda was the real pride of subaltern communities of India who raised the voice of all the marginal sections of society including labours, farmers and the Dalit community.

The struggle and martyrdom of Birsa Munda could be review in the light of the process of colonisation of India where the British, as well as local landlords, were snatching every opportunity of bread and butter from the marginal classes. The elite educated classes as well as the caste-ridden mentalities of pre-independence India both were playing their crucial role to exploit the Adivasi community and displacing them from their natural abode. The taxation system of the British raj was the most destructive issue against which adivasi warriors like Baba Tilka Manzi and other warriors from the Sardari movement fought bravely and got martyrdom. Birsa Munda was born in such a deadly situation when Munda and Santhal territory of Bihar and Orissa were facing the pangs of extreme poverty and inhuman exploitation through bonded labour. Adivasi women's and young girls were seduced by the local hooligans of the landlord. Adivasi areas of those regions were affected by several draughts and famine. Many young generations of the adivasi community could not take their birth because of the malnutrition in those areas. Mainstream history is not going to explore this predicaments of the Adivasi community.

Birsa Munda was born on 15th November 1875 at Ulihatu village. Throughout his childhood, he has witnessed the chaos taking place in Munda territory. He was greatly attracted by the Sardariya movement of the adivasi revolutionaries who were fighting against the displacement, disorientation and marginalisation of the Adivasi community. Sardariya movement was going on in the Munda and Santhal territory for the last of four decades against the marginalisation of adivasi communities brought by British policies and the slavery of local landlords. Sardari's movement has almost come to an end when Birsa Munda was in his childhood. Sardari movement was started by the selective Munda revolutionaries now searching for their new leader in the adivasi heartland of pre-independent India. They got their supreme leader in Birsa Munda.

Birsa Munda was strongly opposed to British power in India. He was learning in a missionary school of *Chaibasa* and was influenced by Christian values and beliefs but soon he came to know to realise that the British Empire is encroaching their adivasi culture through this missionary work. The missionary could raise their voice against the displacement of Adivasi but they were looking to Adivasi only through the lenses of conversion into Christianity. Birsa Munda discarded the missionary values and took his inclination in Hinduism. The several exploitations by the landlord including the ill effects of the bonded labour of Adivasi families through the hands of these right-wing supporters of the caste-ridden mentalities, he came to know the meaninglesness of the Varna system. He abandoned this Varnashram ideology and established his new ideology of *Birsa-Dharma.* He popularised the statement "*Sahib Sahib Ek Topi*". At a very early stage of his youth; his comprehension of the social structure of the Indian society was praiseworthy. Through his *Birsa dharm,* he has given commands to Adivasi people to stay away from bad habits and thoughts. His *Birsa Dharm* was inspired by naturalism and values of environmental protection. Gradually Birsa Munda's religious movement transformed into political mobilisation. Now, this was the phase where the British Empire and local right-wing moneylenders were opposed to Birsa Munda. Birsa Munda's political thought was clear that the *Dikus*-outsiders are solely responsible for the poverty of the Adivasi community, therefore they should be sent back to their non-adivasi territory. Keeping in mind the exploitation of several decades, the volunteers of Birsa Munda started to attack local landlords and other dominant ideologies that were responsible for the protection of bonded labour. These landlords surrender themselves to British power for protection from adivasi revolutionaries. Local landlord and British military made a target to Birsa Munda and arrested him. He was sentenced to imprisonment for two years in 1893.

Birsa Munda now became more silent and mature during his imprisonment. He made contemplation on the duel treachery of British missionaries and the internal colonisation of the local moneylenders. He decided to fight with them on the base of his indigenous ideology of nativism. He believed that the Adivasi community should be given their liberty to decide and implement their self-determination rights. He was opposing the outsider's interference in the internal affairs of the adivasi territory. Birsa

Munda released in 1895 and he started for the groundwork among the Munda and Santhal provinces. He took several corner meetings to declare the self-determination power of Adivasi people in their territory. This transformation of Birsa was appreciated by the Adivasi community. His Ulgulan movement flourished in adivasi areas resulted in a threat to the indigenous community of pre-independence India. He ordered for total incorporation to Britishers and local landlords in adivasi areas. Birsa Munda's popularities and his unstoppable *Ulgulan*-the comprehensive revolt in all walks of life.

Birsa Munda Ulgulan revolution became the biggest source of inspiration to all the Adivasi revolutionary. When Birsa Munda was addressing his volunteers on Dombari hill of Ranchi, he was attacked by treachery and captured along with the volunteers. Birsa Munda was sent to jail and given very brutal treatment by the British administration. Birsa's arrest was the free license to all the feudalists to exploit again the Adivasi community and their natural resources. The revolution which he started now became widespread. People used to meet him at the jail to take inspiration from him. Birsa Munda was infected with tuberculosis and not given proper medical treatment resulting in his untimely death on the 9$^{th}$ of June 1900. Birsa Munda took rest in peace in the soil for which he fought throughout his life. He set the example for the other revolutionary who were fighting for their ancestral claim on natural resources and on indigenous culture. Birsa Munda became a synonym word for martyrdom and sacrifice. In a true sense, he was a national glory and a true symbol of resistance against inequality. Birsa Munda's revolution has shown the mirror to British raj that Adivasi will fight till their last breath to sustain their liberty and self-determination rights in their territory. British government assumed that in upcoming days this ulgulan revolution will take a deep grip in India therefore they tried to make the land reforms and accepted the claims of the adivasi people on land and agriculture. British Government made the land reforms like *CNT (Chota Nagpur Tenancy Act) and SPT (Santhal Pargana Tenancy Act)*.

Birsa Munda's *Ulgulan* movement cannot erase through the memory of the common masses of subaltern sections of India. Birsa Mundas *Ulgulan* movement (Total freedom) is a milestone for other social movements that struggle for social justice and economic equality. After Indian independence, it seems that the role of the

Britishers is played by the handful of business tycoons and multinational corporates in the adivasi territories of India. They have made the worse situation in adivasi areas by displacing and damaging the ecology of adivasi life. This must be admitted that the adaptation of LPG policy in 1992 for the foreign trade and foreign direct investment in India was responsible for the broken identities and disparities in adivasi life. Foreign multinationals are still exploiting the natural resources the ecology through their numerous corporate policies and the resistance of the local adivasi people is to be considered as the threat to nation's progress. Corporate policies are criminalizing the indigenous resistance throughout the world. The situation in Africa and Latin America is almost the same in this regard.

Policies are made for adivasi areas which will provide many benefits to multinational companies at the cost of misery and depravity of original indigenous community. Special economic zones are established to stop the protest of the local communities in the path of the exploitation of natural resources. Every voice of protest against profit mongering mentalities is suppressed by hook or by crook throughout the world. Indigenous countries and communities are again going into the dark phases of recolonisation or in the age of neoimperialism. Still Birsa Munda is having the relevance to protest in democratic ways to unjust and disparity. A big regional indigenous territory of West Bengal, Maharashtra, Orissa, Chhattisgarh is still going on the edge of recolonisation of black skin corporate tycoons. Most of the political parties, many non-governmental organisations are still could not show their proper stand in the public interest because of the fear of state repression. Many intellectuals of the adivasi community still don't want to accept the realism in adivasi areas. They don't understand what capitalism is? Why multinational policies are a danger to the indigenous-aboriginal communities? They simply don't understand the legacy of resistance of Birsa Munda against the colonisation of India and particularly the recolonisation of the subaltern communities. In today's scenario, the history of the Adivasi-indigenous resistance for self-determination rights has been replaced by the popular culture of singing, dancing and other cheap events having no elements of social upliftment.

In such a global pessimistic scenario, only the memories of the *Hool* (Santhal Protest against British Empire), *Ulgulan* (Munda's resistance to internal colonisation) *Bhoomkal* (Gonds rebellion against the British encroachments in Bastar) can stimulate our Adivasi consciousness to give ideological resistance against all kind of dominance, corruption, injustice, violence and disparities. Revolutionary Birsa Munda created a heavy storm of mass mobilisation of Adivasi and other marginalised communities and transformed it into a social movement that could resist the exploitation of identical and existential issues of subaltern communities. Birsa Munda wanted to establish the cultural socialism of the indigenous community throughout the Adivasi territory of India. Birsa Munda is immortal. He should be read in the constitutional democratic framework where his radical thoughts should be given constitutional shape. Birsa Munda was a revolutionary as well as a visionary who dreamed and acted to free his people from the clutches of superstition and illiteracy. He mobilises the people for fulfilling his dream of social equality and political decentralisation. His dream of the Adivasi nation was incomplete but he has shown the path to fulfill that vision by uniting all aboriginal adivasi groups of India and create a big international mass movement of Indigenous communities. He became an international freedom fighter even Native American adivasi groups knew his struggle for the ancestral claims of indigenous people on this earth.

Birsa Munda will always remember by those who want to play their major role in the resistance against the social disparity, cultural hegemony, gender violence and gender inequality including physical-mental violence imposed by caste-ridden mentalities with the help of profit mongering mentalities of several corporate tycoons. Now Birsa Munda is considered as the icon of marginal and displaced communities and a subaltern warrior of broken communities but certainly, he will be studied and analysed beyond the boundary of narrow caste, creed and nationalities and established his identity as the warrior of disposed communities. Presently Birsa Munda is a revolutionary and the heartthrob for each one of the youngsters of India and the indigenous communities across the globe who loves fraternity, equality, brotherhood, democratic values and the saviour of fundamental values honored by the Constitution of India.

# Bibliography


Adiga, Arvind. 2008. *The White Tiger*. Noida. Harper Collins Publication.

Ahamad, Azaj. 2008. *In Theory*. New York. Verso Publication.

Antony, Samy K.S. 2012. *Classical To Contemporary Literary Theory-A Seminal Approach*. New Delhi. Atlantic Publication.

Armstrong, S. 2011. *The Notion of Identity in Indian Subcontinent*. Edt. *Exploring Fourth World Literature*-Raja Shekhar Pateti. New Delhi. Prestige Books.

Bahadur Sanjay. 2013. *Hul-The Cry Rebel*. New Delhi. Rolly Books.

Basheer, M.P. 2015. *The News in Proportion-India Together*, Oct-2002.Web 22.May 2015.

Bhande, Usha. 1994. *Mothers And Mother Dialogues In Indian English Literature*. Jalandhar. ABS.

Bhatiya, Ravi. 2016. *Sustaining the Environment-The Adivasi Way*. Edt. S.N. Choudhary. New Delhi. Rawat Publication.

Bhukya, Bhangya. 2012. *The External Colonial Legacy*, Edt. Nathan/Xaxa-*Social Exclusion and Adverse Inclusion*. New Delhi. Oxford Uni. Press.

Brotherstone, Gordon. 1995. *Book of Fourth World-Reading Native America through their Literature*. Cambridge University Press.

Castle, Gregory. 2007. *Blackwell Guide to Literary Theory*. Oxford. Blackwell Publication.

Chaturvedi, A.K. 2008. *Adivasis In Indian English Novel*. New Delhi. Atlantic Publication.

Chatterjee, Upmanyu. 2003. *The English of August*. London Faber and Faber.

Chauhan, Vibha. 2012. *Crystallizing Protest into Movement Adivasi Community In History, Society and Literature*. Edt. G.N. Devy – *Indignity-Culture and Representation*. New Delhi. Orient Blackswan.

Chakraborty, Deepesh. 1985. *Investigating to a Dialogue-Subaltern Studies* Volum IV. Edt. Ranjit Guha. Delhi. Oxford University Press. p.375. Print.

Choudhary, S.N. 2016. *Social Movement In Adivasi India*. Jaipur Rawat Publication.

Das, Vijay Kumar. 2007. *Critical Essays on Postcolonial Literature*. New Delhi. Atlantic Publication.

Das, Samrendra/Padel Felix. 2010. *Out of This Earth*. New Delhi. Orient Blackswan.

Desai, Kiran. 2006. *The Inheritance of Loss.* New Delhi. Penguin Publication.

Devy, G.N. 2012. *Indigeneity-Culture and Representation.* New Delhi Orient Blackswan.

Devi, Mahasweta. 2003. *Chotti Munda and His Arrow.* New Jersy. Weily Blackwell.

Dungdung,Gladson. 2013. *Whose Country Is This Anyway?* Kolkatta. Advani Publication.

Dungdung, Gladson. 2015. Mission *Saranda-A War for Natural Resources.* Ranchi. Bir Boru Ompay Media.

Ghanshyam, G.A. 2013. *The Voice of Other In Post-Independence Indian English Fiction.* Jaipur. Viking Books.

Gupta Ramnika. 2009. *Adivasi literature-An Emerging Consciousness.* Edt.G.N.Devy New Delhi.Orient Blackswan.

Gavit, Maheshwari. 2009. *AdivasiSahityavichar.*NasikRoad.Vangmay Prakashan.

Hashmi, Miazi. *The Common Mans Tragedy-A Reading of Gopinaths Mohanty's Novel Pajara. JBM*/SSR Vol-03.@014. Print.

Irshad, M.D. *Cross-Cultural Interaction In The Novel of Kamala Markandeya Iyengar,* K.R.2007. Indian Writing In English. New Delhi. Sterling Publication.

Jadhav, Prashant. 2014. *New Man International Journal of Interdisciplinary Studies.* Issues04, Vol-o1, 2014.Print.

Jacob, Asha Susan.2015. *Narrating Adivasi Identity. Edit.G.G.Devy. Voices and Memory.* New Delhi. Orient Blackswan.

Jha, Gourishankar. 2006. *Current Perspectives In Indian English Literature. New Delhi.* Atlantic Publication.

Janu. C.K. 2004. *Mother Forest.* New Delhi. Kali for women Publi, 2004. Print

Jayashree, J.S./Narayan. 2012. *Kocharethi* (Introduction) New Delhi.

Joshi,Arun. 1971.*The Strenge Case of BillyBiswas.* NewDelhi.Orient Blackswan.

Joshi, Ramsharan. 2015. *Yadon KaLal Galiara-Dantewada.* NewDelhi. Rajkamal Prakashan.

Kala, J.S. 2012. *Ecopsycological Perspective of Geeta Mehta's A River Sutra,* Edt. L.C.Khatri- Five Indian Women Novelist. New Delhi. Penguin Publication.

Kankariya Madhu. 2007. *Khule Gagan Ke Sitare.* New Delhi, Rajkamal publication.

Kambale, Pandurang. 2015. *Havasu.* Rucha Publication.Nagpur.

Kapoor, Akash.1994. *It's a Classic, New York Times Review.* New York.

Khatri, L.D. 2012. *World Literature In English-Critical Responses.* Jaipur. Books Enclave.

Kumar, Shiv.2007. K. "Augustya and His English Tradition." *Atlantic Review,* Vol-II, No.02, May 2007, p.23.

Kumar, Vinod. 2005. *Samar Shesh Hai.* New Delhi. Prakashan Sansthan.

Limbale, Sharankumar. 2004. *Towards the Aesthetic of Dalit Literature.* New Delhi. Orient Longman.

Mahanand, Anand. 2011. *Adivasi India in Fiction.* Berlin, Lap Lambert Academic Publication.

Malti, Shubhrendu. 2016. Naxalite *Movement and Involvement of Adivasi.* Edt. S.N. Choudhary-*Adivasi Movement In India.* New Delhi. Raut Publication.

Manzi, Mahua. 2012. *Maram Gomake Nilkanth Hua.*New Delhi. Rajkamal Publication.

Manohar, Yashwant. 2014. *Sahityikanchi Jababadari.* Nagpur, Yugsakshi prakashan.

Malgonkar, Manohar.1963. *The Princess.* New York.Vikings Books.

Mashale Ashok. 2011. *The Postcolonial Perspective in Indian English Novel-Indian Steam Research Journal.*Solapur, Feb2011.p.p.28, 32.

Meena,Ganga Sahay.2016. *Adivasi Our HindiUpnyas.* Newdelhi.Ananya Prakashan.

Meena, Kedar Prasad. 2016 *Adivasi Samaj*, Sahitya Our Rajniti.New Delhi. Anudnya Books.

Mishra, Dinesh. 2015. *Literature and Social Change.* Edt. Pramod Mehara. Delhi. Kalpaz Publication.

Meshram, Bhujang. 2014. *Adivasi Sahitya Ani Asmitavedh.* Mumbai. Lokvangmaygruh.

Mukharjee, Minakshi.1971. *The Twice Born Fiction.* New Delhi Henneman Edu. Publication.

Mohanty. Gopinath. 1997. *Paraja. Noida.* Oxford University Press. 1997. Print. Translated by Bikram Das

Mohanty, Gopinath. 1996. *Dadi Budha (Ancestor).* Kattak.Vidyapuri Prakashan.

Mohanty, Gopinath. 1977. *Amrut Santhan.*Kattak.Vidyapuri Prakashan.

M.Hamid. 2012. *The Marginalisation of Adivasi In India.* Edt. Natha/Xaxa. Social Exclusion and Adverse Inclusion. New Delhi. Oxford University Press.

Mehara, Pramod Kumar. 2015. *Literature and Social Change.* Delhi. Kalpaz Publication.

Mehta Geeta. 1993. *The River Sutra.* Delhi.Viking Penguin Books.

Naik. M.K. 2007. *The History Of Indian Writing In English.* New Delhi. Sahitya Academy.

Nandy Ashish. 1997. *The Future Of Dissent Feminism*-460.December 1997.p.p.42-43.

Narayan. *Kocharethi.* 2012. New Delhi. Oxford University Press, 2012. Print.

Nubili, Clara. 2003. *The Danger Of Gender-Caste, Class and Gender in Contemporary Women Writing.* New Delhi, Samp and Son, 2003. Print.

Padel, Felix. 2015. *Sacrificing People- Invasion of a adivasi Landscape.* New Delhi. Orient Blackswan.

Panday, Manager. 2013. *Bhartiya Samaj Me Pratirodh Ki Parampara.* New Delhi.Vani Publication.

Patel, M.F. 2012. *Postmodern Indian Women Novelist In English.* Jaipur Pointer Publication.

Pateti, Raja Shekhar. 2011. *Exploring Fourth World Literature-Adivasi Adivasi and Dalit.* New Delhi. Prestige Books.

Pathak, R.S. 1999. *Modern Indian English Novel.* Delhi. Creative Books.

Poovilangothai, B. 2016. *Unearthing The Unexplored-A Critical Companion to Fourth World Literature.* New Delhi. Athorspress.

Radhakrishan, Meena. 2016. *First Citizen- Studies on Adivasi-Adivasis and Aboriginals.* New Delhi. Oxford.

Ray, Mohit. 2003. *Studiesin Commonwealth Literature.* New Delhi Atlantic Publisher.

Rao, Shriwas. 2011. *From Margin to Mainstream-A Brief Study of Native American Map.* Edit. Raja Shekhar Pateti-Exploring Fourth World Literature-Adivasi, Adivasi, Dalit. New Delhi Prestige Book, 2011. Print.

Rao, A.V.K. 1983. *A Novel Of Indias Lost Generation-A Bend in The Ganges.* Edt. Hari Mohan Prasad. Bareilly Prakash Book Depot, 1983. p.150-157

Sajeev.2005. *Pair Tale Ki Doob.* Bikaner, Vagdevi Pocket Book.

Sarangi, Joydeep. 2007. *Presentation of Postcolonialism in English.* New Delhi. Authorspress.

Satchidanand, K. 2016. *Word Matters-Writing Against Silence.* New Delhi. Penguin Book.

Sen, Nivedita. 2008. *Mahasweta Devi-An Anthology Of Recent Criticism.* Duncraft International Publication.

Sengupta Amit. 2015. *Mother Forest-C.K. Janus Fight for Adivasi Land.* Tehelka. Sep 11, 2004, Web 26 May,2015.

Shambhunath. 2016. *Rashtra Our Hashia.*New Delhi Vani Publication.

Shekhar Hansada. 2016. *Adivasi Will Not Dance.* New Delhi, Speaking Tiger.

Singh, K.S. 1972. *Adivasi Situation In India.* Simala. Indian Institute of Advanced Studies.

Singh, Rakesh Kumar. 2003. *Jaha Khilate Hai Rakt Palash.* New Delhi, National Publishing House.

.......... 2014. *Utterupniveshvad-Chunoutiya our Vikalp.* New Delhi. Shubhada Publication.

Sharma, S.N. 1983. *Recent Revelation of Indian English Fiction.* Edt. Hari Mohan Prasad. Bareilly, Prakash Book Depot.

Spivak Gayatri. 1988. *Can Subaltern Speak?* Besingtok Macmliien. 1988. Print.

Strumpwell Christian. 2014. *Masking and Unmasking of Adivasi Working Class in Orissa.* Edt.Bates/Shaha-*The Savage Attack.* New Delhi. Social Science Press.

Surana, Pannalal. 2011. *Jagtikikarnane Keleli Fasavnuk.* Pune. Sugava Publication.

Talwar, Veer Bharat. 2008. *Jharkhand Ke Adivasio Ke Bich Ek Activist Ke Notes.*Delhi. Gnyanpith Publication.

Tete, Vandana. 2013. *Adivasi Sahitya-Parampara aur Prayojan.* Ranchi. Pyara-Kerketta Foundation.

Theime, John. 2009. *An Arnold Anthology of Postcolonial Literature In English.* New York. Arnold Press.

Tumram Vinayak. 2012. *Adivasi Sahitya-Disha Ani Darshan.* Aurangabad. Swaroop Prakashan.

Tyson Luis. 2006. *Critical Study Today-A Users Friendly Guide.* New York. Routledge Publication.

Valhekar, Dnyaneshawar. 2009. *Adivasi Sahitya-Ek Abhyas.* Aurangabad, Swaroop Prakashan.

Varma, Anand Swaroop. 1999. *Upniveshik Mansikta Se Mukti.* New Delhi. Granth Shilpi.

Xaxa, Virginias. 2008. *State, Society and Tribes-Issuesin Postcolonial India.* Noida. Pearson.

Xaxa, Virginias. 2009. *Tribes, Conversion and Sangh Pariwar.* Edt. Dharmendra Kumar Proselytisation in India-The Process of Hinduisation in Adivasi Societies. Akar Books.

Yadav, Abhishek Kumar. 2015. *Jharkhand-Andhere Se Sakshatkar.* New Delhi. Media Studies Group.

# Index

## C



## D

**Q**



**R**